SCIENCE EDUCATION IN DEVELOPING COUNTRIES

INTERNATIONAL ENCYCLOPAEDIA OF
SCIENCE AND TECHNOLOGY EDUCATION - 2

SCIENCE EDUCATION IN DEVELOPING COUNTRIES

By

Dr. Digumarti Bhaskara Rao
M.Sc., M.A., M.A., M.Ed., Ph.D.
Dean, Faculty of Education
Member, Academic Senate
Ex-Chairman, Board of Studies in Education
Member, Research Advisory Committee
Acharya Nagarjuna University
D-43, S.V.N. Colony
Guntur - 522 006 (India)

COVERY PUBLISHING HOUSE PVT. LTD.
NEW DELHI-110 002

Published by:

DISCOVERY PUBLISHING HOUSE PVT. LTD.
4383/4B, Ansari Road, Darya Ganj
New Delhi-110 002 (India)
Phone : +91-11-23279245; 23253475; 43596065
E-mail : discoverybooksindia@gmail.com
discoverypublishinghouse@gmail.com
web : www.discoverypublishinggroup.com

First Published: **2001**

Reprinted: **2021**

ISBN: 978-81-7141-569-4

Science Education in Developing Countries

Printed at:
Infinity Imaging Systems
Delhi

Preface

Science and Technology have occupied almost all spheres of human life. The wonderful achievements of science and technology have glorified the modern world and transformed the modern civilization into a scientific and technological civilization. Considering the importance of science and technology, they have been incorporated in every stage of education.

This International Encyclopaedia of Science and Technology Education is developed covering a wide range of aspects related to science and technology education for the benefit of all those who are associated with science and technology education. This Encyclopaedia is consisting of eleven volumes, namely:

1. Science and Technology Education,
2. Science Education in Developing Countries,
3. Organisational Structure of Science,
4. Science Education in Asia and the Pacific,
5. Science and Technology Education for All,
6. Values, Ethics, Talent and Girls in Science and Technology Education,
7. Popularisation of Science and Technology Education,
8. Science, Power and Society
9. Information Technology,
10. Teacher Training in Science and Technology Education and
11. Science, Technology and Society—A Curriculum Framework.

I convey my cordial thanks to UNESCO-PROAP, Bangkok, Thailand; UNESCO-ROSTE, Venice, Italy; UNESCO Paris, France; IIEP, Paris, France; Commonwealth Secretariat, London, UK; UNCTAD, Geneva, Switzerland, Queen's University, Kingston, Canada; and Alberta Education, Edmonton, Canada for their kind co-operation in preparing this Encyclopaedia.

DR. DIGUMARTI BHASKARA RAO
Secretary
Academy of Communication Culture Education
Science and Service
GUNTUR (A.P.)

Contents

SCIENCE EDUCATION IN DEVELOPING COUNTRIES:

ISSUES AND PERSPECTIVES FOR PLANNERS

Keith M. Lewin (1992). Science Education in Developing Countries: Issues and Perspectives for Planners, Paris : IIEP. Reproduced with the permission of International Institute of Educational Planning, Paris.

Introduction

The purpose of this review is to draw together and discuss the experience of science education in developing countries. The analysis offered identified key issues for planning science education in the 1990s. This book forms part of the wider programme of research of the International Institute for Educational Planning, Paris, on 'Planning science education provision in general secondary schools'.

Rationale

Over the last two decades many developing countries[1] have invested heavily in improving access to, and enhancing the quality of science education. Human resource development has become a central feature of most national development strategies and within this the emphasis has more often than not been on the acquisition of scientific and technological skills and capabilities. In many developing countries there is now more than two decades of experience with system reforms, curriculum development, and teacher training for science education at secondary and higher levels. Though much has been achieved, the impact of these initiatives has not always lived up to expectations—labour shortages for scientifically and technically qualified staff have persisted constraining the development of new productive enterprises and hampering the growth of existing ones; teaching and learning practices have been slower to change than many curriculum developers anticipated; and increased access to science education has sharpened awareness of variations in quality and participation associated with urban and rural, and gender differences. What evidence there is of levels of achievement in science suggests that scientific literacy is still a distant goal in many countries, and that the achievement of students who specialise in science falls short of that which is desirable.

There are many reasons for the problems that have arisen. These include inadequate problem diagnosis, lack of skilled curriculum developers, insufficient resources for effective implementation, persistent shortages of trained science teachers, and ineffective planning. Most recently, in a good number of countries, economic austerity within the framework of structural adjustment programmes has placed severe constraints on the resources available for education. Science education, as one of the most expensive areas of the curriculum, has become vulnerable to the effects of parsimonious resourcing.

Radically new technologies of production and access to information are beginning to permeate the developing world. Greater and greater proportions of the labour force are being employed in occupations where scientific literacy is an advantage. Scientific competence and understanding is required for growing numbers of professionals. It is therefore timely and strategically important to undertake a review of the issues raised by the experience of the last two decades.

Scope

This review focuses on secondary science since it is at this level that most initiatives have been taken and human resource needs for development have been identified as most critical. It is recognized that, for different reasons, primary science constitutes an equally important area of concern, especially in the wake of the World Conference on 'Education for All' (Jomtien, Thailand, March, 1990) but it is beyond the scope of this study. So also is higher education where needs are more specialized and participation is available to minorities.

This review examines material judged most relevant to developing countries. It seeks to the selective rather than comprehensive since so much experience has accumulated. The heterogeneity of developing countries' education systems precludes the distillation of a single set of conclusions which are equally relevant everywhere and the review should be read in the light of this. Moreover, choices have had to be made which reflect the accessibility of material (much of value exists in country level documentation and the review has been undertaken from Sussex), the experience of the author (who has worked predominantly in developing countries influenced by British traditions in science education), and the modest resources available. These factors create limitations for the study which are inevitable in an exercise of this kind. Thus most of the literature addressed is published in international journals and English language source material. The perspectives advanced on the development of science education may be considered over influenced by the experience of countries with historic links to the British education system. In many places discussion is restricted by constraints of time, money and access to materials. Nevertheless, it is hoped that within these boundaries the analysis offered is comprehensive and balanced and the responsibility for the judgements made of the material to include is of course mine alone.

Like other recent reviews *e.g.* Wallberg (1991), to singular theme is developed by the review since to attempt this would do considerable violence to the very different historical experience, current conditions and future prospects that exist in different education systems. By identifying issues for policy-makers and planners which appear to have some generable characteristics, based on analysis of the available literature, it is hoped to provoke debate and the interpretation of the arguments advanced in relation to particular policy-making environments. The value of the review therefore lies in creating a framework for subsequent reappraisal, at a country level, of planning and policy questions.

In developing this review a number of different patterns of organization were considered. Since the review is part of a programme of research on science eduction planning which includes country case study and survey elements it was decided to discriminate in the review in favour of those areas where a literature existed of research studies and leave to other part of the programme detailed discussion of areas better suited to empirical enquiry (e.g. discussion of costing, detailed consideration of patterns of enrolment). Additionally, since the review was focused on science education, only limited excursions were taken into the more general literature on educational development (e.g. that on educational innovation and school achievement).

In its final form this review is organized around a number of themes which reflect the main issues identified for future planning and policy-making. The chapter themes are listed below :

1. The Context of Science Education Development in Developing Countries

This chapter offers an account of some of the main features of science education development in developing countries. It traces how curriculum innovations spread throughout the developing world in the 1960s and 1970s, indicates some of their main features, and reviews how the circumstances for further development have changed. This provides a backdrop to the subsequent analysis of the key dimensions addressed in the succeeding chapters.

2. National Science Policy and Science Education Aims

The articulation of science education policy with national science policy and development strategies is the first issue addressed in this chapter. This leads to discussion of the implications of changes in technology and in the international economic system for future science education provision. These condition the environment for future policy-making.

The discussion of policy issues leads to an exploration of how aims and objectives are derived, raises questions about this process and identifies the range of aims and objectives that emerge. A number of more specific interests are addressed: to what extent are terminal (complete learning experience prior to labour market entry) or preparatory (orientated to the demands of science education at the next level) aims and objectives dominant in secondary science programmes? Do they tend to be knowledge or skill oriented? How far are they concerned with attitudes and values? In what ways has the science curriculum broadened to include more concern for social and environmental and technological concerns?

3. Factors Affecting Achievement in Science

This chapter reviews the literature on the achievement of students. It explores some of the problems of method involved in school achievement studies, reviews the various factors that have been advanced as explanations for variations in achievement and comments on their significance. As far as possible the focus is on science achievement though some factors identified are likely to be common to achievement in other subjects. A commentary is included on selected findings from the most recent IEA Second International Science Study.

4. Implementation and Organizational Issues

This chapter briefly considers some of the literature on the implementation of educational innovations. Much of this is not specific for science education but is nevertheless relevant to the main concerns of the review. Implications for effective innovation are noted and also referred to throughout the other chapter. The second part of the chapter explores patterns of curriculum organization for the delivery of science education. It considers one of the most striking trends—that towards the integration of science teaching—in some detail. Other issues touched on include the inter-relationships with other subjects; the balance between the sciences in the curriculum; the time allocation thought appropriate; the conditions under which science is to be taught and which groups are to be taught science. The final part of the chapter describes options in tracking and streaming policy and reviews some of the evidence on their implications.

5. Examinations and Assessment

This chapter reviews common practices in national examining in science education. Some insights are offered into the balance of traits assessed and limitations of particular assessment instruments are noted. The content of science examinations is considered. The consequence of examination orientation are reviewed and some options are explored which might improve the quality and relevance of assessment procedures. Reflections are also offered on practical science examinations and continuous assessment strategies. Science examination data from Pupua New Guinea are used to illustrate a number of points.

6. Teaching and Learning in Science Education

The chapter explores research on teaching and learning in science education. Starting from reconsideration of the issue of educational purposes, which underlies any teaching strategy, it reviews evidence and insights derived from major research traditions including those of the Piagetian and constructivists. An attempt is made to accumulate some insights arising from work on effective teaching methods. As far as possible illustrations are taken from recent studies that relate to developing country teaching and learning environments. Separate sections address work on practical activity, the cultural contexts of teaching and learning in science education, and science education amongst disadvantaged groups which includes some work on gender.

7. Teacher Education

This chapter explores work on teacher education and training and provides some insights into the characteristics of science teachers. It then discusses observations on the control dimensions of science teacher education, addresses the literature on the pre-service training of teachers and concludes with some remarks relating to in-service training practices.

8. Concluding Remarks

This chapter brings together the main issues that emerge from the review and discusses their implications for educational planning.

A Note on Source Materials

This review was compiled using a wide range of bibliographic source material at the University of Sussex and the International Institute for Educational Planning, UNESCO. In addition many individuals in the science education community were consulted and helped to identify source materials.

Electronic data bases were searched for relevant material. Key word searches were completed on the UNESCO data base and on the DIALOG system. The latter accesses the British

Education Index, the Educational Resources Information Centre (ERIC) database of the USA Department of Education and the Social Science database SCI SEARCH of the Institute for Scientific Information. In addition, the Commonwealth Agricultural Bureau's rural education and training abstracts were searched, and entries on science education in the Pergamon International Encyclopaedia of Education were reviewed.

The major science education journals were viewed to identify relevant material. These included the:

1. British Journal of Educational Psychology
2. British Journal of Teacher Education
3. Compensative Education
4. Comparative Education Review
5. Compare
6. Development and Change
7. Education for Development
8. European Journal of Science Education
9. Harvard Education Review Journal of Cross-cultural Psychology
10. International Journal of Education and Development
11. International Journal of Science Education
12. International Review of Education
13. Journal of Biological Education
14. Journal of Curriculum Studies
15. Journal of Research in Science Teaching
16. Prospects, UNESCO
17. Review of Educational Research
18. Science Education
19. School Science Review
20. Studies in Science Education

Some material was identified in regional and national publications from the:

1. African Curriculum Organization Publications
2. Australian Science Teachers' Journal
3. Bulletin of the UNESCO Regional Office for East Asia and the Pacific
4. Canadian and International Education
5. Caribbean Journal of Education
6. Journal of Education for Teaching
7. Journal of the Ghana Association of Science Teachers
9. Kenyan Journal of Education
10. Papua New Guinea Journal of Education
11. Singapore Journal of Education
12. South Pacific Journal of Teacher Education
13. West African Journal of Education
14. Zimbabwe Journal of Teacher Education

In addition the various publications and unpublished reports of a number of bilateral and multilateral agencies were examined for relevant material including those by the:

1. British Council
2. Commonwealth Secretariat
3. Deutsche Stiftung für International Entwichlung, Bonn
4. Institute of Development Studies, at the University of Sussex
5. International Association of Science Education
6. International Development Research Centre, Ottawa
7. Overseas Development Administration of the British Government
8. Science Policy Research Unit at the University of Sussex
9. United Nations Educational, Scientific and Cultural Organization
10. World Bank

REFERENCE

1. Developing countries is used throughout this book as a general category for non-industrialized countries with low to mid-range incomes per capita. There is no assumption that such countries are economically, politically or socially improvised, or that the grouping has homogeneity sufficient to allow indiscriminate global generalizations.

1

The Context of Science Education Development in Developing Countries

1. Summary

This chapter discusses the context of science education development in developing countries. A background section introduces past trends and is followed by a commentary on images of science education which illustrates some of the basic assumptions on which perspectives on science education are based. The development of science education is then considered in more detail in the period since the 1960s. The current climate in which new developments will take place is then outlined and the final section illustrates emergent trends distilled from the literature.

The chapter addresses five main questions:

1. What are the important structural features that condition the development of science education?
2. What are the images that influence the perception of science education in developing countries?
3. What has been the recent historical experience of the development and implementation of new science curricula?
4. What are the most salient features of the current climate for further improvements in access and quality?

5. Which trends have become established and are likely to influence future development?

2. Background

Rapid expansion in school enrolments since the 1960s is a characteristic of the great majority of developing countries. In most the rates of growth have been higher at secondary level, where most science is taught, than at primary. Enrolment growth has been driven both by planned expansion for human resource development and by the exigencies of social demand for greater access to school systems. Science education has occupied a prominent position in the expansion process influenced by aspirations to industrialise, to localise expatriate cadres, and to take more control of production technologies.

In the first instance much expansion built on existing science syllabuses or weakly modified them to remove some of the more obvious distortions inherited from the past with the simple ambition of extending these largely unaltered to greater and greater numbers of students. Little of what would now be called science curriculum development was in evidence in most developing countries during the 1960s. The processes through which science curriculum innovations have spread across the developing world subsequently have been well documented, for example by Baez (1976), Haggis and Adey (1979), Wilson, (1981), and Lockard (1977), Wallberg (1991). These paint a rich picture of how approaches to teaching and learning, materials development and the aims and purposes of science education were exported, transposed and modified as they matured. The special issue of Studies in Science Education (No. 17, 1989), edited by King, also provides a recent overview of contemporary thinking on key issues in science education development in developing countries.

In those countries with a colonial experience that penetrated the fabric of their education systems deeply, science educational practice shadowed that in industrialized countries. Syllabi were borrowed, or perhaps more accurately lent (Little 1990), with the little more than cursory attention to local conditions. They closely resembled those to be found in the more conservative parts of the education systems of the ex-colonial power. Thus in the case of British ex-colonies throughout the world there are many examples of mildly modified General Certificate of Education (G.C.E.) type science rubrics for secondary schools current in the United Kingdom in the 1960s, and even those derived from the School Certificate which preceded G.C.E.

Commonly these courses were assessed by overseas examining boards bound to anglo-centric orthodoxies of content selection and was a relatively difficult object, which often had a substantially lower pass rates than other subjects. Partly as a result it is common to find, in those education systems where standardization and norm-referencing is not used across subjects, that there is a hierarchy of difficulty with foreign languages and mathematics as the most difficult subjects to pass, with science subjects following close behind.

3. Images of Science Education

Science at secondary level in most education systems was generally taught to selected groups of secondary age students both because of the limited resources available and because of the prevalent beliefs that suggested that only relatively small proportions of the school population with a special aptitude for science could benefit. The science programmes were predominantly academic, descriptive, knowledge based and inspired by 'grammar school' traditions. They were introduced by colonial elites who wished to ensure that their children would have access to higher education in the United Kingdom or in other industrialized countries. The extent to which the children of nationals had access to the schools that taught science varied considerably from country to country, with more of less segregation of access depending on the national politics. Primary provision rarely included any science education beyond that associated with nature study.

Alongside the high cost institutions which typically used European languages as the medium of instruction and which represented the apex of many of these systems, vernacular schools were often allowed to develop. Frequently these had support from missionary societies and other non-government agencies. Depending on the country and the culture, formal and non-formal learning systems often co-existed and pre-dated the introduction of colonial school systems. In some of these science occupied a place in the curriculum, but this was the exception rather than the rule.

All this is well known (Lewin, 1985, 1991). Its significance is that in the majority of developing countries it was the curricula and the school practices of elite institutions that provided the basis for post-independence growth. Not only did these schools present models of high status educational practice—in the case of science education the fully equipped science laboratory, the prestige attached to studying pure science removed from its application, the denigration of practical subjects which involved the design of useful objects—but also they were often the ones in which the generation of post independence leaders had their formative educational experiences.

Moreover, unlike in most industrialized countries, there were few if any alternative images of science education to act as models. In the United Kingdom there was a long history of the development of science education. Admittedly this was also dominated by grammar and public school traditions that developed during the nineteenth century and reached maturity in the tripartite system established by the 1944 Education Act. This, amongst other things, enshrined the view that there were three types of student :

> " *pupils interested in learning for its own sake, able to reason abstractly, to appreciate elegance and culture"... "boys whose interests lie in the applied fields of science and art" who have "an uncanny insight into the intricacies of mechanisms"* (girls were not mentioned!) ...and pupils who could *"only deal with concrete things, needed immediate gratification and were interested in things as they are and the realm of facts"*. (Board of Education, 1943)

Hence the development, widely reflected in other countries, of academic, technical/vocational and general secondary schools. In the United Kingdom however, unlike in many developing countries, there were established traditions which acted as a counterpoint to over emphasis on academic science, albeit with different levels of success in different periods. Technological and engineering oriented science education, as well as the tradition of general science provision for the non-specialized students were a nineteenth century legacy. The experience of putting science to work in the 1939-5 war and in the cause of industrial development was deeply noted—not perhaps as much as in the education systems of Germany or the USA but it was there. So also was embryonic concern for the environment and for the social implications of science. These had been given impetus by the invention of nuclear weapons which spawned populist movements and were precursors to the growth of ecology and environmental concern groups which offered a counter balance to technocratic views of the development of science.

In the 1960s most developing countries did not have a scientifically technologically competent cadre outside the minuscule numbers of nationals trained abroad and the expatriate experts who brought science almost as a 'cargo cult' with mystical properties that gave power over the environment and substantial salaries to those who possessed it. Science was an elite preserve of alien knowledge, the practical value of which was not close to the experience of most of the population. Though high educational achievement provided some access to this stage world of the rituals of science, these were narrow conduits with small openings. To understand some aspects of subsequent development, and the continued attachment to externally determined images of the science, it is necessary to asperities these aspects of historical experience. Though certainly different in detail in countries falling under the influence of different colonial powers, the imagery resonates across different systems.

4. The Development of Science Education

Towards the end of the 1960s, many ministries of education took the first steps towards taking a view of the curriculum which was broader than the redefinition of syllabus consisting of a list of topics. National curriculum units or centres began to be established, often with substantial external assistance in the form of buildings, equipment and staff. Inevitably expatriates staff carried with them current orthodoxies of science education as cultural as well as professional baggage. Those trained abroad also absorbed the fashionable wisdom of the times and transposed much of it into local science curriculum development programmes.

Many of the initiatives taken in science education had their inspiration in the explosion of curriculum development in industrialized countries in the 1960s. It is significant that in many countries systematic curriculum development initially concentrated on science education, along with perhaps mathematics and language since these were generally regarded as key subject areas. Thus, for example, one of the first national curriculum development centres was established in Sri Lanka in 1963 with a brief specially oriented towards the development of science education. Projects, programmes and institutions emerged to support by UNESCO and many bilateral donors. The African Primary Science Programme (APSP) developed and become the forerunner to the African Curriculum Organization (ACO); professional associations like the African Association for the Advancement of Science and Technology and the West African Association of Science Teachers (and their analogues in countries throughout Asia and Latin America) were formed and linked to existing international networks like the International Council of Associations of Science Education (ICASE). Many of these developments were influenced by aspirations to see to what extent new approaches to science teaching developed in industrialized countries could be adapted for use in developing countries. A comprehensive review of those supported by the British Council is provided in Chisman and Wilson (1989).

The 1970s saw the coming to fruition of many science education development projects. Large numbers of these were derivative in the sense that they were oriented towards the adoption, and as time passed, the adaptation of what was thought to be good practice in industrialized countries. Thus programmes which drew inspiration from curricula developed in industrialized countries ('Nuffield', PSSC, CHEM Study, BSCS etc.) began to appear throughout the developing world. As curriculum development institutions matured and became more self confident emphasis began to be placed on indigenising science curricula. This it was hoped would make science more accessible and relevant to national needs, would update antiquated material, and relate science education more closely to the needs of modernization and development. The reports of the Science Education Programme for Africa (SEPA) (e.g. Alabi, 1980) and of the International.

Clearing House on Science Mathematics Curriculum Development (Lockard, 1977) illustrate how widespread this activity was and how many projects had substantial international linkages of different forms.

To take one example, Scottish Integrated Science, a programme developed in Scotland in the 1960s, formed the basis for many junior science programmes in Commonwealth countries in West and Southern Africa, the Caribbean, and South East Asia (Chisman and Wilson, 1989). Frequently adaptation concentrated on modifying content without questioning very deeply aims, dominant views of the nature of scientific knowledge, and the prevalent conventional wisdom on teaching methods (Lewin 1981, Williams 1979). Some adaptation and localization took indirect forms—when, for example, programmes were adapted for use in one country and these adaptations were used as the basis for adaptation in a third country. Thus, in Swaziland five curricula were reviewed from other countries and a decision made to adapt the West Indies Science Curriculum Innovation project which itself had a relationship to Scottish Integrated Science (Slimming, 1979). Lee (1990) illustrates how in Malaysia curriculum reforms in science were the result of a complex interplay between international influences and the socio-political context of Malaysian educational development. Bilateral assistance to promote innovations developed in the United Kingdom coincided with local innovations developed in the United Kingdom coincided with local pressures to revise science curricula. She argues that the more countries become integrated into the global networks of information, economic relationship and socio-cultural trends the more likely they are to emulate the educational ideology of the industrialized countries.

Secondary curricula typically took the lions share of curriculum development effort. Much of higher education seemed largely untouched by the flurry of activity at lower levels. Primary curriculum development was almost universally the poor relation to secondary with relatively few examples of substantial projects with a science orientation. The explanation for this probably lies in two directions. First, where primary schooling has become widely available it is secondary school certificates that command access to modern sector jobs—it is at this level that competition is sharpest and demands for curricula improvement the greatest. Second, staff trained in curriculum development disproportionately tend to be drawn from the ranks of secondary teachers whose experience is with secondary level subjects.

Most attention was focused on the design of written materials for schools—textbooks and less frequently teacher's guides. Curriculum development activity related to in-service and pre-service teacher training generally came a poor second. Public examining and assessment systems have generally changed more slowly than curricula—often the localization of the examining system followed rather than preceded the institutionalization of curriculum development activity. Though the content of examination items changed, their style and quality often fell a long way short of comprehensively accessing key aspects of new science curricula. As a result 'backwash' from examinations characteristically undermined rather than reinforced fundamental changes in teaching and learning and the consequences of the 'diploma disease' were widely noted in curriculum implementation (Dore, 1976). By the end of the 1970s most countries had indigenized curriculum materials in schools and had locally designed programmes in widespread use. Several had already embarked on subsequent curriculum renewal cycles.

To bring this schematic story up-to-date is to grapple with the problems of describing heterogeneous circumstances concisely. The account so far has been selective—it has not touched on major influences that some countries have experience (e.g. that of Russian science on the development of science education in India and China) and it has not highlighted differences between the anglophone and francophone traditions. But it does provide an account that should resonate in a good number of developing countries. To bring this story up to date will probably commit similar sins of omission but here is an admittedly personal attempt.

5. The Current Climate

The last decade has provided evidence that development is possible and that developing countries will not always be 'running behind'. Several countries, mostly located around the Pacific rim sustained rates of economic growth far in excess of the mature industrialized countries. Much of their growth depended on their success in producing and marketing products with scientific and technological elements. Electronic products began to figure as more and more important in this process, accompanying the development of more traditional technology intensive products like motor cars. It may have been true that this process was initially supported by copying ideas developed elsewhere. It soon became clear that this was only part of the reason. In any case to argue this perjoratively sounded distinctly like sour grapes to those who studied the history of innovation and industrial development. Science education in the newly industrialising countries was in considerable demand and regarded as of higher status than other subjects.

There is another larger group of countries whose experience has not been so fortunate. In these countries sustained economic growth has been a frequently cited goal which has proved impossible to attain. The reality has been economic stagnation, increased rather than decreased economic dependence and, in a good number of cases, declining budgetary provision for education alongside growing demand. In these countries science education development has probably taken steps backward more often than forward. The resourcing problems are clear, especially in countries experiencing structural adjustment programmes. High population growth rates, and enrolments rising faster than national income have diluted per capita educational resources. Educational expenditures per child have declined to levels below that where anything resembling the science taught in richer countries is a reasonable expectation, except for a select minority. The economic circumstance of these countries have encouraged those who are qualified in science and technology to emigrate to greener pastures. Often public sector hiring practices have contributed to this by maintaining patterns of recruitment and reward that favour the non-scientific, administrative cadres. Why study science, the aspirant youth might ask, (assuming the opportunity is there) when it is more difficult, expensive, time consuming and culturally alien than arts and humanities subjects and it is qualifications in these that are likely to provide a smoother path to the higher reaches of the public service.

Alongside these changes in economic climate, experience with innovatory science programmes has introduced more realism into attempts at curriculum reform. Optimistic hopes that science educational practice could be transformed in a decade or so have proved far more difficult to realise in practice than they had been to conceptualise in theory. With perhaps a predictable sense of *deja vu,* critiques of the implementation of new science programmes introduced in developing countries began to illustrate how difficult it was to change established traditions. The emphasis in the new programmes was often designed to replace teacher centred pedagogy and the teaching of science as an accumulation of facts by more involvement of children in their learning, greater amounts of practical activity, less dependence on traditional textbooks, and more concern for the intellectual skills of scientific problem solving. It soon became clear that many of the necessary antecedent conditions for this were difficult to meet. New methods tended to assume well qualified, motivated teachers working with adequate resources who understood and internalized the new pedagogic techniques. Moreover they assumed that the enthusiasm for change was shared throughout the science teaching profession. This despite the fact that it was invariably difficult to demonstrate that the return on the effort necessary to adopt new practices was rapid in terms of gains in the most readily available indicator of success—examination results. It may have been that new approaches did offer better ways of reaching more comprehensive learning objectives in science education than those that they replaced. But generally patterns of assessment did not change sufficiently to reflect these new learning goals. Crucially, where expertise was in short supply and where the teachers' established role was as an authority within a subject area, open ended questioning approaches making use of discovery learning techniques placed teachers in new relationships with students that required deeper levels of knowledge and confidence in science than many possessed. These kinds of problems are widely documented. (See Lewin 1980; Adamu 1988; Maddock 1981; Yoloye and Bajah 1980).

The 1980s was a period of consolidation in science education in many industrialized countries. The initiatives that were taken built on, rather than tried to break with, the recent past. The most radical departures came with the growing momentum behind introducing more vocational elements into science education and linked school science more closely with the world of work and practical skills. Developments in the United Kingdom illustrate this with many such initiatives. The science education drama took on more of the quality of playing out the debates of the 1970's than of the dislocations of radical innovation. Research on science education during this period was heavily influenced by those studies that explored teaching and learning. These invoked Piagetian schema on the one hand to gain insights into childrens' conceptual understanding of science (Shayer and Adey 1981). On the other hand constructivist approaches stressed the centrality of the learner and their perceptions as a starting point (Driver 1983: Driver and Oldman 1986). Though this research undoubtedly impinged on the thinking of generations of teachers, its impact, at least initially, on the recently introduced United Kingdom national curriculum was small illustrating the power of the political interests over-riding curricula decision making by educationalists.

6. Some Emergent Trends

From the literature some trends in science education that seem most likely to impinge on developing countries in the 1990s can be discerned. These include:

- The tendency towards making science available to all secondary students will continue. This implies more integrated/combined/co-ordinated/modular approaches which balance content from the traditional disciplines.
- Teaching scientific skills and cognitive processes related to scientific problem solving and reducing emphasis on the recall of information will remain the curriculum development orthodoxy.
- Technology will form a new focus of interest in curriculum development complementing or even leading new science curricula with an emphasis on the skills needed to solve real life problems.
- Broader definitions of science education that absorb health education, nutrition, earth sciences etc. will

become more acceptable as will links other curriculum areas. Science and society, and environmental issues will appear more frequently in new curricula as their importance for the preservation of global equilibrium becomes more apparent. These initiatives may be linked to attempts to reduce apparent. These initiatives of global equilibrium becomes more apparent. These initiatives may be linked to attempts to reduce stereotyping of science (as 'masculine', 'foreign', and 'difficult') with a view to improving participation of disadvantaged groups.

- Science teacher training pre-career/in-service/on-service will be enhanced as the teacher is given more emphasis in the light of increasing demands made on the science teacher.
- Science will feature more prominently in the development of primary curricula.

There is a evidence for all these trends. They mirror those identified as early as 1979 in a review of integrated science education by Haggis and Adey (1979). They still cover most of the likely agendas for science education development and suggest that the pace of change has been much slower than anticipated. This indicates that the problems of implementing these ideas demand much more infrastructure and gestation time than has been forthcoming. It might also be concluded, at least in some cases, that the innovatory zeal of the science curriculum developers to change the way in which science is taught and how it is presented has not been so vigorously shared by all groups that have to collaborate in making ideas become a reality—gaps in perception and priority between the science education community and their ultimate clients—the parents, students, politicians and employers—have played their part in slowing down the rate at which changes have taken place.

Several other points emerge from the analysis of the context of science education in developing countries over the recent past. First, since this was a period of consolidation in science education the 'demonstration effects' (of new science course in industrialized countries which suggested that innovation was necessary in developed countries) were weaker than they had been in the 1960s. There was no radically 'new' philosophy or teaching methods to consider. And there were fewer science education development projects in industrialised countries which had natural spin-offs in terms of extension elsewhere. Those that developed were more clearly grounded in domestic concerns which were not seen to resonate so readily with problems in developing countries.

Secondly what was new, in terms of a new vocationalism at second level which stressed employment related and technological skills, was not new to many developing countries. Leaving aside the many colonial experiments in practically orientated and vocationaized schooling which were displaced into the shadows by the expansion of general secondary schooling, many countries embarked on diversified secondary school projects, curriculum development in pre-vocational studies and life skills and other related initiatives. The experience was already there of attempts to introduce a new vocationalism—it did not have to be borrowed or invented. So also was the appreciation of the difficulties of successfully implementing such policies. There were many pre-cursors of this concern to move science education form the realm of sterile facts into the world of action and towards more technological inclined emphases which were thought to increase relevance. Thus UNESCO (1976) noted:

> *"a shift towards greater stress on first hand experience by pupils and their active involvement in the learning process through enquiry and discovery, and on the application of science while incorporating elements of technology".*

Yoloye and Bajah (1980) note the post-independence emphasis in many African countries on ameliorating unemployment through introducing more vocationally relevant material into school curricula. Thus in Uganda science education was to be oriented towards 'job-makers' rather than 'job seekers'; many countries adopted the rhetoric of education for self reliance first promulgated in Tanzania (Mmari, 1977)—technological skill formation for national self-reliance became a live issue in Nigeria; science education for production and the development of socialist ideals caught the imagination of left leaning regimes (Adaya, 1982). A rash of projects were launched with the intention of increasing the relevance of science of the majority of pupils who experienced it.

Third, the participation of disadvantaged groups in science education has become a more important issue than in the past. The lower participation of some groups—girls, rural children, members of minorities—in science is both a concern from the point of view of equity and efficiency. Most education systems adhere to commitments to equality of opportunity though, in science, patterns of participation suggests these continue to be unevenly distributed. In countries which have a shortage of science trained human resources, low participation by disadvantaged groups implies under-utilization of a pool of talent that might ameliorate human resource bottlenecks [United Nations, 1979].

7. Female Participation

The problems of female participation illustrate this. The involvement of girls in science education, or rather the lack of it, has been a growing concern in book developed and developing countries. In the latter group, however, the problem is exacerbated by the under-representation of girls generally in enrolments, though the extent of the problem varied widely from country-to country. In sub-Saharan Africa from example the differential between male and female school enrolments is not pronounced at primary level, but is high at secondary level with girls only accounting for 34 per cent of total enrolments. This figure may be compared with 39 per cent in Asia and 50 per cent in Latin America [World Bank, 1988]. Although great progress has been made in increasing access of girls to secondary education, the trend in several African countries is not encouraging. As early as 1982 it was observed that there had been a decrease in female enrolment since independence in three former Portuguese colonies and stagnation in Benin, Burundi, Rwanda and Togo. [UNESCO, 1982]. Where schooling involves direct costs, and austerity has reduced disposable income, the probability is that family decisions to support children in school in many societies will favour continued enrolments of boys.

It is difficult to find global data on the participation of girls in scientific subjects, but there are many indications that enrolment ratios are often lower and dropout levels higher amongst girls. The magnitude of the problem may be illustrated by two examples from Africa: Eshiwani [1988], in a survey of secondary schools in Kenya, reveals that only 2 per cent of girls take physics and 3 per cent chemistry, although over 50 per cent take biology, and a similar picture emerges from Botswana where Duncan [1985] notes that girls are heavily under-represented in all three sciences, despite the fact that Botswana has one of the highest female school enrolments rates in Africa.

In a recent review of the literature on factors contributing to gender disparities Duncan (1989) identifies the following: the country's level of economic development, the availability, accessibility and type of school, cultural, norms and expectations concerning women's roles, socio-economic background and residence in urban areas, and family-related factors such as perceived marriage prospects and labour market opportunities. Dencan emphasis that none of these factors are simple, and many operate in different ways in different countries. Characteristically they result in lower levels of achievement of girls in science as well as participation. Despite numerous calls for improvements in science education for girls it is evident that education systems in many developing countries continue systematically to favour boys more than girls in education in general and in science in particular, the proceedings of the Gender and Science and Technology Conference (GASAT) from 1981 collect together papers on gender related issues in science education and illustrate both the progress that has been made and the magnitude of the problems that remain.

8. Constraints

Ogunniyi, (1986) has reviewed the nature of science education in Africa and identifies constraints such as rapid enrolment expansion, scarce resources, limited teacher quality and high dropouts as critical. His review of various primary and secondary curriculum innovations of the Science Education Programme for Africa illustrates this. Among the trends in science education he identifies are shift in emphasis from rote learning to inquiry activities and from teacher-centred approaches to student-centred approaches, more subject integration; more emphasis on problem-solving; increased student population and crash programmes for the training of science teachers; tertiary admission policies favouring science students; expansion in the teaching of primary science. Yet despite these efforts progress has been hampered by poor teacher preparation, rapid rate of teacher transfer, shortage of qualified science teachers, lack of a reinforcing home background and the 'conspicuous absence of an active involvement of the scientific community'. Ogunniyi is critical of poor planning and the absence of clear-cut policies and he attributes this to the lack of a scientific approach to planning. He calls for curricula which reflect contemporary and emergent needs of the diverse cultures of Africa; examination reform is needed to support the new emphasis on science as enquiry; more involvement of African scientists in science education; less esoteric tertiary science programmes. Major problems in science education therefore remain. The first international conference of the Forum for African Science Educators drew attention to the most important of these in 1982 (FASE 1982 quoted in Ogguniyi, 1986).

> *"We are aware of the goal of education to produce human beings who are self reliant ... We are aware of the failure in many ways of our current science education programmes to prepare (the drop-out), be it at the secondary school level or at the primary school level, for useful living ... we observe that most African governments have in no way positively supported and sustained action programmes to make science education more functional with a view to replacing or complementing academic preparation ... We recognize that our curricula are deficient of technology, and in particular appropriate technology, for the transformation of rural life. We recognise that our examination system is inadequate, to say the least, and yet its stranglehold on the educational system. We note with regret governments often times institute far-reaching changes in curricula or educational systems at relatively short notice and sometimes without cognizance of professional opinions ..."*

9. Conclusions

In summary from this review it can be concluded that the environment for science education development in many developing countries has changed in at least six ways:

(i) The external 'pull' exerted by science curriculum development in industrialized countries was less powerful as an influence on curriculum development in the 1980s than it was previously.

(ii) Localization of curriculum materials was no longer the highest priority; most countries have developed their own programmes.

(iii) The difficulties of implementing significant changes in teaching and learning in science have become apparent; there have been at least as many examples of failure, as measured against (over-optimistic?) expectations, than success.

(iv) National curriculum development in science has become instructionalized and bureaucratized in specialized units with defined responsibilities.

(v) Science and technology have developed rapidly and, in some countries, have penetrated the social and economic fabric deeply changing expectations of what science education should provide. In other countries, where economic development has been disappointing and austerity has resulted in low and declining resources for education, this process has been very slow. The prospects for improving science education in these circumstances may demand some radical re-appraisal of both goals and modes of delivery.

(vi) There is now greater awareness of disparities in access to opportunities to study science, especially amongst girls as opposed to boys, but also in relation to other apparently disadvantaged group (*e.g.* rural children, minority groups).

10. Implications for Planners

Several implications arise from the review for educational planning. At this stage four points should be noted.

- First, planning the development of science education in most developing countries is not the *tabula rasa* as some many have though it was two decades ago. Science education systems are widely well established, with expectations about goals, traditions of teaching and learning, and patterns of physical provision firmly entrenched. The planning problem starts with these as given and is a much a problem of the optimization of existing provision as it is the development of new forms.

- Second, as the next chapter makes clear, the developmental context for science education has changes as human resource demands evolve to reflect changes in production technologies and increased proportions of the labour force in modern sector jobs that benefit from the possession of some level of scientific literacy.
- Third, the difficulties in achieving and sustaining changes of the kinds promoted by first generation curriculum development suggest both that too many planners may have exaggerated the absorptive capacity of teachers and schools for new methods and materials, and that lack of clarity over goals has been an enduring source of problems.
- Fourth, relatively little attention has been focused on the planning of secondary science education as distinct from secondary provision in general. As a resoled the tendency has been to extrapolate existing practices (standards of laboratory provision, learning goals for different groups of students, training in separate science subjects) despite signs that such practices are unlikely to be inestimable or appropriate to new groups of students

2

National Science Policy and Science Education Aims

The first part of this chapter addresses the key issues in the relationship between policy on science education and national development strategies and considers the implications of changes in technology for future science education provision in developing countries. The second part of the chapter reviews the debate on aims and objectives in science education. This is accomplished first by exploring how aims and objectives are derived and by raising questions on the range of aims and objectives that emerge. Second a number of more specific issues are addressed concerned with the orientation of aims and objectives and the implications that steam from them.

The chapter addresses five main questions:

1. What is the framework within which national science policy is articulated with science education policy?
2. What are the implications of technological changes for science education?
3. Where do aims for science education originate—national policy? subject experts? the logic of science?
4. What are educational aims and objectives orientated towards? terminal or preparatory learning? knowledge or skills? values and attitudes?

5. How have science curriculum aims broadened to include more concern for social and environmental and technological concerns?

1. Science Policy and Development : The Dimensions of Choice

There are good reasons for devoting part of this review to a discussion of national science policy. This is because discussion of the forms science education should take has often ignored this or simply assumed its nature is unproblematic. Yet it is central to the debate. If science education is about the development of human resource and not simply other layer of screening withing the school system than it is critical to ascertain what macro policy perspectives frame decisions on its nature.

2. Technology Transfer

An earlier paper (Lewin 1989) explored some fundamental dimensions of the debate over national science and technology policies as they affect science education in developing countries. It is worth restating this analysis to develop this discussion here. Put simply there are two distinctly different views of the role of science and technology in development. First, there are the kind of analyses which see development as predominantly a problem of *technology transfer* from industrialized countries to those the little scientific capability. This tradition casts the problems of development in a repetitive form. Developing countries, the argument runs, can transform their economies by utilising science and technology developed elsewhere. This will enable them to follow in the footsteps of the successful exponents and acquire the *preconditions for sustained take-off* beloved by the neo-classical development economists of the 1960s (Rostow, 1960). The key to this process is to ensure that technology is transferred, not merely transplanted and that it is adapted to suit local conditions. The difficulties in achieving this centre around proprietary rights, the commercial value of process technology, the different value of factors of production in different environments, and the scarcity of qualified scientists and engineers. This perspective assumes goodwill and some measure of disinterest on the part of the owners of technology and the research and development that is associated with it—viable perhaps in relation to the practices of the leading producers. The optimistic vision has been that in these problems can be overcome the major remaining stumbling block lies in shortages of competent manpower. Suitable education and training in science and technology can rectify this. Technological dependence can then be replaced by technological co-operation that vest some measure of control with the host country. But some authors (Alatas, 1977) stress the difficulty of achieving this:

> *"Technological transfer is hazardous unless there is a truly creative intellectual spirit like that which gave rise to the technology in the first place. Without it such an enterprise will be imitative, cost ineffective, desecrate and disjoined".*

3. Appropriate Science and Technology

An alternative perspective of the role of the science and technology in development, which gained considerable currency in the 1970s, is to stress the qualitative differences in the development of indigenous and appropriate science and technology that cannot come about simply through technology transfer no matter how efficient (Howes, 1979). Proponents of this view stress that the research and development efforts of developed countries are often simply irrelevant to the needs of rural populations where even the simplest technology cannot be maintained and capital is much scarcer than labour. They point to the tardiness and under-funding of research on tropical agricultural as one of many examples of how the development priorities of rich countries have shaped the impact of science and technology on developing countries. Much of the research that has been applied, they argue, is directed towards improving the production of cash crops for export, not meeting the needs of the local population. One of the most well known developments of this case is provided by Schumacher (1973) and his work has spawned a respected development agency (the Intermediate Technology Development Group) and a considerable literature (Carr, 1976; Jequier, 1979). The provision of sufficient competent manpower is also a central problem in this approach. The need is seen to be for those who can create and radically adapt scientific and technological knowledge for domestic application, not simply transfer it. They can then contribute to scientific and technological development domestically and internationally.

Thus, for example, Goonetilleke (1989) attempts to show that there is a reservoir of unexploited ideas relevant to recent developments in such fields as artificial intelligence in developing countries that is often overlooked in the haste of conducting research and development in metropolitan countries. In this alternative view of development technological dependency can be replaced by a judicious mix of appropriate and indigenously developed science and technology which is grounded directly in the needs of the populations it serves and has value beyond it.

"The world is never as simple as the common habit of constructing dichotomies suggests. Both views contain elements of truth and paint incomplete pictures. This is because the problems of development have both local and international dimensions and because science is in a sense universal. It seeks knowledge which is not bound by specific cultural contexts but the utility of its application (technology) is specific to context and need.

4. Policy and Resources

Strategies based on these different views demand an understanding of the room to manoeuvre that national economies have. Small countries with limited access to markets cannot hope to sustain a wide base of technological industries (Cooper, 1980). Even medium and large size countries are unlikely to have the resources to compete globally in most fields. The only strategy that is really viable is to identify affordable technologies where there is a comparative advantage (Stewart, 1979; Roemer, 1981; Seers, 1983; Hobday, 1985). The corollary of this is to emphasize the scientific and technological needs of the population as a whole first, and make special provision to support science and technology in carefully selected areas. For a good proportion of developing countries it will remain much cheaper to buy highly specialized training abroad than develop local facilities for which the demand will be limited and the costs high. The problem of ensuring that expensively trained staff do contribute the fruits of their knowledge to the national economy that sponsors them and do not simply brain-drain themselves away remains, but it is an illusion to believe that training in national institutions prevents this.

Policy on science and technology in most countries is the result of a complex interplay between competing and sometimes contradictory aspirations. Its derivation typically spans several ministries which will each have different perspectives on policy and its purposes *e.g.* industry, agriculture, labour, defence, education. The resolution of these in the political process will determine the extent to which science and technology initiatives are seen primarily as contributing to economic growth of the kind linked to the penetration of global markets for products with a significant science and technology component; as lessening dependence on imported technology and meeting needs to become more self sufficient; as improving the employment prospects of the workforce through increasing knowledge and skill levels; as promoting strong defence capabilities without reliance on imported military hardware; as enhancing the quality of life of the mass of the people through better understanding of their environment and how to make best use of it employing scientific understanding. Which of these is emphasized clearly has implications for the nature of science education that can contribute to such policy objectives.

5. Changing Technologies

The issues discussed above highlight choices that are available in the determination of science policy that sets the framework for science education. There is another important aspect to the policy debate. Science and technology have developed at an accelerating rate. This has consequences for the between the leading exponents of a technology and those that follow in the wake (Pavitt, 1980, OECD, 1983). Mature technologies change slowly with marginal increments in efficiency or quality. Patent protection is likely to have lapsed. Any differences in technical production efficiency are likely to be overshadowed by other factors—the organization of working practices, the cost of labour, access to markets etc. New technologies of production are the obverse to this—they represent order of magnitude improvements in productivity, are patent protected, secret, and competitively lethal to outdated producers. The greater the rate of changes of this kind the more likely the collapse of markets to technological monopolistic with the likelihood of a retreat into protectionism by industrialized countries (Cooper and Hoffman, 1981).

Innovation may also take place with new products as well as new processes., Profitability comes either from the lead years of new product marketing in the absence of competition, or in later incremental improvements in process technology. There have been attempts to analyse the world economy in ways which suggest the existence of 'long waves' related to concentrated bursts of new product innovation followed by movement into phases of mature growth characterized by process innovations driven by Schumpeterian entrepreneurs (Freeman, *et al* 1982). Some argue that the existence of these cycles of economic activity makes it more difficult for developing countries to keep up with the quantum leaps of change embodied in new products (Kaplinsky 1984). Others stress the opportunities that exist on the downswing for catching up using improvements in process technology (Ranis, 1984; Dore, 1984; Freeman, *et al* 1982).

The implications of this for planning science and technology education relate to willingness to carry the risks involved in new product development as opposed to the opportunities for process innovation. The kind of creative individuals educated in science who can conceive of new products and develop them to a marketable form may not be the same people as those who can systematically produce process innovations. To put it another way the kind of education and training that develops the insights that lead to new discoveries may not be consistent with that which promotes incremental improvements in existing technologies. The latter needs the ability to 'search and assimilate' (Dore, 1984) ideas to a greater extent than it may need novel research based on laboratory science proceeding from first principles. It may need flexible learning from a position of relative inferiority, holding in abeyance nationalist sentiments to devalue that which is 'not invented here' and the confidence of vision beyond "the role of humble technology consumers" (Savane, 1973)., More a spirit of *wakon yosai* (Japanese spirit with western ability) than one of dependent acceptance. The 'crippled minds' of Goonatilake (1982) need space to overcome intellectual subordination which may not only be served by the self respect that comes with original invention.

In the light of this framework of issues which influence science policy and development strategies it is now appropriate to consider how the aims and objectives of science education are selected and how they shape science education policy.

6. Sources of Aims and Objectives in Science Education

The aims and objectives given in different national systems have a variety of sources. One of the simplest ways of classifying these sources is in terms of the kind of analysis that produces them. Rowntree (1974) has developed a typology that distinguishes three characteristically different origins. These are:

(i) expectations about future needs in society:

(ii) analysis of the activities of subject matter specialists;

(iii) analysis of the structure of the subject matter itself.

The first mixes those that arise from the science policy debate at the national level with that reflect broader educational concerns with citizenship and broadly distributed scientific literacy. The second utilises a conventional view of educational practice that leans towards training and takes the activities that qualified scientist perform as the end in view. The third relies on epistemological and philosophical discourse to identify the inherent logic of a subject that requires certain selection of content, development of intellectual skills and sequencing of material. In so doing it draws on the work of Hrist and Peters (1970) and Phenix (1964) which argues the existence of "modes of enquiry" and "ways of knowing" that are thought to be embodied in different disciplines.

These different sources result in at least three different types of educational objectives—those concerned with life skills which are of general value to educated citizens (the ability to classify, the power to descriminate according to criteria); those which are methodologically defined (the processes of scientific enquiry, the skills of systematic observation, the design of experiments); and those defined by content objectives (specific content linked knowledge and skills characteristic of the discipline, *e.g.* taxonomic in biology, the periodic table in chemistry, Newton's laws of motion in physics).

Behind these mechanisms for defining educational objectives in science as in other subjects is a long list of questions that need to be answered before the process of establishing aims and objectives for particular programmes or grade levels can be operationalized. Since it is clearly impossible to try and examine how these competing perspectives have weighed in the formulation of educational goals in science in many different developing countries it is instructive here to consider selectively the debate on some key aspects of the debate on aims and objectives.

7. National Plans

First in relation to aims that derive from the national policy making process it does seem possible to identify some the national policy making process it does possible to identify some trends from the most obvious place in which these are stated—national plan documents. A study of 29 plans from 16 countries (Lewin, Little; Colclough, 1982) indicates how plans in the 1960s tended to locate educational aims related to science and technology very much in terms of manpower development rationalize. Typically the purpose of expanding provision was seen to lie in the creation of more graduate level scientists and technologists. It is only in the later plans relating to the 1970s and early 1980s that the rationalise shift to include a broader range of purposes which encompass social as well as economic goals. More commonly in later plans science education is argued to serve needs to redistribute employment opportunities and reduce educational disparities that have consequences for different social groups; in some countries female participation becomes an issue and this is often particularly located in science and mathematics subject areas; nation-building arguments also are used more frequently to justify investment in science education to strengthen local institutions and reduce dependence on imported expertise and technology; and within the economic rationalise used science and technology education are broadened to include rurally relevant science, less academic orientation and more concern, at least in principle, for extending scientific literacy to larger proportions of the population.

8. Subject Matter Specialists

Second, concerning those aims that derive from the activities of subject matter specialist the key question for science education in developing countries is which specialists? These problem has at least three dimensions. The first issue is whether the scientists that are taken as role models are those to be found in the research laboratories of institutions in the countries of the North working within a highly specialized, resource intensive environment and occupying themselves with the pursuit of fundamental insights into the nature of physical reality. Even this image is misleading as it is well established that most qualified scientists and engineers in the North do not have such jobs (see for example Ellis, 1969). More frequently they are to be found in posts which require technical expertise but where the nature of the job is fairly routine and removed from the image that 'pure' science has established for itself. They are more often the puzzle solvers of Kuhn's 'normal science' than the paradigm breaking geniuses of 'revolutionary science' (Kuhn, 1970). Routine problem solving is a much more common activity than fundamental reconsideration of basic principles most of which are taken for granted most of the time.

The second aspect of this issue is that even if subject specialists can be identified in what do they specialise? The dominant specialities familiar to school science (Physics, Chemistry, Botany, Zoology) are themselves early twentieth century artefacts which came to replace the traditions of natural philosophy of the early nineteenth century and before where science was more commonly studied as a whole. These distinctions have begun to look even more arbitrary as science divided and sub-divided into more and more specializations, some of which have begun to impinge on curriculum reality in schools. Environmental science after a false start in the 1960s is now re-entering the curriculum in many countries; earth science is rationalized as linking with the 'other' sciences and integrating geographical knowledge into science; hybrid subjects—bio-chemistry, bio-physics, bio-technology are increasingly at the centre of the development of new products which have direct consequences for development strategies. Which kind of scientist should be emulated if the main purpose is to prepare learners for careers in those fields? And if universities, which in most countries act to legitimate and define the nature of school subjects, are encumbered by colonial legacies of subject compartmentalization, what prospect is there of yielding genuine status to science education defined in ways other than the traditional three sciences. The strategy of 'counter-penetration' advocated by Masrui (1975) depends for its success on the development of a capacity to innovate independently which in itself requires the courage to challenge the existing structure of academic knowledge.

The final dimension of this problem is that the idea of subject specialization presuppose that the 'realms of meaning' and 'modes of enquiry' really are separately distinguishable. As we shall see in the discussion of curriculum issues below this looks less and less compelling as an argument the more science is defined as a learning activity which results in process skills and enquiry strategies rather than content based knowledge.

9. Subject Logic

Aims that are based on the 'logic of the subject' are familiar to science teachers world-wide. Basic understanding of the laws of motion is a pre-requisite for more advanced consideration of the motion of projectiles or the importance of momentum; the periodic table allows order to be put into the properties of elements and compounds; taxonomic classification is necessary to explore theories of evolution. But there are many aspects of science that do not require the same kind of cumulative and sequential study that may be logically essential in some branches of mathematics. Some content selection and the order of its teaching is relatively arbitrary—optics does not have to be taught before or after thermo-dynamics except where the two inter-relate. It does not have to be taught at all—choices have to be made to include and exclude content on the basis partly of what serves overall learning aims best. Indeed optics, as traditionally taught with a strong dose of geometric optics has increasingly fallen out of favour as a school level topic as other fields have been considered more important—*e.g.* electronics. There has been little debate that geometric optics provided something of educational value for science that could be achieved through other routes.

10. Consensus

Another aspect of the debate of aims and objectives for science education addresses the question 'whose aims'. The problem here is evident and not easily resolved. Each group with an interest in science education will have different perspectives on purpose linked to particular interests. This is not to suppose that consensus is not possible, merely to remined the reader that the ease with which it is achieved is often greatly exaggerated. It is not a coincidence that Havelock and Huberman (1977) identify consensus as one of the three key elements in the determinants of success or failure in implements educational innovations. Their accounts of unsuccessfully implemented educational innovations also identify lack of understanding of project goals as an important factor in contributing to failure. This may conceal the real problem; namely that the goals are indeed understood but are not accepted and internalized by those with the responsibility for putting ideas into practice.

To unpack this problem a little it is worth elaborating on some likely conflicts of interest. Governments have frequently seen science education as a vehicle for human resource development to meet scarce manpower needs. If this is in their interest the science education aims that will be emphasized are those which seem to offer most prospect of providing predominantly high-level graduates with international comparable levels of qualification. Employers in the modern sector may share some of these concerns but often have at least as much interest in the basic skills that the bulk of the workforce bring to specific jobs that require some scientific skills and the ability to employ them in day-to-day production activities. Hence the complaints from employers in many countries about the inability of school leavers to perform basic tasks of measurement, observation, and use reasoning skills on-the-job. High-level scientific manpower can be bought, or licenses for technology acquired, often at marginal cost to the enterprise; the workforce cannot be substituted so easily.

Teachers and curriculum developers have other interests, not least their own professional identity which may cause them to emphasize aims which promote specialization and the status that accompanies it, and which emphasizes the intellectual and academic at the expense of the practical. Thus Adamu (1988) illustrates how aspects of the Nigerian science curriculum were ambitiously specified and often not fully operationalized in his study of science schools in Kano State. Parents and students will have the mixed motives that are associated with schooling everywhere; the aims for a good number will be to ensure success through study which leads to access to higher grades, the substance of the study being less important than reaching an acceptable level of achievement. For some, no doubt, what is learned will be of importance independent of its value for selection, but the pressures arising from restricted access to modern sector jobs where these are scarce, may make what is learned of secondary importance.

Despite these differences in interests it is worth noting that at one level, the importance attached of different content in the sciences, there does seem to be substantial convergence. At least in the 23 countries sampled by the IEA study (Postlethwaite and Wiley, 1991) it appears there was general consistency in ratings assigned to the importance of different content at different levels. Some content tended to have consistently high rating and other content consistently low ratings. Moreover, they argue, that since ratings tend to increase from level to level content treated at one level is generally treated more intensively at the level above suggesting to them that 'concyclic' patterns existed across countries.

11. Orientation of Science Education

The range of aims and objectives given for secondary science programmes in different in systems is vast, as might be expected. The reports of the International Clearing House on Science and Mathematics Education (*e.g.* Lockard, 1977) list project objectives for hundreds of projects which cover as wide a spectrum as can be imagined. At the most general level themes recur about which there is a certain universality. Typically science course at the lower secondary level will include knowledge of basic scientific facts and some ability to apply them, the development of basic measurement and observation skills, some practice of the psychomotor skills involved in conducting experiments, and affective objectives designed to encourage positive attitudes to science. At the upper secondary level in addition to these there are more likely to be objectives which seek to develop theoretical understanding and formal reasoning skills, the ability to utilize physical and mathematical models, facility with experimental design and data interpretation. The content intensity of programmes also typically increases in the higher grades with more material being included.

The situation is made even more complex by the fact that the same aims can be achieved, at least in principle, through many different routes. Thus curricula which share educational aims in large part may differ considerably in how they are presented and taught. Though Swaziland Integrated Science utilises the bulk of the aims for the West Indian Science Curriculum (which was itself adapted from Scottish Integrated Science) there is considerable deviation in the materials produced (Williams, 1977). Malaysian upper secondary science materials developed in the 1970s shared many common goals with those of Nuffield programmes in the United Kingdom but the form of the materials that were developed differed considerably form the Nuffield courses.

A comparative review of aims and objectives across countries is beyond the scope of this chapter. We confine out attention to the issues raised by different emphasis on different types of aims and objectives. The main dimensions chosen for this discussion are identified in the introductory paragraph.

12. Terminal or Preparatory?

Science education programmes at secondary level can be roughly classified into those intended for selected groups who will continue to study science to higher levels, those for whom science as thought to be an essential part of a general education but whose experience of science will terminate at or before the school leaving age, and those which attempt to satisfy the needs of both groups simultaneously. In making this classification we should not forget that a good number of education system allows secondary children to give up the study of science at an early stage in favour of other subjects. In order systems although science appears on the curriculum throughout the secondary years, the form it takes limits in practice the nature of the experience for many students to minimal levels.

The dilemma in orientating science education to the needs of different groups of students is a fairly universal problem in planning science education and it mirrors a broader problem of the conflicts between early specialization with concentration of a limited range of subjects and broad based general education that exposes all children to a balanced diet of educational experience. This has been problematic in most countries whether industrialized or not. Thus it was an issue in the development of Science for Every Student in Canada (see discussion Layton, 1986) as it was when integrated science was being introduced into Malaysia (Lewin, 1981).

The most common patterns are for introductory science to be taught to all children in lower secondary programmes without strong differentiation between those who will not (UNESCO, 1986). This usually involves treating science as a whole and attempting to develop the same range of basic skills and knowledge in all students through similar educational experiences. The main difficulties in this approach seem to arise from the pressures for selection that generally accompany that are associated with the study of science to higher levels.

Five factors can be identified that have often oriented lower secondary science programmes away from emphasizing their value to those who leave school and study no more science.

First, continuity in the curriculum creates pressure to see lower secondary science as preparatory for higher levels. 'Backwash' from the demands of higher levels of science study militates against the inclusion of material and learning goals which only have direct relevance to school leavers. Hence the inclusion of topics that prepare the ground for their subsequent study rather than topics related to the science aspects of common economic livelihoods.

Second, to incorporate much material which deals with the science of everyday things often has low status. The development of science historically was indeed often influenced by social and economic concerns, but the way this is understood often stresses the latest innovations and the concerns of 'rich country science' rather than those of pre-industrial societies.

Third, those involved in defining the subject are themselves successful products of science education in so far as they have become professionally qualified and oriented towards modern science and technology. They have an interest in maintaining its status and part of this process is to ensure that the modern science is promoted.

Forth, science is an important selection subject in most education systems. Conventionally educational selection based on academic knowledge has found more favour than that based on practical knowledge. This augers in favour of the abstract and the mathematical treatments of science which are widely recognized as means of discriminating between pupils' abilities.

Fifth, the more relevant to the needs of school leavers science becomes the more it may be difficult to find within the existing cadre of teachers staff with experience, insight and expertize in the science aspects of traditional economic activities. Involving local practitioners in teaching is as widely canvassed solution to this problem but it may be resisted if it is seen to deprofessionalize teachers. Some forms of science knowledge that might be relevant also have an economic value that it is not in the interests of skill exemplars to share (*e.g.* the science of gem processing in Sri Lanka where family businesses have transmitted specialized knowledge from generation to generation and have no economic interest in extending access to such knowledge). Parents also may resist the idea that schools are places where students learn about the science of local production activities when parents have aspirations for their children which run beyond remaining in the same socio-economic environment.

Partly as a result it is rare to find lower secondary science programmes that are designed on the basis of any extensive exploration of the needs of school leavers for whom this experience of science education is terminal. Though there have been many attempts to do this the resulting programmes run into an enduring contradiction. If they are genuinely terminal and include the achievement of aims and objectives of most direct value to those who leave school, those who achieve most highly on them are least likely to become school leavers. For them emphasis on rural science, science for living and practical skills of direct economic value are of less importance than selection. For those whose futures lie in the direction of employment or self-employment their experience of science is that of the relatively low achiever.

There are curriculum alternatives that go some towards ameliorating the consequences of the contradiction outlined. Science basic skills can be taught to a wide range of students through examples which are locally based. Thus basic ideas in fluid dynamics can be illustrated using models of boats, kites and windmills rather than aeroplane wing surfaces; acceleration can be illustrated without using the experience of travelling in an elevator as a starting point. At a more sophisticated level of curriculum organization different pathways can be followed through curriculum materials that provide different learning experiences for students who progress at different rates and whose needs are different. Thus some curricula provide optional enrichment material available at the choice of the teacher depending on progress and local environment. But these require quite high levels of resourcing, organizational flexibility and teacher expertise.

If relevance and the orientation of science towards the needs of most students who leave school is a problem at the lower secondary level it can be even more so for upper secondary children. The extent to which it is, will depend partly on how many are selected to follow science at this level. The more restricted a group this is at the upper secondary level the more reasonable it is to define the curriculum in terms of the needs of those who will continue to higher levels since the majority are likely to continue if they have been highly selected.

Aims and objectives defined for upper secondary commonly assume that most if not all lower secondary science has been mastered. Unless selection is draconian this is unlikely to be a very secure assumption. There is a danger that 'cycles of cumulative ignorance' can develop where there will be many pupils selected who have achieved and internalized only a proportion of lower secondary learning objectives (Lewin 1985) As a consequence they may quickly drift out of touch with teaching at the next level since it starts from assumed knowledge and skills that are not possessed. The longer they attend the less they master of what is supposed to be mastered.

Upper secondary science education is also closer to university entrance examinations than the lower secondary school. Universities in most countries exert their own special influence on the science curriculum in most countries. As they represent the pinnacle of achievement for students, and reflect the ambitions of many parents for their children, their nature exerts strong effects on the science curriculum as intended, and the curriculum in action. And university entrance requirements, an university undergraduate courses, tend to have a direct relationship with international conventions on standards and content for different science subjects. This cap on the system favours conventional academic definitions of science rather than those relevant to school leavers below university entrance level.

No neat solution to the delemma posed between the needs of specialists and the general population has been identified yet this is a critical area—meeting the needs of the non-specialist majority are likely to be at least as significant as ensuring an adequate supply of graduate scientists. Commentators like Layton see the relationship between two types of outcome—trained specialists and a scientifically literate population—as inherently conflicting and not compatible pulling the curriculum in opposing directions. Fensham (1984) has argued for a three stage policy to resolve the tension and create a balanced science curriculum which can meet the conflicting demands. He argues first for containment, where elite, academic science is deliberately restricted to upper secondary grades for a selected proportion of population most of whom will study science to high levels. Below this containment level science should be taught to all students in an accessible way which is not over academicized. Second, because academic science is restricted to selected groups is needs to be intensive and it should not be placed in direct competition with 'second class' science for the rest of the student population. It should be clearly distinguished as science for those intending to pursue occupations with a scientific base. Third science should continue to be taught above the containment level to non-scientists in ways which provide clear differentiation from academic science curricula. They should not simply be watered down versions of academic science.

Though these suggestion do go someway towards a constructive response to the dilemma Fensham does not really address the problems of changing the preconceptions that are likely to block changes of this kind. Parity of esteem is an elusive chimera when academic science is an important selection subject. Containment will only offer assistance if boundaries are maintained and this may be difficult in many systems.

13. Knowledge or Skill Orientation?

The science eduction debate over the relative importance of aims and objectives that are more or less knowledge or skill oriented is long standing. Some aspects of it have already been touched on. The historical experience of the development of science as a school subject generally placed more emphasis on science as a body of knowledge with the 'scientific method' raised on a pedestal in the background as a mechanism to achieve such knowledge rather than as an end in itself. The development of many guided discovery, heuristic and pupil centred programmes which swept though the science education community in the 1960s shifted the emphasis at least at the level of intent away from a view of science based securely on facts to be learned towards one where the process of investigating the natural world was to be given pride of place. Science education was to develop thinkings skills that would provide learning which would endure beyond the usefulness of the discrete facts that enquiry might lead to.

The debate over knowledge or skills is often framed in terms of process *versus* content or concept based learning. The former stresses the view that students should acquire scientific attitudes and problem solving skills as a priority and that concepts and content have a second order importance. Scientific attitudes include scepticism, curiosity, open-mindedness, suspended judgement until evidence is available. Process skills include observation, interpretation of data, inference, testing of hypotheses, prediction, classification skills. This view of science learning values an inductive approach Harlen (1986) where students accumulate experience based on observation and analysis that leads them to generalizations that can be tested.

Concept and content based views of science argue that science is essentially a body of knowledge which consists of the insights scientists have discovered about the physical world. Thus science students should be required to internalize these concepts first through encounters with specific content and examples based on conventional sub-division of science knowledge—mechanics, acids and bases, photosynthesis. The emphasis is on the concepts not the means through which they were developed or can be understood. The underlying approach to learning here is deductive—generalizations, scientific laws, principles are to be learned first and than hopefully applied. Since secondary education in many countries has been heavily subject compartmentalized the latter view has been the dominant one. Most of the new science curricula of the 1960s and 1970s promoted process views in one form or another but they have not been as fast to take root in practice as they have been in principle amongst science educators.

The IEA's (Postlethwaith and Wiley, 1991) attempts to classify process skill objectives and analyse the emphasis placed on them in different national systems conclude that the emphasis on process skills increases at higher curriculum levels. Of the nine process objectives they consider observation, measurement, problem solving, and interpretation of evidence have the greatest emphasis. Generalization and model building the least. The limitations of science, and the applications of science were also not weighted as emphasized much, the latter perhaps surprisingly so given increased concern for the technological dimensions of science education. They note that some countries in their sample had not considered process aspects of their curricula and therefore did not respond.

Content does influence the use of process skills. A well known example of this occurs when students use microscopes to draw biological materials. What students 'see' and draw is very much dependent on the cues provided by teachers as to what they are supposed to see. If you are told two contrasting lines represent a cell wall then that is what you will label the image—but what is inside and what is outside? Might they be holes? And in the classic Brownian motion experiment particles are identified that move under the random impact of air molecules—but that tends not to be the observation made by students when looking at this experiment unprompted—it is only when attention is drawn to this effect that it becomes apparent to most. For others the swirling of bright specks is as important, the drifting of particles in a similar direction, and the colours and changing contrast may be as noticeable.

More programmes are developing as reconciliation or balance between process and concept or content based approaches, and are by implication seeking to resolve the crude polarity between skills and knowledge. Scientific skills have come to occupy a central place in the rhetoric of science curriculum development. Most recently increasing emphasis on technological aspects of science has heightened this trend though some would argue that this is balanced by emphasis on 'back to basics' that is to be found in some countries. It is important to separate the aspirations of governments and politicians and curriculum developers, from what actually happens in the science curriculum. It is important also to understand the conservatism of many science educators who see their first loyalty as to their subject and whose career interests canonised with maintaining the integrity of separate science subjects. The boundary maintenance required to differentiate physics from chemistry and form biology generally emphasizes content based differences rather than those related to the science skills involved.

There is another dimension to the debate over aims and purposes which is germane to the questions of knowledge and skills. Increased emphasis on the technological aspects of science education necessarily leads curricula to greater concern for skills, both intellectual and psychomotor as well as perhaps aesthetic. Technology defined in terms of the processes through which needs are identified, solutions to problems designed and artefacts created to produce durable responses to needs, essentially couples the skills of doing with those of conceptualising. Few would accord 'technological facts' with comparable status as 'scientific facts'. Practical work orientated to functional devices—and hence skill which applied and psychomotor as well as intellectual—has been of low status in much science education for the historical reasons explored earlier in this review.

From this discussion we can conclude that the division between content and process perspectives is to some extent exaggerated. Science learning that consists of the accumulation of isolated scientific facts is unlikely to lead to any durable internalization of science constructs. Without procedures to select and employ relevant knowledge and adapt it to new situations the knowledge itself has little value. Simply rote learning the periodic table without a deeper understanding of its significance for the properties of elements has no particular virtue. Similarly, process skills cannot be taught in a vacuum. Problems have to be meaningful and directed towards real problem, if problem solving skills are to be applied to them. But there certainly remains a question of balance between the approach and it is widely argued that too much of what passes as science education in practice is dominated by the acquisition of facts that are not coherently related to conceptual frameworks—consequently this learning proves fragile once the immediate need for it is taken away.

14. Values and Attitudes Orientation

Any review of secondary science programmes introduced over the last two decades will show increasing emphasis on aims and objectives related to values and attitude changes. There are several reasons for this. First, the view that science as a school subject is somehow value free has become unfashionable. This of course follows on from the more academic discussion amongst philosophers and historians of science concerning the ways in which values enter into the activities of scientists (Jevons, 1973; Ravetz, 1971). Though there are aspects of science that appear universal in terms of understandings of the natural world—the kinetic theory of gases as useful in predicting the behaviour of gases in the United Kingdom as it is in Zimbawe—science does have values embedded in it and scientists as human beings have values. The things which are identified as of interest to science are partly culturally determined as the history of science shows very clearly; the uses to which science is put are very much influenced by the values of scientists and others. In the areas where science interacts with politics and religion values emerge as important.

Second, it has been increasingly recognized that the motivations and interests children bring to science education and develop through studying it are important in the extent to which they achieve in the subject. Head (1985) explores this in depth arguing that students subjects choices are heavily influenced by social psychological factors bound up with the development of self identify during adolescence. He also reviews the literature on the images that students have of science and scientists. This displays strong stereotyping which attributes scientists with having to work long hours, being competitive at work, not being very sociable and having a conservative life-style—attributes that may not appeal to many adolescents in the United Kingdom. Entwistle and Wilson (1977) found that successful science students at university were more syllabus bound, more conservative and less neurotic than students from the humanities and the social sciences. Personality factors do seen important in attracting students to, or alienating them from, science. Some have seen this understanding as creating opportunities to make science more appealing to students by changing its presentation to take advantage of aspects that are attractive to particular groups. This has been a theme in the literature on girls participation in science some of which makes suggestions as to how to make the teaching of the subject more 'girl friendly' (Kelly, 1981). Duncan's study of gender-typing in Botswana [1989] found that school science was perceived as a masculine subject and that gender typing is considerably more salient in the achievement process for girls than for boys, through its influence on attitude to school subjects. Her study also found that girls who favour a divided family role and have a feminine self-image are more inclined to see science as a male area of activity and have less positive attitudes towards school science. Lin and Crawley (1987) studied attitude differences in relation to gender, ability group and school socio-geographic location among rural and urban junior high school students in Taiwan. It this case perception of learning environment was independent of gender or ability group. Students in metropolitan schools reported more positive attitudes towards science, but also reported highly competitive learning environments. Rural students were just as interested in careers in science as their metropolitan counterparts.

Third, science is seen in many curricula as a subject which can promote rational analysis and inductive and deductive reasoning. It represents par excellence a field of study in which evidence can be collected and interpreted according to explicit principles. To encourage this is to place a value on the development of these skills in the population—and by the implication to subscribe to some of the ideas of modernization theory (Inkeles and Smith, 1974). These stress the importance of changing individuals values in traditional societies from the parochial, the egocentric, and the concrete to those which involve seeing other points of view, which are universalistic, and are abstract and not bound by the experience of the present.

Fourth, although many programmes introduce effective elements into the objectives for science programmes few articulate this in ways that assist classroom teachers in converting these general aims into specific learning experience. The danger is obvious—that the congnitive aspects of learning science take precedence on a day to day basis and that the cumulative development of attitudes relevant to science is ignored or down graded. It is important here to distinguish between those values that might be thought directly part of science—*e.g.* scepticism, curiosity, open-mindedess, critical scrutiny of evidence; and those that might be promoted through the teaching of science but which also have a more general character—honesty, respect for others, tolerance.

Important problems in relation to values and attitudes seem to circulate around two themes in a particular. For number of commentators 'western science' carries with it embedded value assumptions that are culturally bound. These values are thought to inter-relate with social and economic aspects of development and thus carry implications for what science should be taught and how. 'Western science' is variously categorized as being concerned with the problems of rich countries, fundamental science rather than that with direct utility, 'big' science not 'small' science. The implications of this need careful consideration in any development activity based on the adaptation of materials from one country to another.

In addition many studies in developed countries seem to show that children's attitudes towards science deteriorate as they move through school to higher grades—and circumstantial evidence suggests this may well be the case in many developing countries. Thus in the United Kingdom physics and chemistry show steep declines in popularity from grades 9 to 11 (Whitfield, 1979). Biology increases marginally in popularity as a result of increased interest amongst girls. This mirrors similar findings on attitudes to school which also show deterioration. This also seems to be a particular problem for girls (whose attitudes to physics and chemistry are much less favourable than boys in the United Kingdom). Insofar as children antagonistic to science will not be motivated to study it, this creates a problem for science education. The more values are seen as a cross curricula concern and the product of experience in different subjects the greater challenge is to explore how discussion of values may be introduced into science education and how substantial a dimension of the curriculum engagement with value issues should be.

15. The Broadening of the Science Curriculum

The final aspect of this discussion of aims and objectives of science education concerns the broadening of the curriculum. Many countries have embarked on programmes to provide a more balanced diet of science to secondary school students. This has several elements and is reflected in at least three types of development. These are concerned with movement towards broad balanced science; the inclusion of science and society issues and the incorporation of environmental perspectives; and the introduction of technology into the curriculum.

First, complementary to the adoption of more subject integration already noted, there has been a general movement towards seeing science as a whole and giving more equal emphasis to its component parts. Historically a good number of systems have emphasized the physical sciences at secondary level and given less emphasis to the life sciences. With the increasing importance of developments in bio-technology and the growth of agribusiness the case for redressing this balance has been strengthened. In those countries where choice between subjects is permitted it has generally been the case that biology has been preferred by girls and boys have opted for the physical sciences. The consensus in the science education community has moved towards considering this pattern unbalanced. The 'science for all' movement has embraced the idea of broad and banished science, as have many developments of national curricula (*e.g.* in the United Kingdom). 'Science for all' has formed part of basic policy in science education in a number of developing countries [see e.g. Goswami 1984 (India) and Deutrom and Wilson 1986

(Papua New Guinea)] and is generally associated with the idea of balanced science. So also are programmes which stress 'scientific literacy.'

Second, it has been increasingly common to find science and society material appearing in secondary science curricula. This has been an accelerating trend though it has proved unpopular with some science teachers and policy-makers who have taken the view that this dilutes the science that is taught. Several reasons for this seem influential. The work on attitudes has suggested that environmental concerns were popular amongst children and introducing more of this material has been used as a device to attract more students to study science. Growing public concern with environmental issues has played a part as public participation in the debate over these has grown in a number of countries (*e.g.* Ziman, 1980). Attempts to increase the relevance of school science to students, especially those who leave school during or after secondary education, have also led in the direction of including more of this kind of content. The Discussion of Issues in School Science Project (DISS) based at Oxford has been running for two years in the United Kingdom and is one example of the many programmes designed to contribute to increasing the public understanding of science which have been introduced in many countries. In a number of developing countries presaging environmental problems (erosion, deforestation, desertification, etc.) have resulted in the inclusion of environmental science in the curriculum (e.g. Environmental and Agricultural Science in Zimbabwe and Man and the Environment in Malaysia). Sawyerr (1985) has argued for increased environmental aspects to the science curriculum in Sierra Leone. Ahmed (1979) also argues that in developing countries the social objectives of education must take precedence over those concerning the development of the individual student. With respect to science education this means greater emphasis on environmentally-based integrated science. Knamiller (1984) suggests the development of issues-based biological education in schools can help bridge the gap between purely academic schooling and education for relevance.

Science and society issues, though much broader than environmental concerns, have increasingly penetrated new science curricula and most innovations now include material of this kind. The development of environmental education has also been stimulated by realization of global interdependence as issues like the depletion of the ozone layer become prominent. Thus a number of authors have argued like Knamiller (1981) that mutual interests between the industrialized North and the developing South are satisfied by extending the environment orientation of science. Concerns of more widespread scientific literacy have been repeatedly voiced (see *e.g.* Klopfer, 1985). This has been defined in terms of a basic understanding of science in order to make informed decisions in daily life and to function effectively as a citizen which can be subdivided into, (i) survival needs in a physical environment pervaded by science derived products, machines and devices; and (ii) the need to participate responsibly in formulating policy and making decisions concerning public issues having technological components which involve a basic understanding of science.

Third, and perhaps most significantly for the next decade, there has been a resurgence of interest in technology as a school subject. Sometimes this has been expressed in terms of technologizing the science curriculum, and sometimes it has been seen as a separate subject. This perspective has been stressed in several recent publications (Layton, 1978, British Council, 1990) and it seems to have a growing momentum. 'Privileging the practical' is one of the catch phrases used to encapsulate the thinking behind this. Many have argued the central importance of science with a technological dimension for development (e.g. Kumar, *et al* 1987). Technological skills take the process of problems solving from conceptualizing, through consideration of alternatives, the design of proto-typing and their testing, to the development of artefacts to meet needs identified. It is thus very much concerned with the tasks of putting of useful purpose the skills towards which many science education programmes are directed towards. In principle, it provides an answer to critics who see academic science education as a sterile theoretical exercise that develops arcane intellectual skills but does not result in useful skills of making and doing. Technological education is differentiated from the older practical subject traditions—woodwork, metalwork, etc.—since it encompasses a broader range of intellectual skills and is concerned with a wide spectrum of types of problem. It may approach textile design and production as readily as it addresses the problems of water pump design. And much of the knowledge and skills which underlie it are scientific in character—fair tests of performance of prototypes have to be developed; scientific knowledge of the properties of materials is important; physical and biological principles are likely to influence design. Technology also has an aesthetic dimension since good design also incorporates ideas of elegance, attractive and functional products, and aesthetics which widen the attractions of the subject to a larger group of students. It may therefore be a mechanism to encourage more students of acquire some science concepts. It is also consistent with increased integration between subjects and the need for this has been explored in a variety of curricula situations (Commonwealth Secretariat, 1985).

16. Implications for Planners

In short, the issue at the policy level is the development of a clear view of the role science and technology play in national development strategies so that implications for science educational policy can be identified. This was a qualitative dimension, as has been argued above, and is not simply a problem of getting the numbers right in filling available and anticipated occupational niches. New balances may need to be struck between emphasis on design and discovery, and maintenance and incremental improvement that reflect strategic choices in economic and educational policy for science education. Implications can be identified for the planning process in relation to science policy, the impact of austerity, and the definition of aims for science education.

17. Implications for Science Policy

From the above several issues for planners can be identified. These are concerned directly with national science policy and requires the identification of those aspects of policy that have direct implications for science education. These need to be analysed in terms of how these have been changing to reflect developments in labour markets, the technology of production in science based industries, and in the markets for the products of such industry. It may then be possible to arrive at some reconciliation between developing an indigenous science and technology base and maintaining efficient access to science and technology developed elsewhere.

Some dimensions of policy problem with every likelihood of being relevant are:

- *What are the basic assumptions of science and technology policy?*

  Is it directed towards establishing science based industry as a whole or in selected fields?

  Is innovation seem to flow from basic research or from borrowing and adapting ideas?

  How important is the design and control of new technology seen to be and how realistic are aspirations to achieve these things?

  How, if at all, are the developments of new technologies seen to affect policy and the needs for changes in the education and training systems for science and technology?

- *What is the policy orientation for science and technology?*

  Is it that of the 'leading edge consumer' which allows the use and adaptation of technology developed elsewhere; or is it an orientation towards new insights from fundamental research that will have spin off that will increase agricultural and industrial productivity?

  Is there any evidence from the recent past that the policy employed has resulted in developmental gains or losses? If so why?

- *How is overall policy on science and technology related to education and training policy?*

  Is it logically consistent?

  Have changes in the pattern of provision for science and technology education at school level been a result of strategic decisions or have they reflected other considerations unrelated to macro policy e.g. social demand for places?

18. Responding to Austerity

Many developing countries have suffered from the impact of global recession, especially in Africa. The general characteristics of this problem need no repetition her and are the subject of an earlier book (Lewin, 1987:a). Science and technology education at all levels tend to be amongst the most expensive curricula areas to resource. Many countries continue to suffer from a lack of scientific and technological personnel. Shortages at the highest levels of qualification are often matched and exceeded at intermediate levels and these may compromise the impact of expensively trained professional staff at graduate level on development problems. Even where the numbers of graduates stand in a satisfactory relationship to demand the quality of individuals' capabilities in science and technology is often considered a problem. The exigencies created by austerity require a reappraisal of priorities. This needs to explore whether conditions of budgetary stringency can be accommodated by new approaches to education and training in science and technology that would make better use of scarce resources and the pool of talent that exists within a given population. Possible options include:

- greater attention to equitable and efficient selection of those who may benefit most from science and technological education;
- assessing the feasibility and desirability of concentrating resources in well founded institutions when it is impossible to provide these for the whole student population;
- re-examining the structure of incentives that may make it difficult to attract and retain science students in employment related to their special skills;
- exploring reasons for aversion to the study of science (especially amongst females, rural students and other disadvantaged minorities) where this is a problem;
- establishing more efficient ways of developing science based skills in the education system and through job related training;

- ensuring that opportunities to acquire science based literacy and numeracy in the population as a whole are not over shadowed by the needs of the minority who acquire specific high level skills in science.

19. Reconsideration of the Aims for Science Education

The issues that arise for planning from the discussion on aims and objectives of science education can be summarized in terms of the need for:

- clear appraisal of the purposes of the science education curriculum; this need to specify what is to be achieved, by which group of students, for which purposes. Only then can choices be made between curriculum delivery strategies;
- recognition that aims and objectives may not be shared by all the participants in the science education process in equal measures; without a degree of consensus on these implementation will be problematic;
- there are different pay-offs involved in selecting different emphases on aims and objectives; different mixes may be appropriate for different groups though the over-riding trend is towards common specification for all students—at least at the lower secondary level;
- shifts towards integration, more recognition of the needs of those who leave school, the importance of attitudes and values, and the boarding of the science curriculum all carry resource implications that need careful consideration. These depend in part on pedagogical and epistemological questions about the nature of science and the nature of learning.

3

Factors Affecting Achievement in Science Education

This chapter reviews the literature on the achievements of students. It explores some of the methodological problems involved in school achievement studies, and reviews the various factors that have been advanced as explanations for variations in achievement and comments on their significance. The IEA Second International Science Study is discussed drawing attention to some of its findings in as much details as space allows. A concluding sections comments in particular on some aspects of gender differences.

The four main questions addressed in this chapter are:

1. What is the general background to attempts to identify the factors associated with school achievement?
2. What can be learned from recent school effectiveness studies?
3. Whigh findings from the IEA science study are of most interest to the issues raised in this review?
4. What insights can be gained from studies on gender disparities in science education in developing countries?

1. Background to Research Studies on Achievement

There are now a very large number of studies on the factors that affect school achievement. Most of the earliest examples of these were conducted in the USA and the United Kingdom and were initiated by concerns to understand why children from unfavourable soico-economic backgrounds failed to achieve comparable levels of performance to their more favoured peers. They were thus heavily influenced by sociological analytical traditions and borrowed varieties of production function analysis from economic theory to partial out the influence of different factors on a dependent in terms of some combination of test results (e.g. Coleman, *et al* 1966, Jancks, 1972). These studies were accompanied by a developing literature which offered a critique of the methods used and which also became entangled in the debates about nature and socio-economic background in the developments of intelligence, school achievement and subsequent success in the labour market (Bowles and Gintis, 1976, Little, 1975). Much of the concern was a explore to what extent meritocracies functioned as such and to what extent education achievement behaved as an intervening variable explaining why in these societies socio-economic status of children continued to be linked closely to parents' socio-economic status (Halsey, 1977). These studies tended to show that schools were less important determinants of scholastic success than home background factors. It was, however, misleading to draw the conclusion, as some popularises did, that this implied that not much of importance went on in schools. It was differences that were being studied not absolute effects— as a weary commentator observed "students don't imagine algebra". Neither do most of them idependently establish Newton's laws of motion.

Subsequently, studies have began to appear which extended the analysis offered to a whole host of in-school factors and these began to demonstrate that school effects were important (e.g. Rutter, *et al* 1973). The studies also began to be extended in significant numbers to developing countries where the initial results seemed to confirm that school effects were more important than had hitherto been anticipated (e.g. Heyneman; Loxley, 1983).

2. School Effectiveness Studies

Heyneman and Loxley's (1983) study of science achievement in 16 developing and 13 industrialized countries examined a range of school variables and regressed science achievement scores against them (obtained largely from IEA instruments). This study found relatively little variance explained by school factors in the industrialized countries but much larger amounts explained in the developed countries (27 per cent of the variance in achievement explained in the developed countries (27 per cent of the variance in achievement explained by school quality in Indian children and only 3 per cent by social class; 25 per cent by school quality in Thailand and only 6 per cent by social class). Note however that the total variance explained in the cases studied was typically around the 20-30 per cent level leaving much that was not explained. *A priori* findings that school effects are important might not be wholly unexpected in science since it is a subject which is removed from everyday experience and its systematic study is often only accessible through schools.

The very large literature that now exists on school effectiveness is difficult to summarise. More than 50 multivariate or experimental school effect studies now exist relating to developing countries. Fuller's (1987) comprehensive review identifies several studies which have used science achievement as the dependent variable (e.g. Heyneman and Loxley, 1983; Morales and Pinellsiles 1977; Arriagada 1983; Comber and Keeves 1973. However most school achievement studies use other subjects or a combination which includes science. We will consider the Second IEA Science study separately below.

The studies are methodologically diverse; vary in term of the specification of the dependent and independent variables, use a range of sampling techniques, and have been undertaken in very differently structured education systems. The problems involved in research on factors which effect school achievement are well known (see Fuller, 1987). They include problems with the cross-cultural transferability of notions like social class (even if this is portable, few studies grapple with the problems arising for comparability from the constrained range found in weakly differentiated societies where wealth and education are concentrated in small elites); the difficulties in specifying the dependent variable i.e. achievement (should the level of analysis be individual or school level? which type of test results are reliable and valid? how does this type of achievement reflect the full range of curriculum goals?); the realization that often large parts of the total variance remained unexplained after the effects of independent variables have been accounted for; and the rarity of studies that are capable of controlling for the entry characteristics of students. Not surprisingly a universally applicable set of conclusions does not emerge from this literature.

Synthetic reviews like Fuller's (1987) and that by Schiefelbein and Simmons (1981) have additional problems of aggregation that make it different to decide what importance to give to findings that appear true in some systems and not in others. What can we conclude from the 11 analyses cited of school expenditure and achievement, six of which confirm a positive relationship, and five do not?; or of Hanushek's review of more than 150 studies which concluded that there was no systematic relationship between expenditures and student achievement; attitudes and drop-out rates and reduced class sizes and more trained teachers were also unlikely to make much difference to achievement (Hanushek 1986)? Common sense suggests that, in the limiting cases (of close to zero, or at levels comparable with industrialized countries), level of expenditure must have some relationship to achievement; nevertheless it is unlikely to be a sufficient condition alone. And perhaps those studies that failed to demonstrate a link were in circumstances where systems were already well resourced and additional expenditure was at the margin. Laying behind these difficulties we note that in any case these were not parallel studies; many of the parameters varied simultaneously between them. One of the earlier studies (This and Carnoy 1973) conclude that there was no relationship between expenditure per pupil and achievement at primary level but such that they claimed raising national examination scores by 5 per cent would require a 50 per cent increase in expenditures per pupil. This serves to illustrate the limitations of this kind of analysis. There are many ways of increasing achievement and each will have a different cost structure. Simply redistributing existing resources towards at least favoured schools (which would have little or no direct cost) is likely to have a much bigger effect on those schools and little or no effect on those which already enjoy surpluses of qualified teachers, materials, etc. The incremental rate of return or investment to raise achievement in schools which have no books or facilities will be much greater than similar inputs in well-funded institutions.

Another example of the kinds of problems that arise from taking a macro view of school effectiveness studies can be illustrated by the well publicized literature on the effect of textbooks on school achievement. Fuller's review indicates that 16 out of 24 studies show positive effects of texts and reading materials on achievement—not perhaps as overwhelming a trend as might be expected from the fashionable wisdom on this subject. Again, though the general measure was textbooks/ students the independent variables that were controlled for in the studies varied. But perhaps more important is the lack of insight into whether the studies related to the first pieces of reading material available or the additions to an existing stock (though one study (Heyneman *et al* 1983) does show no gains resulting from a change in the pupil/book ratio from 2:1 to 1:1); neither is the qualitative relationship explored between the types of reading material and the demands of the tests used to measure achievement—do comics have the same effect as well constructed reading materials? Some of the violence done in the search for global generalizations is illustrated by the finding the improvement in achievement attributable to book provision in the Philippines (Heyneman, *et al* 1983) is twice the impact that would be gained by lowering class size from 40 to 10 students. But this finding uses evidence from an experimental study in the Philippines and data on class size effects from the USA. This presumes that the range of variation in class size considered and teaching methods are indistinguishable between the two systems which is unlikely to be true. Interestingly a more recent study (Lockheed *et al* 1989) fails to find any relationship between class size and student achievement in primary science in the Philippines.

3. Possible influences on achievement

Fuller and Heyneman (1989) have attempted to identify effective and ineffective factors that influence school achievement. These turn out to be:

Effective parameters	*Percent of studies showing positive effects*
Length of instructional programme	86%
Pupil feeding programmes	83%
School library activity	83%
Years of teacher training	71%
Textbooks and instructional materials	67%
Ineffective parameters	
Pupil grade repetition	20%
Reduced class size	24%
Teachers salaries	36%
Science laboratories	36%

Simple conclusions of this kind are dangerous. The effects of repetition on academic achievement are difficult to measure for a number of reasons. In many systems repeaters have a disproportionate tendency to drop out. The medium-term effects of repetition are then difficult to ascertain. Since in most systems repetition implies just that—repeating the same material often with the same teacher without any special treatment—it might be surprising to find strong effects from repeating an experience of failure. Since few if any of the achievement tests are age corrected maturation effects will further complicate the interpretation of any achievement gains. As a policy issue repetition is not as serious problem if it only effects the marginal student with particular learning disabilities. It represents a serious inefficiency in systems where repetition averages 20 per cent or more and this is really the policy issue, not what effect it has on achievement.

It may be that within a wide band achievement is not related to class size but this does not mean there are no limits. Intuitively the significant factor is when teaching practices change—practical group work is difficult when class sizes exceed 40; it may not be practised below this number; a lecture is likely to be as effective with 20 students as with 80 if the space is available. And class size does interact with other variables—if textbooks/pupil are correlated with achievement large class sizes given a fixed stock of books (which is a realistic assumption in a rapidly expanding system) will diminish it.

Teachers' salaries, at the level of individual teachers, are unlikely to be directly related to achievement for the simple reason that achievement is unlikely to be the result of the teaching of a single teacher—students will experience several teachers over their careers in school. Moreover it cannot lead to the conclusion that paying teachers better is unlikely to have an effect on achievement—it may be that the most effective teachers do not get the highest rewards in a given education system; it may be that all teachers are paid so poorly that what variation there is not reflected in performance. Given the fairly universal belief that income should be related to effectiveness the challenge is to change the reward structure so that they are.

And the obvious comment to make about the effectiveness of laboratory provision is that is science achievement tests do not test the skills developed in laboratories (which frequently they do not) it should surprise no-one that they do not have a large impact on achievement measured through pencil and paper tests that often emphasize recall and the abstract application of principles. The reasons for incorporating practical work in science have been thoroughly explored by Haddad and Za'our (1986) who argue its benefits whilst recognising the difficulty of measuring its impact. A study of university entrance examinations in China (Lewin and Wang, 1990) illustrates how the science papers do not assess experience of practical science in much depth. The most recent IEA study (Rosier and Keeves 1991) is complex to interpret on the subject of practical work and achievement; it does suggest that where students' views of teaching indicate more practical in five out of nine cases. The weight of opinion seems to lie with those who are sceptical about the measurable benefits of laboratory science for achievement as conventionally measured, and who stress its high costs (Wallberg, 1991).

The First IEA Science study noted positive effects of reported laboratory use in three of the four developing countries in their sample. Heyneman and Loxley's (1983) study found no such effect. Lockheed *et al* (1989) did find positive effects arising from teaching primary science in laboratories but note that the magnitude of this was much less than the effect of frequent group work and of frequent testing. That those who are tested frequently perform better on tests is perhaps not surprising. Whether the reasons why younger teachers make more frequent use of group work than their elder colleagues in an attempt to offset difficulties encountered by large classes, as is claimed, or whether it arises from other considerations remains an open question in the study. A Nigerian study by Okebukola (1987) which examined achievement in chemistry did find that participation in laboratory activities as an important factor in determining achievement. In order of importance, student attitude towards chemistry, teacher attitude towards laboratory activities and availability of chemistry laboratory materials made significant contributions to the variation in achievement. Mutsune's (1983) study of the correlation between the practical and theory components of the Kenya, A-level Biology examination found low correlation between practical and theory achievement which is attributed to lack of coverage of practical work by many students.

On the positive side length of time spent on instruction is reported widely as having an impact on achievement. Heyneman and Loxley (1983) note this in relation to general science in India, Thailand and Iran. Fuller (1986) counts 12 out of 14 analyses supporting this proposition. There are wide ranges between countries in the amount of time allocated to science at different levels—by a factor of two or more in the IEA countries. Comparisons between countries are dubious since so many other factors vary simultaneously so the more useful comparisons are within the same system. The difficulty with this is that the largest variations generally stem not from official policy but from practice in the schools. In some countries as much as 30 per cent of the official teaching days are not utilized for their intended purposes as a result of teacher absenteeism, school functions, excessive examination practice, natural events and casual holidays. Given that science is taught in lessons, clearly the more lessons there are the more is likely to be learned, but there is no reason to suppose that the relationship is necessarily linear and the most recent IEA data, whilst supporting the general proposition that time studying science is related to achievement, recognises limitations in its data that make more precise statements of the relationship difficult. It may well be, as Wallberg (1991) observes that 'Mathew effects' operate in education—such that initial advantage are multiplied. He argues that improved instruction (including greater time allocations) may benefit all students but will benefit the more able most.

Feeding programmes are an established way of enhancing enrolment and increasing retention. *A priori* they will serve this purpose for science as much as other subjects. School libraries also offer the prospect of providing more relevant sources of information for teachers and students though the existence of these in relatively well endowed schools must not simply lead to the conclusion that they have a causative relationship with achievement. Those studies which relate use of the library to achievement do seem to indicate that frequent users benefit from the access they enjoy.

Pre-service teacher qualifications and training do show up in many studies as positively related to achievement. The magnitudes of the effects are often moderate however. They are in any case difficult to measure—children experience different teachers—should recent training be given the same weight as training ten years ago?—and the number of years of schooling completed before training may be at least as important as the training itself. One recent study (Lockheed *et al* 1986) suggests that other inputs *i.e.* textbooks can be substituted for additional training since textbook use and training did not interact in their data and the effects of textbooks were greater. Very little evidence exists on the effectiveness of in-service training. Those studies that do exist are generally positive but often have no means of controlling for the effects of training as opposed to the traits of the teachers who choose to take advantage of it—those involved are generally the more motivated and skilled in the first place. Of course it is also likely to matter what teachers are being trained to do and what kind of students they are teaching though this also is largely unresearched.

There is little doubt on the margin that textbooks do have a major impact on achievement in most subjects, and probably in science more than most since they are likely to be the only source of authoritative information relevant to achievement tests in poor school environments. Unfortunately, beyond the level of their existence in reasonable quality there is little research to indicate at what point additional written material ceases to have an effect (the Philippines study mentioned above is an exception); or what the relative impact of different types of material is—teachers' guides, student texts, worksheets, reference books. And every teacher has opinions, often well founded, about 'good' and 'bad' books. Every textbook is not the same—some have inappropriate reading levels, some are poorly structured, some contain factual errors, some are produced with poor quality and uninteresting design.

Four other observations are pertinent before moving on to discuss the Second IEA Science Study. First, in an interesting study in Zambia, Mulupo and Fowler (1987) compared achievement, understandings about science and the scientific attitudes of learners at the concrete and formal levels of cognitive development. Subjects were an equally weighted sample of concrete and formal reasoners in 11th grade chemistry classes assigned to one of two teaching method groups for 10 weeks. Results showed that among formal resoners discovery method teaching was more effective than traditional methods on understanding science; for concrete reasoners that mode of instruction made no difference; overall the traditional group out-performed the discovery group in achievement but the discovery group scored better on attitudes. This draws attention to the way the characteristics of learners are likely to influence the effectiveness of different inputs which is largely lost in most school achievement studies. Second, Hamilton (1982) draws attention to how the attitudes to science of 11th and 13th grade Jamaican students influence achievement. Attitudes appeared to play a vital role in achievement, particularly as far as girls are concerned. This it is argued demonstrates the need for more role models for science achievements for girls and reinforces findings in industrialized countries. The importance of dispositions towards science is also rarely accounted for in the school achievement literture. Third, Tuppen (1981) compares examination performance of secondary students in ten high schools in Purua New Guinea to an Index of Educational Opportunity (IEO) in the student's province of schooling. The IEO is defined as the percentage of the age group enrolled in high school. The study reports that the index, parental eduction levels and interest in schooling are important in explaining variation in examination sources. Some school factors were also reports a 0.5-0.6 correlation between examination performance and internal school assessment in English, Mathematics and Science perhaps suggesting that the skills tested in different subjects overlap considerably. Fourth, Maundu's study in Kenya (1988) explores student achievement in Mathematics and Science and relates it to parental education and occupation and to type of school. This study argues that socio-economic factors such as family background are important in determining student achievement, but are reinforced by teaching and learning resources available which are interactive variables.

4. The Second International Science Study of the IEA

The most comprehensive data on science achievement are to be found in the Second IEA Science Study (Postlethwait and Wiley, 1991). This includes data from 24 countries of which China, Ghana, Nigeria, Papua New Guinea, Thailand, the Philippines, and Zimbabwe can clearly located as developing countries. Hong Kong, Singapore, and Korea might also be classified in this way albeit that their economic development has reached a different level. The IEA studies have been conducted on three populations, broadly speaking 10 year olds, 14 year olds an those in the last year of schooling before university entrance. Our interest in this review is in secondary science which falls within Population 2 (14-15 years old) and, to a lesser extent, Population 3 (final year of formal schooling) of the IEA classification.

The interpretation of the IEA findings is very complex since various asymmetries arise in sampling, curricula emphasis, test participation between the samples in different countries, etc. These preclude the possibility of making simple comparisons between countries. At this stage it is only possible to draw attention to some of the main findings which seem to be of interest, especially as they relate to the developing countries in the sample. Even this is tentative since the variations in the data sets are important for any comparison between countries and all of the overall findings should really be contextualized in detailed ways which cannot be attempted here. Within country analysis is beyond the scope of this review. We note also that what may be true in the lowest scoring developing countries as a group is often not true in the other developing countries in the IEA studies. This further strengthens our concern that the most useful interpretations of this data are likely to be at the intra-country level. With all these caveats some of the main findings are described below for the Population 2 data which are of most interest to this review.

In terms of total score Ghana, Nigeria, the Philippines and Zimbabwe have the lowest scores on the science tests. This is true in aggregate and different areas. Other developing countries—*e.g.* Papua New Guinea, Thailand and China have means that are comparable with industrialized countries like England, and the USA. Hungary and Japan score consistently well above most other countries. In general there is a high inter correlation between scores at the Population 2 level and those for Population 1 suggesting that low performance is compounded through the system. Though there are considerable changes in the ranking of mean scores by country at the Population 3 level, these are heavily influenced by the selection practices of different countries which, to a greater or lesser extent, concentrate resources on the most able science students.

In general the proportion of schools scoring below the lowest school in the highest scoring country (Hungary) was high in the low scoring developing countries in the Population 2 sample Ghana 64 per cent, Nigeria 88 per cent, Philippines 87 per cent, Zimbabwe 80 per cent of students tested indicates that they have learned very little science. This is particularly worrying when it is realised that the Nigerian students were from a higher grade, and the Ghanaian students were from selective elite schools. The IEA data suggest that the bottom 20 per cent of students in Ghana, Italy (Grade 8), Nigeria, the Philippines and Zimbabwe are 'scientifically illiterate' and that the United Kingdom, Hong Kong, Singapore and the USA are borderline cases. Interestingly the USA has a higher proportion of schools scoring below the worst school in Hungry than does Thailand.

Of particular interest is the finding that the teaching group or class that pupils are in its considerable significance to the scores that they achieve in some countries. This effect is particularly prominent in Ghana, the Philippines, Italy and the Netherlands. By contrast in Japan and the Noridic countries at this level the effect is very low indeed at the Population 2 level. This changes dramatically in Japan at the Population 3 level probably because of the increase in the number of private schools. One of the implications of this appears to be that in some countries differences between schools are considerable and it does matter a great deal in which school or class students study science, in terms of their achievement. In other countries school and class effects are much smaller and have much less influence on achievement. This is not simply a function resource level; rather it seems to depend more on selection and streaming practices and organizational features of education systems.

The IEA authors have developed a yield coefficient that modifies the distribution of scores by the proportion of the age group in school. This is intended to indicate how many children know how much science. It highlights differences between countries and shows that yield coefficients tend to be much lower in those countries with the lowest proportions in school which are mainly the developing countries at Population 2 level. This raises a dilemma for countries with low yields wishing to improve them—should numbers enrolled be increased or should low levels of achievement be improved first?

At Population 3 level in the IEA data inter-country comparisons are even more hazardous than they are at Population 2 level. There are wide disparities in the percentage of the age group studying at this level (from 1 per cent in Ghana and Papua New Guinea to 89 per cent in Japan). The average age of this population spans 23 months. There was a 2-year grade difference in the level to which the test were applied. The average number of subjects studied varied from 3 to 9 or more with concomitant variations in the time spent on science.

Generally the United Kingdom, Singapore and Hong Kong and Hungary have the highest scores in Population 3 with some variations between subjects in this. These countries also have small numbers enrolled and highly specialized curricula. In general the IEA found no relationship between the proportion studying science and the achievement of elite students defined as the top 3 per cent of the age group. There was no significant tendency for the number of subjects studied to influence science achievement except in chemistry. Positive age effects were noted with older students scoring better.

5. Some Additional Evidence on Science Achievement of Girls

The IEA study demonstrates that sex differences greatly favoured boys in the countries with the lowest overall scores in terms of the performance of both the bottom 20 per cent and the top 20 per cent. Though in Hungary sex differences were minimal, in Japan, the other high scoring country, boys outperformed girls consistently at all levels of ability. Typically sex differences in performance are greatest in physics and least in chemistry.

A review of the Papua New Guinea School Certificate Examination reports [MSU, 1986-1990] shows significant difference in science examinations. In this case male scores are typically about half a standard deviation lower for girls. The pattern is not universal however; in Trinidad and Tobago girls perform consistently better than boys in all types of schools and at all class levels in science [Kutnick and Jules, 1988]. Similar findings have been reported for African-Americans, and West Indians in the United Kingdom [Duncan, 1989]. Analyses of O-level examination results for Kenya, Zambia and Botswana demonstrate that girls perform less well than boys in almost all subjects, but particularly in the physical sciences. And unpublished evidence from Sri Lanka suggests that differences in performance between boys and girls in science are generated largely from the performance differences between relatively low achievers—differences between high achieving students are small.

A number of factors have been suggested in an attempt to account for gender disparities in levels of achievements in science. Duncan (1989) and Eshiwani (1988) categorise these factors according to whether they relate to the societal context, the attitudes and aspirations of students, or to the school environment. The first group involves socio-cultural explanations which are supported by the variations in magnitude of the disparities across countries, and socio-economic explanations such as social class, family background and level of urbanization.

The second group of factors suggested to explain under-achievement of girls arise to the hypothesis that girls hold less favourable attitudes towards science and have lower aspirations for science-based careers. This results in a lowering of motivation to work in science and a consequent reduction in levels of achievement. Duncan [1989] in Botswana found that only six girls out of her sample of 650 girls aspired to technical occupations [outside medicine] which would require academic science knowledge. Eshiwani (1988) cites studies which show that in general girls find science more difficult than any other subjects, a conclusion supported by the large number of girls who drop science at the earliest opportunity. Lack of self-confidence, particularly in laboratory work, was found to be a major factor contributing to negative attitudes towards science.

A number of research findings maintained that the school environment is a significant factor in influencing and reinforcing gender disparities in achievement. The staffing structure of schools may contribute towards gender stereotyping, especially in Africa where the vast majority of teachers in secondary schools, particularly in science, are men. Furthermore, women head-teachers or principals are extremely rare. In Nigeria women constitute a large proportion of the teaching force but a negligible number of them are in headships and only then in low status schools and girls schools. Of 150 secondary schools in Tunisia only 12 had female Principals and women were totally unrepresented in the inspectorate [Davies, 1986]. Biraimah (1982) in her study of a Togolese secondary school found that while the teaching staff appeared balanced in terms of numbers, men occupied all the positions that exercised authority and women were assigned to domestic or secretarial roles. Biraimah relates these disparities to a whole pattern of differential expectations and attitudes and argues that they convey female observance especially to girls who view women teachers as role models. Gender stereotyping is also reinforced through teaching materials and textbooks of science which may rarely provide female characters or situational examples with which girls can identify.

The type of school appears to be a significant factor affecting the performance of girls. Eshiwani (1988) reports that in secondary schools in Kenya there were very limited opportunities for girls to study science, with several girls' schools having their laboratory facilities in nearby boys' schools. Co-education is not necessarily the answer to this problem as Kutnick and Jules (1988) report that girls attending single-sex schools scored higher than girls in parallel co-educational schools. Similar findings are reported by Eshiwani (1983) who demonstrates that girls in single-sex schools in Kenya performed better in science than both boys and girls in mixed schools, and suggests that:

> *"any intervention strategy for the improvement of science education among girls should steer clear of co-education"*. (1983, p. 47).

It is not uncommon to find single sex schools out-performing co-educational ones. Often this is partly a result of selected intakes—such schools are disproportionately drawn from those with a long history, established reputation, and elite urban catchment areas as, for example, in Malaysia. This in itself does not constitute a case for single sex schools in general. It should also be remembered that sex difference in performance exist in other subjects and movements away from co-education may be detrimental in performance in these for boys or girls. In any case decisions on co-education should not be determined by science performance alone. Great care should be taken to establish whether, in particular systems where single sex schools perform well, this is the result of intervening variable unrelated to sex.

6. Implications for Planners

It has proved very difficult to review the literature on achievement. It is massive and frequently contradictory. It often exists at a high level or generality with little accessibility to the detailed specification of which effects are being compared to which dependent variables. Aggregated reviews deepen the confusion by mixing together wide ranges of studies as if simply counting the direction of findings tell us of something of value to policy. All the school quality indicators used in the various studies—material inputs, teacher quality, teaching practices, classroom organization, and school management practices—are measured in ways which prevent easy comparison or aggregation. The research results really only take on meaning in the context of the particular systems—what is of critical importance for achievement in one part of one school system may or may be elsewhere and that is what is of most direct concern to policy-makers in science education. While the sincerity of the researchers who have painstakingly constructed the studies is not in doubt there must be reservation about the wisdom of attempting to package all these kinds of findings into easily digestible 'bind alleys and promising avenues' (Lockheed, *et al* 1990) as if they were global prescriptions that are context free.

For the reasons outlined above it is not possible to arrive at a list of universally valid generalizations concerning the factors that effect science achievement. It should be clear from this review that there are many different factors in different circumstances, seem to have causal relationships with achievement. Which ones are significant will depend on which characteristics of the particular system, school, teachers, students are of interest. Thus we can conclude that the kind of insights that come from achievement studies are important, but have to be approached with caution and full understanding of their derivation. They may carry important implications for planners if rigorously established and able to point the way to more and less cost effective strategies towards enhancing science achievement.

4

Implementation and Organizational Issues

This chapter briefly considers some of the literature on the implementation of educational innovations. Much of this is not specific for science education but is nevertheless relevant to the main concerns of the review. Further implications for effective innovation are distributed throughout the other chapters. The second part of the chapter explores patterns of cirriculum organization for the delivery of science education. It considers one of the most striking trends—that towards the integration of science teaching—in some detail. Other issues touched on include the inter-relationships with other subjects; the balance between the sciences in the curriculum; the time allocation thought appropriate; the conditions under which science is to be taught and which groups are to be taught science are also considered. The final part of the chapter reviews issues raised by different tracking and streaming policies for science education.

The chapter addresses for main questions:

1. What are the main perspectives on educational innovation in developing countries?
2. How have patterns of organization for science education developed?
3. What are the key features of the organization of secondary science.

4. What variations are there in tracking and streaming policy and what are the implications of these?

1. Theories of Educational Innovation

There are many reviews of the educational change literature which need no repetition here (Slater, 1985; Fullan and Pomfret, 1977; Fullan 1982; Papagiannis, Klees and Bickel, 1982; Bolam, 1978; Dalin, 1978; Hurst, 1978; Huberman, 1973; Hoyle, 1970). Much of the early work developed in areas outside formal education systems and was based on the experiences that were beginning to a accumulate in development projects which sought to promote planned change. Thus for example Rogers and Shoemaker, (1971) explored social system innovations cross-culturally using many examples drawn from different fields in the development literature. American perspectives on innovation and the linking of research and development with practitioners were heavily influenced by the development of the Land Grant Universities and agricultural extension practices. Another strand in the innovation literature was inspired by psychological studies with a utopian (Skinner, 1948), group participatory (Lewin, 1947) or psycho-analytic basis (see Chin and Benne, 1968). Organizational psychology and sociology have provided other inspirations (for example, the 1930s Hawthorne studies, Roethlisberger and Dickson 1939), the Mayo Human Relations school (1945) Likert's work on organizations (Likert, 1966) and that of Katz and Khan (1964).

The most accessible educational change literature ralates to experience with education system in industrialized countries. Thus much seminal work (*e.g.* Gross *et al* 1971; Smith and Keith, 1971; Havelock, 1973; Huberman and Miles, 1984; Becher and Maclure, 1978) reflects the organizational ecology and social system characteristics of educational institutions in the North. Case study accounts (e.g. OECD, 1973) are often drawn from industrialized countries. As Havelock and Huberman (1977) note in their analysis of the problems of innovation in developing countries:

> *"These problems (of educational innovation) have given rise to a considerable theoretical literature in which research workers have tried to explain change phenomena in order to help practitioners better to organise for change. However, most of this work relates to industrialized*

countries, and tends to reach a degree of abstraction or complexity that reduces its applicability ..... the case study literature and the impirical research that we expected to find in rich abundance were not really there ...".

Recently more studies are becoming available which address the problems of educational innovation in developing countries (Adams and Chen 1981; Lewin with Stuart 1991) but the accumulation of experience based on independent evaluations of projects is still relatively thin. Chisman and Wilson (1989) are the last in a long list of academics who have commented on this lack of disinterested evaluation specifically addressing their comments to science education projects. There appears to be little or no independent development of theoretical perspectives which relate to science education innovations that is separate from that of the bulk of educational innovation theory. Science projects may have special features related to the nature of the subject but the reasons they are judged to succeed or fail seem to fall largely into the categories that apply to educational innovations as a whole. Further, when surveying the embryonic literature on these problems in developing countries it becomes clear that few if any studies exist which chart the fates of a variety of innovations in science within the same systems where key organizational, infrastructural and cultural factors remain broadly similar. Any attempts to compare the importance of factors across these boundaries are problematic.

Many models have been developed from for different phases of the innovation process. At the most general level there are those which identify over-searching theories encompassing initiation, development, implementation, and evaluation of outcomes. The models which have most currency in the literature and are most widely quoted are those related to the work of Havelock (1969), and Chin and Benne (1969). The former initially identified three dominant patterns in approach—research development, diffusion; social interaction; and problem solving. The latter classified innovation strategies into rational-empirical; normative, re-educative; and power-coercive. Thus has led to several subsequent formulations and attempts at synthesis (Havelock and Huberman, 1977). Lewin (1980) in his work on science education development in Malysia and Sri Lanka traces the innovation process through five key phases, the (i) project initiation; (ii) contextual constraints, (iii) course development process, (iv) implementation strategy, and (v) examining assessment policy.

Decisions and events in all these areas influence the way innovatory programmes are introduced into the schools and the extent to which they are put into practice as intended. Different styles are identified in the two case studies—internal and external initiation, science for all students or science for selected groups, writing groups involving extensive consulation and those involving little, phased implementation with a gradual build up or national implementation in all schools simultaneously, examination reform to reflect new curricula goals or minor adaptation of existing examining structures. These are used to develop some explanations of the effectiveness of implementation. In a later development of this work, Lewin with Stuart (1991) identify six approaches to innovation with distinctive features. These can be characterized as *systems, bureaucratic, scientific, problem solving, deflationist, and charismatic.*

System approaches which view educational institutions as sub-systems which are part of a wider system that has formally specified goals. Innovation from this point of view is initiated as a result of a commitment to achieve these goals are generated by systems (political or otherwise) outside the education system and the innovators role is to design and implement programmes that will achieve these goals. Poor goal achievement requires remedial action to ensure that elements in the system behave as intended.

Bureaucratic approaches to innovation are directed by goals identified at the system level and are related to systems approaches. Unlike a systems approach they tend to have static rather than dynamic characteristics. In particular, directive circulars, rules and regulations, agreed procedures, and legal obligations provide the benchmarks against which innovation is judged and the needs for it are identified. As these change, innovations may be appraised against criteria which are more administrative than educational. Innovation than takes place to satisfy approval processes where the regulatory process is given prominence.

Scientific approaches to innovation claim that research and evaluation on the needs of learners, the learning process, and curriculum effectiveness are at the centre of the initiation of change. The curriculum developer in this model must undertake basic and applied research on teaching and learning to arrive at the more effective design of learning materials and curricula. More sophisticated versions of this model have feedback built in to them so that formative experiments feature prominently and development is planned as a meticulous process of trial, evaluation and revision.

Problem-solving approaches offer a fourth alternative. In these 'organizational plan' and individual dissatisfaction are important. A problem may be experienced within educational institutions and the innovators' first task is to find out what problems have arisen and what their causes are. Alternatively problems may be recognized by individuals in their own practice. The problem-solver diagnoses the difficulty, searches for a solution which may or may not involve innovation, and then offers it to the organization, or applies it to their own practice for trial and refinement.

Diffusionist approaches place the stress on the processes through which innovations are disseminated and adopted. This is seen characteristically as the result of social interaction between actors existing within networks of communication that provide access to information. This model assumes that behaviour is heavily influenced by the social networks which actors are linked to; that position in these networks is a good predictor of acceptance of innovation; that personal contracts are central to the spread of innovation, and that diffusion of new practices will follow an S-curve of growth with early adopters and laggards.

Charismatic approaches are difficult to classify since their nature makes them unique to individuals and circumstances. Strong beliefs, convincingly articulated by those in influential positions, are often the initiating activity. When they succeed in carrying other people with them they can generate development activity which reflects their educational philosophy. Their motivation comes from conviction rather than research; their goals may not be those of the organizations in which they work but which they may seek to change.

Examples of all these approaches can be found in descriptions in the literature on science education innovations. Commonly elements of more than one approach co-exist. Though lip-service is often paid to scientific and problem solving approaches, these are rarely used in a systematic way, with research and development and problem diagnosis often being short-circuited by the exigencies of political demands for rapid change. Systems views of eduction systems tend to dominate much public decision making on policy despite wide recognition that system malfunctions may be so common that there is a wide gulf between what is intended to happen and what actually does. Bureaucratic structures are often very powerful in explaining the events that take place during implementation when responsibilities for change more from professional developers to the administrators with day-to-day responsibilities for school systems. Many science education projects can be linked to charismatic 'curriculum entrepreneurs' who play key roles, especially in the initiation process. Much actual change takes place as a result of the planned and unplanned diffusion of ideas through the social and professional networks of practising science educators.

There are a number of studies of aspects of implementation in science education which raise important issues. These include the work by Lillis and Lowe (1987) in Kenya. Early difficulties identified in the School Science Project (SSP) were seen as staff rather than course related. SSP was never truly localized because it did not begin with a needs analysis but assumed transfer from a western context and produced an inherent role conflict between the heuristic approach implicit in the curriculum and the rote-teaching norm in African classes. There was insufficient sensitivity to the interface between culture and knowledge and between culture and pedagogy:

> .... *"curriculum development in the third world over the last two decades has assume(d) complete transferability in content and methods ...an atmosphere of cultural neutrality is assumed."* (Lillis and Lowe, 1987).

Warf (1978) earlier argued that there was a need for more effort to adapt science teaching to the classical ways of learning of the indigenous populations, so lessening the contrast between science and traditional culture. At a national level there is a mismatch between educational objectives and development activities; there is little merit in imparting a technology more rapidly than it can be absorbed into the economy he asserts. Ingle and Turner (1981) reinforce this view suggesting that school science education in some developing countries has been closely modelled on that in the United Kingdom and USA. The wholesale adoption of syllabuses and textbooks also implies the transfer of objectives, yet these may be inappropriate to the environmental, employment, cognitive and pedagogical situations into which they are implanted. Ogawa (1986) takes the problems of science education innovation cross culturally to another level suggesting that science education in most developing countries is a foreign culture to most non-westerners. He presents a model to explain conflicts between traditional views of man and nature and ways of thinking and the science education view. He goes on to suggest one of the aims of science education in non-western society should be to compare the traditional and scientific views of man and nature and ways of thinking, and to explore similarities and difference between them. There are number of other studies reported later in this review that also argue that science education innovation has suffered from inadequate cultural adaptation (Maddock, 1981, 1983; Collison, 1976; Ogunniyi, 1988; Hornett, 1978; Eiseman, 1979; Watson, 1980; Swetz and Merah, 1982; Pottinger, 1982).

Amongst other studies on science education innovation are those which highlight human and physical resource availability problems, training inadequacies, gaps between intentions and curriculum reality, and the paucity of timely and insightful evaluation. Thus Lutterodt (1979) describes the evaluation planning undertaken for the Project for Science Integration in Ghana, which highlighted the limitations arising from characteristics of teachers, students, authors, materials, and finances. Jegede (1982) evaluated the Nigerian Integrated Science Project and found that teachers were not favourably disposed towards some parts of it though the majority of students had positive attitudes. Low achievement was attributed to problems with textbook readability and lack of training to teach integrated science which were compounded be equipment shortages. Brophy and Dalgety (1981) scrutinized the implementation of a new science curriculum in Guyana. They found that there was a wide gap between practice and officially stated intentions. For instance, what are intended to be student-centred, laboratory-based activities were in practice teacher-centred and textbook oriented. In-service teacher education involving the use of distance education methods was being used in attempt to improve the situation. Vulliamy (1988) discusses the lessons that might be learned for other developing countries from the Secondary Schools Community Extension Project (SSCEP) in Papua New Guinea, which included science curriculum development as part of an attempt to increase the relevance of secondary schooling to rural development. This work emphasized the importance of appreciation of cultural differences, the potential for using the examination system to support desired teaching and learning strategies, and the necessity for a careful planning and monitoring. Chisman and Wilson (1989) in their review of the experience of 25 years of attempts to innovate in science education single out more effective evaluation as possibly the most important factor in improving implementation of new science curricula.

As might be expected the international literature includes other studies which focus on the role of external change extents, agents. Thus Nichter (1984) discusses some of the problems faced by technical advisers implementing projects for the improvement of science education in Africa. Reasons for these problems include institutional under-development, underestimating the process of reform, inadequate finances, personality conflict and lack of motivation, and opposition from key groups. Lillis (1981) focused on expatriates and curriculum change in Kenya and explores curriculum entrance; the complex inter-relationships between local and metropolitan actors; and the assumptions of universality. He uses three perspectives—the adoption perspective, the implementation perspective, and the politico-administrative perspective to reflect on the Africanization of formal decision-making, curriculum decision-making and of the curriculum itself. Maybury (1975) reviewed a range of science curriculum projects which have involved international aid through the Ford Foundation. He argues the most successful have been those where the foreign specialists were resident in the country and had acquired a wide knowledge of local political, social, economic and educational conditions. Crucial to success is the ability of the members of curriculum development groups to discern the world-view held by children, particularly those from the more deprived sectors of society. These kind of findings cannot be see as definitive—if only because there are successful projects supported by international donors that do not involve foreign specialists on a large scale. There is very little literature that explores in depth the tensions that arise in technical co-operation and assistance related to science education and not much in general. Leach's (1991) recent study is an exception which highlights the kinds of perception gap that may develop, the different organizational and procedural assumptions of key actors, and the strategies that project staff develop to accommodate these. In so doing she illustrates that many projects develop goals that go beyond those formally negotiated and these may have more importance for the actors involved than successful goal achievement of that originally agreed. Zainal (1989) notes that in the reform of the science curriculum in Malaysia decision-making at the adoption and adaptation levels involved a very small group of key actors who were influenced by external change agents. The latter mobilized arguments to suggest that the planned changes would meet needs for continuity, feasibility and relevance. However, at the implementation stage, none of the planned innovations were fully implemented by classroom teachers. Pedagogical aspects in particular were modified or rejected. Whilst content changes appeared more durable. The centralized decision-making system failed to appreciate fully the extent to which this would happen as teachers adapted the intended curriculum to reflect needs and constraints of particular teachers in particular schools.

2. The Historical Context of the Organization of Science Curriculum

The debate on the organization of the science in the curriculum has a long historic (Jenkins, 1979). This is intermingled with the history of the development of science itself. In brief, it was only in the nineteenth century that science began to strongly differentiate into what are now recognized as the three main sciences—physics, chemistry and biology. Since the 1950s other specialities began to emerge at University level and filter down into schools systems which were sub-divisions or extensions of these three sciences. Additionally the more prestigious science became as an activity in the curriculum the more substantial became attractions of making more scientific other disciplines. Thus geography and earth science increasingly became seen as sciences suitable for study at school level and environmental studies curricula moved towards environmental science.

In terms of the origin of the science curriculum three broad patterns can be traced. First, the *classical tradition* of pure science reflecting the development of the separate subjects and to a degree rivalry between them. Historically physics, closely allied mathematics had the earliest claims to be considered the core of science. The natural philosophers of the sixteenth and seventeenth centuries used mathematical and scientific concepts with their roots in antiquity to explore the physical world and it was these that largely defined science. This was period when the nature of the cosmos provoked sharp debate (the Galilean controversy) and much scientific effort was directed towards problems of navigation and warfare. Subsequently the successful development of chemical concepts in the eighteenth and nineteenth century opened a new window on the world through the systematic understanding of the properties of elements and the ways in which they combined with each other. The economic implications of this became important as it became possible to synthesise new materials, starting most notably with synthetic dyes whose properties could be predicted. Chemistry became respectable and lost its alchemist's image (Isaac Newton, it appears, was both a supreme rationalist, when developing the laws of motion and mathematical calculus, but a part time alchemist and quasi-mystic when delving into the properties of materials). Later the biological sciences grasped the popular imagination in the Europe of the nineteenth century as the travels of Darwin and Wallance revealed the wealth of *flora* and *fauna* on the planet and began to developed theories with far reaching implications. The economic advantages of understanding how biological resources could be exploited by colonialists played an important supporting role.

The second tradition was *utilitarian*. There was losing tradition of useful science removed from academic science in the elementary schools of the United Kingdom. This always remained of much lower status than the real science which had more classical than utilitarian origins. Thus the 'Society for the Diffusion of Useful Knowledge' in the nineteenth century in the United Kingdom was an early precursor of the general science movement of the mid twentieth century and the science for all movement of the late twentieth century. In this tradition the ideas of science were to be made available to a broad cross-section of society to assist them in their occupations and in everyday living. Thus elementary objects and simple skills of observation, measurement and experiments, mixed with a modicum of basic scientific knowledge, than with the more profound investigation of the scientific laws, the nature of matter and the evolution of species.

The third tradition that can be traced is *technological*. It appears most strongly in the nineteenth century in Germany as well as the United Kingdom and USA. The development of large scale industry and the infrastructure that depended on sophisticated engineering skills created a need for the technological skills of making and doing in the cause of new products and structures to serve particular purposes. Systematic knowledge of the strength of materials was required, design became important, and though trial and error remained an important feature of technological development with many economically significant developments depending on a certain amount of serendipity (Goodyear reputedly discovered vulcanization of rubber by trial and error well in advance of any molecular theory that explained why it worked), there were comparative advantages to those who used scientific ideas to create technological artefacts. All this stimulated the growth of technical institutes and schools, often of lower social status than academic institutions, that taught practical knowledge related to engineering skills.

All these three tradition have their current analogues in the development of science education internationally and have had an influence on the development of science curricula. Dominant have been the academic and classical traditions science these in the majority of school systems have continued to occupy the high ground of teaching in elite institutions which yield access to the most attractive jobs. Science for all, with its utilitarian emphasis has come to new prominence as more and more school systems teach science to most if not all of the school population. The intrinsic difficulty and lack of relevance of fundamental science to the majority of school populations has forced curriculum developers to consider providing more accessible science related to the experimental world of students. Most recently technological approaches to science have became fashionable as a way of teaching economically useful skills that takes advantages of some of the strengths of both of the other two approaches.

3. Patterns of Organization in Science Education

The overall trend over the last two decades is clear. Most lower secondary science teaching has become integrated, at least in the sense that science is treated as whole and not as separate subjects. UNESCO has been instrumental in encouraging this trend (see Richmond, 1970, 1973, 1974; Cohen, 1977; Reay, 1979). The same trend exists at upper secondary though less well-defined. It is uncommon at the pre-university level. There is some evidence that these tendencies have been less pronounced in Francophone countries than in the rest of the world (UNESCO, 1986). It is also the case that the physical sciences are more commonly integrated than are all three traditional sciences. The IEA data (Postlethwaite and Wiley, 1991) also support this picture and shows that integrated or combined courses are most common below grade 9 in the 23 countries sampled. Above this single subject teaching becomes more common.

There is no single commonly accepted definition of what constitutes integration beyond the practical consideration of whether science is time-table as one subject. Integration can be conceived of as *thematic,* taking themes like energy transformations and examining them from physical, chemical, and biological perspectives; it may be *topic based* choosing a topic like water and similarly treating it from the three disciplinary perspectives in a coherently inter-related way; science may be conceptually integrated by stressing science *process skills* which are common to the three sciences and emphasizing these in the teaching of content located in the three disciplines. Examples of all these approaches can be found. What lies behind them are the philosophies of science education and curriculum development that are discussed elsewhere in this review.

There are practical reasons why integrated science has become more common as well as those based on changing epistemological and pedagogical perspectives. Lower secondary school systems almost everywhere have expended rapidly and schools have become less selective as greater proportions of the age cohort are enrolled. At the same time in many systems more subjects have been introduced into the compulsory curriculum squeezing the time available for science. Rapid expansion also creates severe problems of teacher supply. The attractions of integrated science in theses circumstances are clear—textbook production and teacher training can be simplified by concentrating on producing science teachers and materials rather than three varieties for each of conventional science subjects; science taught as three subjects is generally thought to require four to six periods a week for each subject—totalling about 15 in all. This time is unlikely to available if there are seven or more other compulsory subjects. Integrated science is usually allocated four to six periods a week. Integration might also be thought to reduce overlap in teaching between the three sciences and economise on scarce resources (laboratory space, equipment, trained teachers).

De facto, therefore, integrated patterns of science teaching are becoming the norm at lower secondary level, with similar trends at upper secondary in many countries. The literature contains few examples of attempts to compare the effectiveness of teaching science in an integrated way with the teaching of separate subjects. It is generally very difficult to find comparable groups that have a choice between single subjects and integrated programmes; where they do single subject science is invariably allocated more time. Other common problems of this kind of research (*e.g.* variable teacher effects, inter-school differences, non-parallel learning objectives) make it elusive to reach simple conclusions. It does appear true that, for example, students taught in integrated science are less aware of the differences between the sciences, but this kind of finding does not contribute much to decisions on whether or not to adopt approaches. The decisions are usually made for other reasons like the advantages noted above. It must be remembered that the relative attractions of single subjects teaching rests largely on hearsay, casual empiricism, and the attachment of teachers to the disciplines that they were trained in (Gunstone, 1985). They are most frequently advanced in relation to students who may subsequently follow careers with a science base for whom in-depth knowledge is thought essential and who are in a minority. The IEA Second International Science Study does suggest that the performance of those studying single subject science is not related to the overall percentage enrolled in secondary education, and it is negatively related to the proportion enrolled in science subjects; The latter might be expected as the size of the cohort following science increases and selection becomes weaker.

The epistemological and pedagogical arguments for specialization into separated subjects become more convincing at higher academic levels. Here, if conventional assumptions are retained about the depth in which science is to be studied, more time is required and some selection is inevitable. The differences in achievement across groups of students become wider and more prior knowledge is assumed to have been mastered. If it has not, learning at the level of meaning becomes extremely difficult in the science since the subject is cumulative in nature. At lower secondary level however, the cognitive skills and assumptions of antecedent knowledge should not be seen as barrier to integration. There are examples of successful integrated science programmes up to and beyond upper secondary school and there have been many initiatives with inter-disciplinary degree courses. The reasons why they have not become a dominant mode of provision probably owe more to the entrenched conservatism of science educators and organizational limitations on resources, than to inherent epistemological or pedagogical weaknesses.

Curriculum organisation in secondary science has many other aspects in addition to the debate on integration. These include the inter-relationships with other subjects; the balance between the sciences in the curriculum; the time allocation thought appropriate; the conditions under which science is to be taught and which groups are to be taught science, Practice varies widely on all of these.

It is not difficult to find examples of curricula planned with scant regard to the mathematics curricula on which some abstract manipulation and data analysis are likely to depend. It is rare to find science curricula, except those with a conscious science and society orientation, that make direct connections with learning in history, social studies or languages. This is not a problem specific to science since similar things can be observed in relation to other subject areas. Its significance is that where there is some inter-dependence (science and mathematics) co-ordination is obviously desirable; and where few links are made between science and other subjects the separateness of science is emphasized and this may discourage some children and reduce the appeal of the subject.

Policy varies on science subject emphasis. If tentative generations can be made than biological content is more heavily emphasized at the lower levels and physical science at the higher levels. There is no great universality to this pattern however. To talk of emphasis at higher levels is to be confound by the complexities of option choice where different numbers of students take different subjects often in an unknown pattern of overlap, and this is further complicated by the differential allocation of study time to the different subjects. In an exception to the common pattern in China biological sciences were virtually eliminated from the secondary curriculum at one time—reflecting perhaps the influence of Russia orthodoxies on content selection. Physical science has been given most emphasis at secondary level for many years (Lewin, 1987:b) though this is now changing. But in many countries emphasis in more equal. It is also true that the only science subject that many girls study at upper secondary level is biology in those systems where a choice is available.

The time allocated to teaching of science varies greatly as the IEA data show. But so does total instructional time. If there is any consensus it appears to be that science should occupy between 10 and 20 per cent of curricula time for most secondary students—any less and it will be a shallow learning experience, any more and the competition for curriculum time with other subjects will become fierce but there is enormous variation in practice (UNESCO, 1986).

Most systems have ideal images of the conditions under which science should be taught characterized by graduate science teachers, well-established science laboratories, adequate textbooks and enlightened teaching methods. Many of the studies cited in this review indicate these conditions are not met in the majority of schools in developing countries. One consequence is that whatever the policy on streaming and tracking (see below) the common reality is effective science education for the few under appropriate conditions, and relatively poorly executed science for the majority.

4. Tracking and Streaming Policy

Tracking and streaming policy have both resource and pedagogical implications since it will determine how many students study science to which levels. It will also influence what types of science students experience in schools. This chapter outlines some of the most common options and discusses some of the consequence of adopting them.

There is an extensive body of research on the effects of different methods of grouping students. Most of this research has focused on primary and the lower reaches of secondary education where practice has varied widely within and between countries. Much less work relates to upper secondary where commonly some selection takes place, either as a result of student choice or as a result of schools deciding to treat more and less able children in separate groups. First we should consider the range of options that exist in organising groups of students at any given level. These cover a spectrum broadly defined by the following practices.

5. Options for Grouping Students

Streaming and Tacking by Ability

- children are segregated into different institutions depending on achievement scores and/or
- children are divided into groups on the basis of their achievement and grouped into classes accordingly.

Setting

Groups of children electing to follow a particular subject are placed in teaching groups which are streamed so that sets in the same subject are of recognisably different achievement.

Banding

Groups of children electing to follow a particular subject are placed in teaching groups that are broadly comparable in terms of achievement.

Mixed Ability

Children randomly assigned to schools and class groups independently of their ability and the full range of ability is represented.

6. Grouping and Achievement

The extent of homogeneity in achievement in teaching groups reduces from the first to the last of these options. The reasoning used to defined each of these practices differs. In its simplest form the argument in favour of streaming suggests that the narrower the ability range the more the class can be taught as a whole without losing contact with the very able or very slow. Opponents of this view argue that this is not convincing as all classes are mixed ability in some sense and that teaching methods can be devised that allow students to progress at different rates.

What evidence there is generally fails to show consistent achievement gains for children in streamed classes over and above what would be expected of more able children in any case. In particular some studies draw attention to the negative consequence for low stream teaching groups on achievements and suggest that, if a view of achievement is taken which includes effects on the cohort as a whole, any gains that may accrue for the best students are likely to be compensated for by deterioration in performance of the least able. The phenomenon of the 'sink set' is a part of teacher folklore in many countries—failure reinforces itself as motivation falls and peer group sub-cultures begin to develop anti-school attitudes (Lacey, 1970).

Another consequence of streaming which is widely recognized is that schools that stream students often stream teachers too. That is, the most well qualified, senior and effective teachers tend to teach the most able groups and the older students most of the time. This might partially explain the deterioration in performance of low stream groups. It seems undesirable unless the philosophy being teacher allocation is unashamedly elitist. A recent study in Zimbabwe (Lewin and Bajah, 1990) confirmed that teachers of Environmental and Agricultural Science of the lowest grades generally had the lest number of years of formal schooling and the lowest level of science achievement. Those with the highest professional qualifications were concentrated in the highest professional qualifications were concentrated in the highest grades. Where classes are stream it is also often the case that the better qualified and more experienced teachers teach the most able students. An on-going research study in Malaysia also suggests that this pattern prevails. Though this ensures that the more demanding science contracts are taught by the most scientifically competent, it creates a situation in which the most competent teachers may spend a considerable amount of teaching time trying to overcome the effects of poor quality teaching in lower grades.

Streaming by ability creates another dilemma since it always implies a mechanism to separate the more from the less able. Though it may be more fashionable to take a genotypic view of human abilities than was the case a decade ago it is still widely recognized that children's achievement is complex and not necessarily stable or unidimensional. Thus any selection process will risk misclassification—learners develop at different rates, especially during adolescence in the secondary school, and may be misclassified; the type of achievement on which selection is accomplished is usually based on a number of core subjects and/or attempts to tap an underlying general ability factor (the G of the intelligence test constructors) which may or may not correlate closely with since achievement. As we have seen there is little unanimity as to what kind of attributes are especially suited to science education since the question begs the issue of what kind of science education we are talking of.

Whilst there appear to be no convincing educational arguments that can be made across the board about the benefits of streaming for achievement there is more convincing evidence that streaming by ability has social consequences, at least in the industrialized countries where studies have been completed. Thus rates of delinquency, truancy and misdemeanours appear to increase amongst low ability children when they are grouped together. The peer group sub-cultures that form are antipathetic to school norms and to status acquired through school achievement. Admittedly these effects may not be the same when projected cross culturally and where the calculus of reward for school achievement is very different to that in societies where alternative opportunities are available to those without education qualifications that provide reasonable standards of living.

There is a considerable amount or research on the interaction between teachers expectations of pupil's abilities, pupils self concepts and actual achievement. From this emerges a consensus that teacher's images of children are likely a create 'self fulfilling prophecies' which enhance the performance of favoured students and suppress that of the less favoured, though not perhaps in the simple way implied by Rosenthal and Jacobson (1986). This is not the place to enter into this literature in detail, but it is worth highlighting some findings that emerge from research on grouping practices (which are themselves a source of teacher expectation). Pidgeon's analysis of the IEA pilot tests in 1970 showed that standard deviations on test sources tended to be higher in England and Wales than in other countries. This he attributed to streaming practices more prevalent in these schools than in those of other countries.

The most recent IEA science study also notes that the proportion of the variance attributable to the class and school attended is much greater in some of the developing country samples than it is in most industrialized countries though there is considerable variatioin in this. Where it is high e.g., Nigeria and the Philippines (Population 1 data) and Ghana, Italy, the Netherlands and the Philippines (Populations 2 data) it suggests that the class and school attended make a considerable difference to achievement in science. A well known United Kingdom study (Rutter *et al* 1979) compares performance amongst 12 secondary schools on an aggregate measure of scholastic achievement. This study indicates strong school effects after verbal reasoning score on entry and socio-economic background have been controlled. The effect is so strong that the most disadvantaged students (lowest verbal reasoning, lowest socio-economic background) in the most successful school are as successful as the most advantaged students in the worst school. There is no reason to suppose that these effects are not reflected in science in particular though evidence on this is not presented.

If generally true, these kinds of findings suggest that where there is a significant range in institutional types (as is the case where institutional tracking exists) there may be improvement of students in performance in favoured institutions, but this is accompanied by deterioration in performance of similar students in unfavoured institutions. This of course ceases to be an immediate problem from the point of equity if the achievement of concern (e.g. science) is not available to those selected out of elite institutions, *i.e.* the mass of the Population do not compete for similar levels of achievement in science. In such cases equity tends to be defined more by fair competition for entry into selective institutions than by equal participation in curriculum options.

The Second IEA Science Study indicates that the performance of elite students (the best 3 per cent) is unaffected by the proportion of the age group studying science, when examined cross-nationally. This suggests that elite students do not suffer in general from broader access to science. To what extent this may be a result of particularly grouping strategies is, however, not explored.

There is another dimension to the streaming debate that turns to two stands of arguments for its defences. On the one hand it is argued that some subjects have relatively high 'entry prices' and are cumulative. That is to progress with them to ideas that are of interest and can be applied, a certain amount of persistence and systematic study is required. Since some learning has to be sequential— '*y*' cannot be understood until '*x*' has been mastered—it follows that the subject itself requires differentiation of students since they will not all progress through these sequences at the rate, nor will they have they motivation to do so. If the view of some psychologists is accepted, namely that what really differentiates learners achievement is not intrinsic inabilities to master concepts but differences in the length of time that it takes to acquire them, it follows that student groups should be sub-divided to reflect these differences. For some students the length of time will be so long as to be unavailable and they will never master the ideas—but this has different educational consequences than a view which holds that they could not do so under any circumstances.

On the other hand cognitive development studies are cited in science (Shayer and Adey, 1981) which show that in school populations only a minority of students consistently perform at Piagetian levels of formal operations whilst in secondary education. If the view is taken that concrete reasoners find formal thought intrinsically unavailable to them this limits what kind of science can be taught effectively. Many of the ideas of science require formal reasoning. This then reinforces the previous argument that science students should be grouped to reflect their rate of progress towards the acquisition of formal reasoning skills. This is an issue we will return to in discussing teaching and learning.

7. Implications for Planners

Implementation Issues

One of the reasons why it is difficult to tease out common factors that lead to problems in implementation is that perspectives on what these are depend very much on the analytic framework employed and the nature of the innovation attempted. Thus those within a functionalist sociological tradition will take a very different view of the nature of problems, there causes and the action necessary to overcome them to those within the traditions of conflict theory in organizational analysis (Lewin and Little 1984). What may look like the failure to communicate the purpose of an innovation in science education requiring better public relations from one perspective could be interpreted as the inevitable result of conflict in interests between different groups expected to implement the innovation which is not based simply on ignorance of purpose. The six approaches to curriculum development identified—systems, bureaucratic, scientific, problem solving, diffusionist, and charismatic—all have different implications for implementation strategies and their likely effectiveness which will be context specific.

At the risk of over-generalization, some of the most important implications for planners arising from the analysis seem to be :

- The careful consideration of the source(s) of innovations. Why is it needed?—system disfunction? administrative fiat? basic research findings? problem diagnosis? diffusion of new ideas on practice? charismatic enthusiasm? What the status of these are carries implication for the most appropriate development and implementation strategies.
- The identification of information needs to improve decision-making as the innovation takes shape. In particular, a tenacious pursuit of antecedent assumptions on which the implementation strategy may depend. Are they demonstrably sound?
- The systematic appraisal of options to achieve desired ends, using wherever possible, realistic pilot projects that are capable of extension to scale.
- Flexible adaptation to evolving goals as events unfold and the limitations and possibilities of implementation strategies become apparent.
- Serious commitment to the aftercare of innovations designed to support durable changes and discourage regression to previous patterns of provision.

8. Organizational Issues

Organizational questions are clearly of importance to planners science they carry implications for resources and some options will be more expensive than others. However, from what as already been argued it is clear that the number of possible permutations is very wide and cannot be reduced to simple algorithms. This is because organizational decisions have to take into account existing traditions, and the established development of resources, as well as the nature of the goals towards which science education is directed. Often there are real choices to achieve the similar ends at different costs but inevitably not all patterns of organization are appropriate to different circumstances.

In planning science education the resource implications, as well as the pedagogical ones, must form an integral part of the decision-making process. Relevant questions are likely to include:

- What are the resource implications of moving from single subject to integrated science curriculum patterns?
- How can best sue be made of the existing trained science teachers stock? What curricula patterns will enable this?
- How can the facilities for practical science be utilized in ways which maximise opportunities for the least some students to experience practical work in which they are directly involved? How extensively should these opportunities be made available given the costs of so doing?
- How should science be time-tabled to allow the sequential development of the subject over the secondary school cycle for all students?

9. Tracking and Streaming

Tracking and streaming policy in science education has implications of costs and internal efficiency. The evidence suggests that early selection does not have every substantial impact on achievement—especially when gains for the selected group are balanced against possible deterioration amongst those not selected for special treatment. The behavioural consequences of streaming seem a matter of concern, at least in those developed countries where these have been shown to be negative in character. At higher academic levels some forms of streaming and tracking are inevitable for several reasons—the increased difficulty of the science to be learned, the preferences of students to study science, the difficulties of resourcing science adequately. What form this should take has no generally appropriate prescription and must be examined at the country and school-levels. Key questions for planners include :

- On what basis should science education resources be concentrated on selected groups as opposed to being distributed across all students?
- What range of unit costs are justified in teaching science to selected groups or in selective installations?
- How will the quality of science education for those not selected to study science to high levels be protected?

5

Examinations and Assessment

This chapter reviews the nature of public examinations for science education. It discusses technical aspects of the quality of examinations and comments on analyses of the content of science examinations. The status of practical examining is reviewed. The effects of patterns of public examining on teaching and learning are explored; and the potential and problems of adoptiong continues assessment are debated. The last part of the chapter uses data from Papua New Guinea to reflect on relationships between internal and external assessment.

The six questions addressed in this chapter are:

1. What are the most common forms of public examining for secondary science?
2. What do content analyses of examinations in science indicate?
3. What is the status of practical examining in science?
4. What is the evidence from studies on the effects of examination orientation?
5. What has been the experience with continuous assessment systems?
6. What can be learned about the relationship between internal and external examinations results in Pupua New Guinea?

1. The Nature of Examination Systems

The form and structure of examination systems are widely recognized as key determinants of educational practice. Well known expositions of the reasons for this can be found in Dore (1976) and Oxenham (ed. 1984). Many others have commented on the significance of examinations for educational development and quality improvement (e.g. Fletcher, 1973; Heyneman, 1987). Wherever opportunities to enter modern sector employment are scarce and the rewards of doing so are great, selection mechanisms will adopt great importance in the minds of teachers and learners. Most commonly educational qualifications are used to regulate flows into career jobs and science is often a key subject for selection. In China the examination system is known as the baton which conducts the schools (Lewin and Lu, 1988) and this is a common perception in many other developing countries.

The industrialized countries often exported and imposed their own national examination systems on their colonies and the traditions established by these boards linger on. However, most developing countries now have their own examination systems without any apparent lowering of standards at least as determined by the percentages of candidates passing the examinations each year (Kellaghan and Greaney, 1989). Thus West Africa, the Sudan, East Africa, Malaysia, and more recently Cyprus and the Commonwealth Caribbean have instituted regional or national Public Examination Councils. Local examiners have been substituted for expariate ones. The World Bank has shown a particular interest in the recent past in the use of examination reform to improve academic achievement and has invested in the strengthening of examination systems in a number of developing countries (World Bank, 1988). As long ago 1973 Fletcher warned *'the musicians were changed, not so the music,'* suggesting that localization of examination boards would not be itself overcome the criticisms of their effects on teaching and learning.

Typically secondary level tests do not appear to cover the range of educational aims and objectives that are usually associated with secondary science course. There may the both structural reasons for this and those which are concerned more with traditions within subjects as to what as examinable and what should be examined. The first observation is that since assessment in most secondary school systems in science is undertaken through written test this immediately places boundaries around what can be assessed. Further, much testing is constrained by the use of multiple choice formats which are very limited in the extent to which they can assess powers of expression, communication skills etc. on teaching it the assessment pattern of the classroom minors that of the examination (de Souza Barros and Elia, 1990) rather than that of the curriculum and its goals.

The reasons assessment is often limited to written papers and to multiple choice items are practical as well as pedagogic. Written examinations and multiple choice in particular offers relative reliability, objectivity, economy, and ease of administration over most other methods. These are also the methods that many teachers, pupils and parents have become familiar with. The restrictions placed on assessment of curricula goals by written examinations are well known and need no extensive development here. It is worth noting that some rather more subtle processes are at work in electing for such formats.

Multiple choice examinations as conventionally constructed from pre-tested items, select items which have proven reliability, a restricted range of facility values, and which discriminate between students positively in terms of overall score. They will also be selected using a table of specifications that tries to ensure coverage of a range of topics across the curriculum tested at different levels of cognitive demand. Reliability is essential if confidence is to be placed in results for selection and the associated error score will be minimized in part to achieve this. A technical reason for restricting the range of facility values for items is to ensure that discrimination remains high since the two interact—very easy or very difficult items cannot discriminate highly. Moreover, in selecting only those items that discriminate well the assumption is made that the attribute being measured is uni-dimensional—if an item measures an attribute on which performance does not correlate with overall score it will be rejected, though it might be a valid measure of that attribute. Without delving too deeply into the technicalities of examining the point to be made is that different selection criteria for items could produce different patterns of performance. They could also covney different messages back to teachers as to what constructs and capabilities in science were most important. Emphasizing discrimination emphasized those things where there are the largest differences in performance between candidates, not those things which may be most useful or fundamental to the understanding of science.

To put things more concretely there is evidence from internal studies by various examination boards that both facility values and discrimination indices for items very between sub-populations. There may be, for example, some items which are completed relatively well by rural students despite the fact that their overall performance is inferior to that of urban students. And so for boys and girls, linguistic minorities, etc. This is important since it implies both that a different mix of items might produce different patterns of performance, and because it illustrates that differences between groups may not be stable across the curriculum as a whole but the result of particular difficulties in certain curriculum areas. If the latter is so, planned intervention to improve performance and reduce disparities would be well advised to focus on those areas where differences in performance are most marked. And it also acts as a reminder that in principle, it should be curriculum goals, not assessment criteria, that should define the curriculum in action and that the assessment system fails in an important sense if it does not reinforce the full range of curriculum goals to which teaching and learning is intended to be directed.

2. Examination Content

There is little in the literature specifically on science examinations in developing countries. Kellaghan and Greaney (1989) provide a study of the examination systems of five African countries—Ethiopia, Lesotho, Malawi, Swaziland and Zambia. They identify a number of key issues in examination reform such as improving the efficiency of examination administration; improving the quality of examinations by reflecting more of the curriculum objectives; providing information regarding examination performance both for policy decisions at regional—and national-levels and as a diagnostic basis for class room teaching. These writers also discuss the implications for examination reform.

In the early 1980s as part of the ILO Jobs and Study skills Programme for Africa school examination papers were analysed in eight African countries—the Gambia, Ghana, Kenya, Liberia, Sierra Leone, Somalia, Tanzania, Zambia, and (ILO 1981). These studies used the Bloom taxonomy to classify the skills tested in public examination papers in different subjects. The results yield insights into what were than common examining practices in science. Though practice may have changed in some countries since these reports were produced evidence from the literature suggest that many of the basic findings remain valid.

The general picture that emerges is of examining in science dominated by recall items that test the ability of candidates to reproduce factual knowledge about science. This is overwhelmingly the case for the lower secondary examinations analysed, and strongly but less emphatically true of the upper secondary papers. Other features of the examinations worth noting are the extensive use of multiple choice items in the format of public examination papers. These are by far the most common approach used and few countries now examine science at secondary level without their use. Despite there being many excellent examples of multiple-choice items testing higher order skills there is evidence that they are perceived as being more associated with the testing of lower order skills. Lewin (1981) reports that 58 per cent of a sample of Malaysian students agreed or strongly agreed with the statement *"to do well on objective tests all you need is a good memory"*. A number of other formats are used which include blank filling, shorter answer items that require brief explanations or comments and interpretation, longer answer items that require substantial written responses for example describing experiments but these generally have declined in popularity. Across all the papers analysed in the ILO study it was the exception rather than the rule to find many items which directly draw on life experiences, especially those of rural children, in their construction and situation. It is characteristic of most national examinations in science at secondary level that few if any attempts are made to measure affective outcomes. Yet affective objectives are included in most new secondary science curricula and are sometimes argued to be as important as cognitive ones.

The ILO examination analyses showed that it was generally biology that had the highest number of recall based items, reflecting the way this science subject is often interpreted in the curriculum. The more descriptive the treatment the more likely that its assessment will favour the recall of information. Physics tends to be the least the recall dominated of the sciences, though this may be partly because the mathematical demands of it are generally more extensive. Most items that have a mathematical component are likely to require more than recall for their successful solution. Health science, agricultural science, home science and other electives appear in the examining systems of different countries. These subjects also tend to have a high proportion of items that appear to be directed at the level of recall. In a minority of countries trends to reduce the number of recall based items have been apparent. Thus the proportion of higher cognitive level items in the science certificate of primary education did increase from about 17 per cent to more than 70 per cent over the period of the 1970s in the Kenya Certificate of Primary Education. So also did the number of items with a rural bias which used material familiar to rural children as a vehicle to assess science learning outcomes. A recent analysis of secondary science examinations (grade 10) in Papua New Guinea showed that in recent papers more than 25 per cent of items were intended to operate above the level of comprehension and test higher process skills; the majority of the remaining items were testing comprehension, not simple recall (Ross 1990). Possibly foreshadowing a contrary trend Deutrom and Wilson (1986) expressed concern about academic standards in Papua New Guinea which seemed likely to lead to greater emphasis on more traditional science content in examinations. Low academic standards at grades 10 and 12 are attributed to the deliberate policy of 'containing' traditional science in grade 11 and above, and giving grades 1 to 10 a 'science for all'.

A Brazilian study (de Souza Barros and Elia, 1990) of university entrance physics exams found that the level of attainment, as indicated by item facility indices, was very low

(23 per cent—32 per cent), over a seven year period. This analysis revealed an over-emphasis on mechanics problems and little attempt to present problems in an everyday rather than scientific context. It was also found that mean facility followed the hierarchical order for the taxonomy level dimension of analysis, with recall items showing the highest facility values and therefore being easiest for most students. Items which used a concrete context had higher facility values than those with an abstract scientific context. Lewin (1981) found average facility values in the Malaysian LCE/SRP Science examination of 60 per cent, 56 per cent and 52 per cent for knowledge, comprehension and application items, respectively, and comments that these differences were less than he had been led to expect from assertions that more higher level items could not be included since they would reduce mean facility values to unacceptable levels. In another study of Chinese entrance university entrance examinations (Lewin, 1991) it seems clear that recall questions are common even at upper secondary level, though less so in physics than in the other sciences.

Other types of item are still used in science examining in addition to multiple choice. These include various kinds of short answer and structured items, with or without grade difficulty within them, essay question, and still on occasion the traditional description of an experiment followed by the calculation of some results. Of the newer types perhaps the most widely used are short answer items with structured stimuli—graphs, diagrams, tables of results, photographs, etc.—and tasks to undertake based on the stimuli. These can test a wide range of skills though they are often time-construct.

Though, with imagination and investment of suitable resources in training and development it is possible to test a much greater range of learning outcomes than is typically assessed in public examinations, the format itself is inevitably restrictive. This may be one reason to encourage the growth of school based assessment where there are no contra-indicators that suggest that such developments will overburden teachers who do not have the skills or motivation to operate such systems effectively.

3. Practical Science Examinations

Practical examinations are no longer a feature of much public examining at secondary level in science. The costs and logistic difficulties of maintaining practical examinations have proved beyond the capabilities of many countries. Items are used in some countries which describe experiments and ask students to comment on what has been described in terms of the conclusions that can be drawn and/or the flaws in the experimental procedure described. Where practical examinations remain they are generally only held at the highest levels of the recent movement towards more school based examining opens up the possibility of more assement of practical skills. However, these developments are much more common in industrialized countries than in those developing countries with highly centralized examination systems. There are some alternatives to practical science examinations the use of slides, photographs, thought experiments, critiques of experimental and many ideas about the best ways to test practical skills. They have not been widely adopted however since they generally require individual or small group working situations and multiple sets of equipment and are time consuming.

Fairly typical of many developments is the Zimbabwe Junior Certificate Examination which is locally set. Although there is no practical examination the syllabus emphasizes practical experiences—there are 29 such subjects, *e.g.* demonstrate how to wire a 3-pin plug—to be learnt by arranging an extensive range of simple practical experiments for each student in the laboratory. The new Zimbabwe O' level (1987) was to have included a practical examination consisting of a series of short practical exercises testing specific science skills with instructions provided to candidates and a circus style of test administration (with students moving around several experiments).

> *"Examiners are looking for evidence that candidates can apply basic skills such as handling apparatus, recording observations and displaying data in graphical form"*.

By circulating around a set of tests a balanced coverage of skills was planned and the possibilities of using teacher assessment are being investigated. (Sibanda, 1990). However, the practical examination has so far not been implemented.

The university entrance examination in China (Lewin, 1990) does not have a practical component in science. It does include a small number of items which described experimental procedures and ask a series of questions about the reasons for the methods used and pose question about the reasons for anomalous results. Practical work by students in uncommon in Chinese schools and it is generally only in well resourced 'key-point' schools that there is sufficient apparatus to allow individual experimentation. Even in these most experimental work appears to be undertaken through teacher demonstrations.

Where there are practical examinations, it is commonly the case that performance on them accounts for a small proportion of total marks—rarely more than 15 per cent. Moreover, the variance in students scores that arises from practicals is generally smaller than that on test scores as a whole. Thus they tend not to contribute much to the discriminating power of the test as a whole and may actually reduce it. Strategically practical examining is important science in its absence it is likely that teachers would arrange even less practical work than they currently do.

4. Examination Orientation

Life chances depend on educational qualifications in developing countries to a much greater extent than in industrialized countries. Because employers in the labour market use educational qualifications in the recruitment and selection of personnel students and teachers will follow strategies of learning and teaching which will maximise their chance of gaining the qualifications which will secure them a job, i.e. students and teachers will become exam-oriented. Based on a secondary analysis of the 1971/72 IEA Survey of Science achievement data, Little (1978) reports on differences in exam-oriented teaching styles between countries. She reports a greater tendency in developing countries to view the education system in terms of examining orientation towards jobs in the modern sector, and discusses the historical reasons for this. Schools themselves belong to the modern sector resulting in a greater disjunction between what goes on in school and what goes on at home. High examination orientation is characterized by frequent use of standardized and objective tests and greater importance of external exams and official syllabus as teaching criteria. The analysis revealed that the four developing countries in the study (Chile, India, Iran and Thailand) ranked in the first 6 out of a total of 15 countries on the frequent use of tests indicator, and in the top half on the exam/syllabus indicators. For many teachers in developing countries examinations appear to be very important even at the primary stage.

A hypothesized link between examination orientation and teaching which emphasized rote learning was investigated by analysing sub-scores on the IEA achievement tests. Rote-learnable items in the tests tended on average to be easier than those testing higher order skills but the difference was insufficient to justify concentration by teachers on rote-learnable items. Although recall items may not be that much easier for students to answer they are easier to teach towards, to revise for and to practice. The overall finding of the analysis is that factors affecting problem-solving sub test scores affect simultaneously rote-learnable scores. This suggests further thought is needed about the balance between rote and problem-solving items in exams given the likely backwash effects on the curriculum of the types of learning outcome emphasized in public examinations.

The Student Learning Orientation Group (SLOG) is investigating the hypothesis that highly examination dominated schooling induces in students certain values and attitudes which influence behaviour in the workplace. Six countries (India, Japan, Malaysia, Nigeria, Sri Lanka, the United Kingdom,) were involved in the study. The initial study was directed towards developing measures for describing profiles of learning orientation and planned to follow up with developing measures for workplace behaviour. Questionnaire items were developed to measure orientation to assessment, task interest, personal development, achievement and significant others of form 4 and form 6 students. At the intra-country level of analysis assessment domination was clearly evident in Malaysia and Sri Lanka but less so in India and Nigeria. At the Inter-country level of analysis three main dimensions of motivation were evident: orientation to examination and assessment results, orientation to the task of learning for personal development, orientation to the expectations of parents, teachers and peers. The relative distinctiveness of the three dimensions was found to vary by country. (SLOG, 1987). These findings point to the need for more research on the classroom observation of science teaching to understand more comprehensively the nature of the link between teaching and learning orientation and achievement.

5. Continuous Assessment

Continuous assessment spread out school-based assessment over a period of years and can thereby enhance the validity of assessment, improve the integration between the curriculum, pedagogy and assessment. It can also cover a broader range of assessable outcomes. Several countries have introduced various forms of continuous assessment into secondary schools to allow schools to play a greater role in assessment procedures and to take more control over the single most important determinant of teaching and learning. Pennycuick (1990) reports on the continuous assessment policies of Papua New Guinea, Sri Lanka, Seychelles, Tanzania, and Nigeria, and finds a variety of practices including to total replacement of external exams, parallel and separate systems of continuous assessment and external exams, and systems where continuous assessment forms a component of final results, together with examination results. In all the systems teachers are much more directly involved in assessment than in conventional public examining. But there has been a wealth of difference between the systems as planned, and the procedures adopted in practice as the Nigerian experience illustrates (Nwakoby, 1988). She highlights major problem areas in the introduction of continuous assessment as inadequate conceptualization by teachers, doubtful validity of test items, and inadequate structural and administrative support. Though the planned system looks in many respects laudable its operationalization has been hampered by many unsatisfied conditions that are necessary for its effective implementation, not least at time for teachers to understand and absorb new practices and the timetable time to make it feasible to operate them.

As well as teacher inexperience and increased workload Pennycuick (1990) identifies technical problems related to moderation. There moderation procedures are identifiable—statistical, visitation and consensus—the selection choice depends on context. Statistical moderation, for example using national tests results to moderate school based ones, is probably the simplest assuming data are collected in a timely fashion since it can be accomplished centrally in an examination department. Visitation and consensus require negotiation and agreement which may be both expensive in time and travel costs and may not be easy to achieve. School based examining moderated by national examinations has been tries in Papua New Guinea and this offers one possible solution to the problem of reconciling the need to locate assessment in schools if it is to be closely linked to curricula experience and the need to ensure comparable standards between schools. In this system continuous assessment occurs over the year and the national end of year test is used to moderate the continous assessment scores, which count for 50 per cent of the final marks. The extent to which school scores differ from rankings produced by national exams any illustrate that a wider range of attributes are being tested in school based examinations (Ross, 1981).

Attempts to introduce continuous assessment schemes in other countries have floundered in the face of practical problems and the opposition of groups seeing few real benefits emerging and much extra work (e.g. in Sri Lanka continuous assessment has now been abandoned in the face of widespread dissatisfaction with increased workloads and inadequate infrastructure to maintain the reporting system).

If school-based assessment related to the particular characteristics of curriculum at the school level is to flourish than its relationship to the national examination system has to be carefully considered. It does imply a degree of curriculum diversity, and local control over the curriculum, that is not common. Its advantage is that it can be more valid, and it can support local curriculum development and adaptation to make science more attractive and useful to different groups of students. Mathews (1985) distinguishes between the assessment of *common* criteria determined nationally, and *particular* criteria determined by individual schools. As Mathews points out:

"...public examination boards as we know them will find it extremely difficult to promote both national standards in the curriculum and an individualization of the curriculum".

In some national circumstances where a common curriculum is seen to be of over-riding importance, substantial variations at the school level in what is taught and assessed will not be attractive. Neither will it by where levels of teacher expertise are such that designing learning experiences in science and appropriate assessment takes are beyond the reach of most teachers. But where it is possible it offers one avenue to reduce the adverse effects of examination backwash in teaching and learning.

6. Continuous Assessment and Science Examinations in Papua New Guinea

Papua New Guinea provides an interesting example of a country which has recently introduced several examination reforms. It is relevant to examine this in a little more detail. In 1982 the lower secondary examination system changed from one based exclusively on internal school assessment moderate by external examination scores to one which combined moderated internal assessment scores with national examination scores. As part of the changes the syllabus-free items which had been used in the moderating examination were replaced by items which were based on the science syllabus objectives.

Internal assessment data are moderated according to school performance on the School Certificate Examination (SCE), held at the end of grade ten, and the results of both components are combined in equal weighting to give an aggregate score which determines final SCE rating on the basic of the national rating allocation; distinction grades are awarded to the top 5 per cent, credit to the next 20 per cent, upper pass to the next 25 per cent, pass to the next 40 per cent and fail to the bottom 10 per cent. Since the examination is norm-referenced the standardized score determining the various grade cut-off marks various from year to year.

Table 1 shows basic statistics on science exam performance over the period 1984-1990, compiled from information provided in annual SCE Reports (MSU, 84 : 90). The maximum score in each exam is 50.

It is not possible to estimate changes in standards of achievements since the abilities of the population of candidates in each year cannot be assumed to remain constant, and the specification of papers varies considerably each year. The cut-off mark range for Upper Pass is between 50 per cent and 60 per cent. Detailed examination reports provided schools with school and provincial level results (a 'league table' often criticized by teachers) as well as analyses of the largely multiple-choice exam papers. However, there is little centrally organized follow-up to the report findings such as teacher in-service work on areas of weakness identified by the exam largely due to lack of resources.

The annual Examination Reports published by MSU provide no information about the quality of school assessments, although correlation data are provided to show the relationship (Person *r*) between the exam scores and internal assessment scores. The values for '*r*' show wide variation across the country. For example in 1989, values for '*r*' ranged from 0.54 to 0.87. Each year well over half of the schools have co-efficients greater than 0.71, i.e. where variance in the school's internal assessments marks accounts for more than 50 per cent of variance in the schools' examination marks. A high correlation, say of 0.8 or more, might suggest that a school has internally tested similar areas of content and skill to those tested by the national examination, perhaps even using similar forms of assessment such as written multiple-choice tests, or even old exam papers. This can be explored a little more by a further analysis of the inter-correlations for different schools grouped by overall achievement.

A rating index (RI) can be used as an indicator of overall school performance in science. RI is defined as the percentage of students in a school who obtain SCE grades of Upper Pass or better on a nationally examined subjects. At a national level 50 per cent of students can be expected to obtain Upper Pass grades or better in science. Thus an individual school with RI of 50 has performed at the national level; while those with RI greater than 50 and less than 50, perform better and worse than average, respectively.

Schools at the extreme ends of the exam performance spectrum were categorized as high performance and low performance on the basis of rating index in science, as shown in *Table 2.*

High performance schools are defined as those whose Rating Index in Science is 70 per cent or more, indicating that 70 per cent or more the students in these schools were awarded ratings of upper pass or better. In 1985, 11 schools were in this category. Similarly, *low performance schools* are defined as those with rating indices less than or equal to 30 per cent; in 1985, 14 schools were in this category. Inspection of Table 2 shows that in each year except 1989 the low performance schools exhibited higher levels of correlation between the external exam scores and internal assessment scores. *Graph 1* further illustrates the relationship.

Table 1. School certificate examination (SCE) performance 1984-1990

	1984	*1985*	*1986*	*1987*	*1988*	*1989*	*1990*
Candidates	8,423	8,846	9,432	9,508	10,021	10,163	10,120
Mean examination score	25.1	28.2	25.0	24.0	22.9	23.7	27.0
Standard deviation	5.2	6.6	6.8	6.1	7.7	7.0	8.2
Reliability[Horst]	0.67	0.82	0.78	0.74	0.83	0.81	0.84

Upper pass range

1984	1985	1986	1987	1988	1989	1990
49.4–56.9%	56.0–65.1%	49.8–59.4%	47.5–56.0%	44.9–56.5%	46.5–56.8%	53.8–66.19%

It can be seen that school performance on SCE Science appears to be inversely related to the strength of internal: external correlation. Higher performance schools tend to exhibit lower correlation.

The evidence from this analysis suggests that the more closely a school's assessment pattern matches that of the national examination, the less likely the school is to perform well overall. It is possible that schools in the high correlation group (and low performance) concentrate their efforts on the lower taxonomical levels using items from the national exam in classroom assessment.

Table 2. Average correlations for high performance and low performance schools

	High performance schools					
Year	*1985*	*1986*	*1987*	*1988*	*1989*	*1990*
RI >=70 per cent	11	12	15	16	14	13
Average correlation	0.70	0.69	0.67	0.62	0.73	0.69
RI <=30 per cent	14	8	12	11	8	11
Average correlation	0.71	0.75	0.71	0.74	0.70	0.76

Graph 1. **Mean internal: external correlation versus performance group on SCE Science, 1985-1990.**

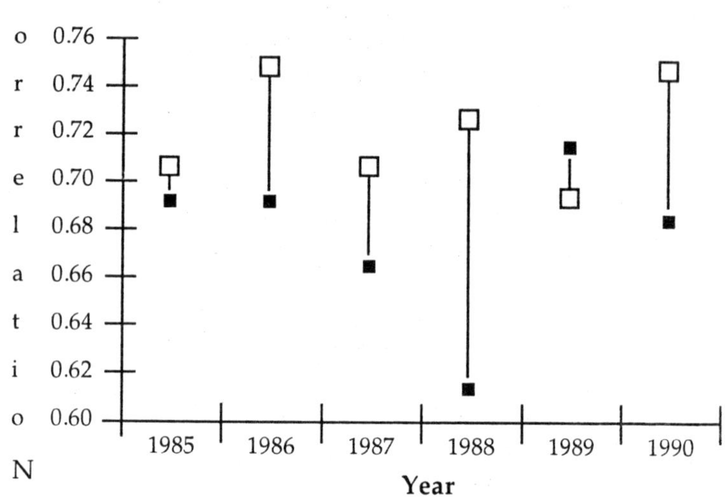

Those schools which provide more practical work in science and provide more opportunity for a more analytical command of subject matter may test internally a different range of outcomes than those tested by the external examination.

If this is true it suggests that teachers who test a variety of content and skills using different types of assessment techniques obtain better overall student results than teachers who confine assessment (and teaching) to the items which appear in public examinations. These observations are tentative since it has not been possible to verify through school case studies whether internal assessment does vary in the way suggested.

Papua New Guinea provides its science teachers with considerable assistance in the construction of classroom test in science by including item banks of suitable test material in the curriculum package, teachers' guides for classroom assessment techniques, and a degree of training in assessment for teachers participating in annual item-writing workshops for the national examination. The examination reports provide schools with detailed information and item performance and overall examination performance each year at the system level. Over past decade a considerable effort has been made to ensure a closer matching of curriculum objectives and the examination items. The science examination now samples more of the content of the curriculum than it did ten years ago, writing the restrictions imposed by its written and fixed-response format. There is much greater teacher participation in the final certification of students than there ever was as a result of the continuous assessment.

Yet, many problems remain. It is becoming more and more difficult to generate good quality multiple-choice items testing at the higher process level: written multiple-choice items reflecting the needs of school-levers are difficult to design and are often rejected because they trial badly; the final selection of examination items after trials have be undertaken is still determined more on the basis of psychometric principles than on the basis of curricular validity; marking of open-response items is unreliable, and this limits the cognitive level at which such items can be set; opportunity to learn varies widely across schools; teachers have limited and training in assessment; the norm-referenced nature of the examination precludes its use in the monitoring of standards of achievement in science. Although teacher assessment contributes 50 per cent of the final student assessment in science the national centrally set examination still has dominating influence on what is taught and what is assessed in the schools.

7. Implications for Planners

Examination systems represent low-cost levers for educational change. Experience from Kenya (Somerset, 1982, 1988) and elsewhere illustrates how curriculum reform can be reinforced by changes in examination items which closely reflect learning goals that are stressed by the curriculum. Conversely overlooking examination reform in implementing innovations in science education is likely to be counterproductive science, at least at those levels where there are public examinations, curricula in action are likely to reflect that demands of the examination for learning outcomes rather than the learning objectives contained in curriculum materials. There are several avenues that can be explored to increase the match between examination systems and the curricula they assess and introduce positive feedback that reinforces teaching and learning objectives. These have been explored in the various publications of the Institute of Development Studies Education Project [see Oxenham (ed.) 1984], and are listed below.

- *Curriculum Sensitive Item Writing*

  There is a need to balance technical criteria for item selection with curriculum goals. Item writing is a highly skilled task which should involve teams of curriculum and examination specialists working closely with experienced teachers to develop item banks of examination material. The task is hampered where curriculum goals are poorly defined and where there is a rapid turnover of staff. Properly resourced examination development groups are essential to improving the quality of assessment instruments.

- *Provision of Diagnostic Information*

  Examination performance analysis at the individual item level should be feed back to schools to indicate what types of items students are performing badly on.

It is insufficient to merely distribute examination reports to schools which only contain data at the highest level of aggregation. Analysis of performance characteristics of low scoring schools and low scoring students can identify which elements of the curriculum are most difficult. It when be used in designing intervention programmes (in-service course, enrichment materials, etc.) targeted at areas of special need.

- *School Based Examinations*

  The introduction of school based examining can extend the range of types of performance assessed, particularly if combined with an appropriate moderation system. This requires careful appraisal of the antecedent conditions which need to be satisfied for this kind of innovation. The additional demands on teacher time and competence should not be underestimated. If statistical moderation is employed examination boards need resourcing for this purpose.

- *Regional Examination Groups*

  The possibilities of supporting regional examination systems are worth exploration, especially in large countries. This might reduce some of the difficulties associated with centrally set written examinations which by their nature cannot reflect regional variations in educational experience. Even where there is a national curriculum, in practice there will be variations in how it is implemented and which material is most valuable to different groups of learners. This could be reflected in different mixes of assessment items which could draw more heavily on the real life experiences of students and enhance curriculum relevance. The additional costs of moving in this direction are significant, but would be small compared to other recurrent costs. The benefits could be considerable.

- *Standards*

  Norm-referenced national examinations can provide little information on changes in standards of achievement in science. There is a need to develop systems for monitoring standards using a more criterion-referenced approach to assessment. Re-analysis of national examination data, where data are retained from year-to-year, has considerable potential in assessing the impact of attempts to improve quality and access in science education.

6

Teaching and Learning in Science Education

There are many different approaches to the teaching and learning of science and a massive literature on the subject. This chapter selectively explores research studies starting with a review of different perspectives on science education science these are central to any teaching and learning strategy.

Cognitive development research on science education is considered and juxtaposed with constructivist views of learning. Different approaches to the teaching of science in developing countries are then considered and a section developed on the role of practical work. A separate section addresses work on the cultural contexts of science education.

The five main question address in this chapter are:

1. What are the major perspectives on science education?
2. What are the implications of research on cognitive development?
3. What do constructivists have to say about the teaching of science?
4. How is science taught in developing countries?
5. What insights does research on the cultural contexts of science education provide?

1. Perspectives on Science Education

Central to problems of teaching and learning is the issue of whether science education should emulate science practice. We have touched on this in the earlier discussion of aims and objectives. Yoloye and Bajah (1980) argue:

"Science is an activity carried out by scientists. As a result, any modification of the approaches used in the schools that were already found wanting was to be taken by scientist ... Science, the architects of the APSP (African Primary Science Programme) approach maintained, should be taught in the way scientists operate".

And Burner (1961) is often quoted for his view that:

"... intellectual activity anywhere is the same whether at the frontiers of knowledge or in the third grade classroom ... the difference is in degree, not in kind. The schoolboy learning physics is a physicist, it is easier for him to learn physics behaving like a physicist than doing something else".

As already noted, even if it were easy to identify which kinds of scientist we had in mind when basing teaching and learning on the sorts of things that they do, we would still have difficulties in arriving at a clear view of their activities. The argument continues as to whether science is an essentially creative exercise where divergent thinking should be encouraged and this is what defines successful science, or whether it is essentially convergent and rule bound. This dilemma was neatly put by Medawar (1969):

"According to the first conception science is above all else an imaginative and exploratory activity, and the scientist is a man taking part in a great intellectual adventure. Intuition is the mainspring of every advancement in learning, and having ideas is the scientist's highest accomplishment; the working out of ideas is an important and exacting but lesser occupation. Pure science requires no justification outside itself, and its usefulness has not bearing on its valuation.

The alternative conception runs something like this. Science is above all else a critical and analytical activity; the scientist is per-eminently a man who requires evidence before he delivers an opinion, and when it comes to evidence he is hard to please. Imagination is a catalyst merely: it can speed thought but it cannot start it or give it direction: imagination must at all time be under the censorship of a dispassionate and sceptical habit of thought".

Some studies of children seem to indicate that it is covergent rather than divergent thinkers who are attracted to science subjects. Thus Hudson's (1963, 1967) well known work illustrates how senior school students in the United differentiate between the personalities they associated with science and arts students and are themselves differentiated into 'covergent' and 'divergent' thinkers. Science students are relatively 'convergent' (*i.e.* excelling in closed ended reasoning tasks, practically oriented, conventional in behaviour, relatively unimaginative and more fluent with numbers and patterns than in the use of language) when compared to arts students.

Two kinds of implications arise from this work. First, the balance between creative and critical/analytical views of science is relevant to decisions on educational purposes and on science policy. The kind of curriculum that may promote the one is not necessarily the same as the kind of curriculum that will promote the other. Second, if students are predisposed by individual psychological traits to be attracted to science, and if the study of science requires these traits, then there are considerable implications for curricula and for selection policy.

2. Science Education and Cognitive Development

Many science programmes have implicitly or explicitly adopted a view of science education based on emulating the activities of scientists. Some of the problems this has led to have been widely researched in so far as they arise from mismatches between the level of cognitive development of students and the tasks that they are asked to perform. Indeed one of the major developments in research on the teaching of science has concerned the application of cognitive development scheme to understanding the acquisition of science concepts. An example of this is the well known work by Sheyer and Adey (1973). This work developed from the Concepts in Secondary Mathematics and Science Programme at Chelsea Collage in London. In summary it takes Piagetian scheme of cognitive development and uses them to classify different aspects of secondary science teaching in terms of their cognitive demand. Amongst other things, this work confirmed the view of many teachers in the United Kingdom that the first generation of Nuffield 'O' level curricula were likely to be too demanding of students too early and that a number of specific concepts, like the Mole in chemistry, were shown to require reasoning that was unlikely to be accessible to most of the students that the programmes were intended for. Indeed when science reasoning tests were applied to a sample of the British school population it transpired that even at the age of 16 years the majority of students were performing at late concrete operational rather than formal operational level in Piagetian terms. This observation reinforced the need to look again at the reasoning levels required in science curricula to ensure that difficulties were not arising from teaching material that was too demanding too soon.

A lively debate has ensued as to whether it is possible to accelerate progress through Piagetian levels through the use of specially designed intervention strategies which encourage students to make leaps in their thinking. This research has not been very conclusive so far. It has exposed some problems surficially interpreted as developmental which may be determined as much by language and familiarity as with terminology. Thus students may understand the meaning of a variable in an experimental context without being able to use the correct terms to explain what they are doing.

The ideas being the research have been of significance internationally and many similar studies have been conducted in other countries (Archenold, *et al* 1980). Adey (1979) extended his work to the Caribbean and confirmed that science curriculum development in the Anglophone West Indies has been largely an empirical process, lacking a theoretical psychological framework which might explain low achievement and guide the selection of curricular activities and objectives. His analysis of the West Indies Science Curriculum (WISC) determined the stages of cognitive development that seem to be necessary to succeed in each of its activities. The data reflected that few of the students reached the stage of formal operations before the fourth year of secondary education, whereas many WISC activities seem to demand formal operational thinking. Nyiti (1976), working in Tanzania with children in the 8-14 age range on conservation tasks on substance, weight and volume, found that while performance improved with age, surprisingly formal schooling had no independent effect. This could be as much a comment on the effectiveness of the schools attended in assisting the development of science constructs as on the stability of the underlying developmental process.

Some cross cultural studies illustrate how concept acquisition may take place at different rates between populations. Dasen (1975) worked with children aged 6-14 years old from Canadian Eskimo, Australian Aborigine and Ivory Coast African cultural backgrounds. He found that nomadic, hunting, subsistence-economy people develop spatial concepts more rapidly than do sedentary, agriculturalist groups, whereas the latter attain concepts of conservation of quality, weight and volume more rapidly than do the former. Shea (1985) reviewed research dealing with problem-solving abilities amongst Papua New Guineans using individual intelligence tests, group intelligence tests, achievement tests, conservation measures, classificatory skills, and formal operational thinking. Comparisons are made with the performance of Papua New Guinean children and adults with people elsewhere, and with foreigners resident in Papua New Guinea. Shea notes important differences within Papua New Guinea related in particular to schooling and language culture-group. By contrast to some previous conclusions about the cognitive skill development of Papua New Guineans, he concludes that while there are differences between some Papua New Guinean groups and groups from English-speaking countries in problem-solving performance, developmental patterns appear to be similar. Thus, educated Papua New Guineans achieve the highest levels of formal thinking though not necessarily at the same rates.

Otaala and Ohuche (1980) accumulated research on the cognitive development of African children and Peterson (1981) reports on a South-East Asian project to establish patterns of cognitive development in the region. Others have examined science process skills and cognitive performance styles in Singapore and Malaysia (Wong and Yeoh, 1987; Dekkers and Allen, 1977), spatial ability (Cox, Brynant and Agnihotri (1982) and depth perception amongst Nigrian secondary students (Ross, 1977) and mental maps of Jamaican children (Webb and Brissett 1986) to name but a few studies with links to the literature on cognitive development and science education.

3. The Constructivist View of Science Education

The other prominent strand in research on teaching and learning developers from the work of 'constructivists' who argue that science education should start from the child's understanding of natural phenomena, not from attempts to emulate the reasoning of professional scientists, who have developed adult understandings of casuality, formal reasoning etc. The strategies and antecedent experience scientists bring to problem solving are unlikely to be the same as those mobilized by lower secondary children. Most of the research on students learning science suggests that students bring their own concpetions of science to explaning the natural world (Driver and Erickson, 1983), Gilbert and Watts, 1983), Tiberghien, 1986) Osborne and Freyberg, 1985). Ausubel's (1968) thoery of cognition argues that:

> *"... the most important single factor influencing learning is what the learner already knows".*

The conceptions that students bring to science education are often misconceptions. Moreover it seems that they are often resistant to direct experience which contradicts them and therein lies the challenge to teaching and learning. By way of example we might consider some common misconceptions that are held by many children—and adults. Metals, glass and stone are generally thought to be colder materials than wood and fabrics with a lower surface temperature because they feel cold. Pressure in liquids and gases is thought to act 'downwards'; electrical currents are thought to be 'used up' by devices in a circuit. The fallacy of these ideas is easy to demonstrate and many people who hold these views have seen this done. They have often also been taught the 'correct' facts but the beliefs continue to exist because underlying structures are resilient enough to resist change. In a recent evaluation of an environmental and agricultural science project in Zimbabwe one of the most difficult units identified was that which dealt with the Sun and the Cosmos. Why was this so difficult for most teachers? Part of the reason seems to lie in unfamiliar terminology; but another lies in strength of everyday 'commonsense' beliefs drawn from traditional cosmology that simply do not utilise the same frameworks to explain the changes of the seasons and the disposition of the planets.

What the alternative conceptions of students are in different countries remains to be fully researched. Some literature already exists and is discussed in relation to cultural contexts. Few countries have anything approaching a comprehensive research base that would be sufficient to design curricula that built outward from students existing understandings. It would be dangerous to assume these are the same everywhere though there are likely to be commonalities between countries. The constructivists have a powerful argument that this kind of research needs to be undertaken widely if learning difficulties in science are to be better understood and more effective and learning strategies planned.

4. Approaches to Science Teaching

Statements of desirable approaches to be teaching of science can be found in many different official publications. Typical of the last two decades are statements like the following taken from teaching notes for and environmental science curriculum in Africa. Science should:

> *"... develop an attitude of self reliance ...based on understanding skills and confidence in man's ability to solve problems himself. It is not the purpose of the course that pupils should be made to learn large numbers of facts, though basic knowledge is important. It is much more important that pupils develop an active and enquiring attitudes towards their environment and this is only possible it the pupils do experiments, keep records of observations and draw conclusions from clear discussion sessions".*

But equally commonly criticisms are made concerning the persistence of recall dominated teaching and learning that stresses factual knowledge and largely ignores higher levels of cognitive outcomes.

> *"These of us who are concerned about education in Africa and indeed in the third world countries in general, recognise rote learning as our greatest set back in educational transactions".* (Kamara, 1983)

The intended stress in practical activity, on enquiry, on process skills and problem solving is clear. Avalos and Haddad (1981) in their reviews of research on teacher effectiveness in developing countries claim that discovery learning approaches are likely to have significant effect on higher levels of cognitive outcomes. Also of relevance is the findings from teacher effectiveness research that didactic methods of teaching seem to be appropriate for low level cognitive skills whereas discovery or problem-solving approaches are better for higher cognitive skills (Dove, 1986). If these things are so, there are important implications for science teaching. There have been a number of attempts to research the use of discovery approaches in developing countries, and much discussion on the appropriateness of such methods in the context of referred teaching styles, cultural norms and availability of resources. Little of the research seems to consider the relationships between teaching method used and the content of the science lessons however, nor is it usually able to reach firm conclusions about its relative effectiveness since adequate control groups are rarely available. Even where it appears effective, the generaliability of the experience is often in question since most frequently it is selected groups of teachers who are involved in undertaking experiments with teaching methods. Some relevant studies relating to the relative efficacy of guided discovery and activity based teaching approaches are summarized below.

Mulopo and Fowler (1987) compared achievement, understanding about science and the scientific attitudes of learners at the concrete and formal level of cognitive development taught with different approaches in Zambia. Subjects were an equally weighted sample of concrete and formal reasoners in 11th grade chemistry classes assigned to one of two teaching method groups for 10 weeks. Results showed that among formal reasoners discovery method teaching was more effective than traditional methods for understanding science; for concrete reasoners the mode of instruction made no difference; overall the traditional group out-performed the discovery group in achievement but the discovery group developed what were judged more favourable attitudes to science. Okpala and Onocha (1988) used experimental and control groups (fifth year secondary) and ascertained that students taught physics concepts through active enquiry have less difficulties in learning the concepts than students taught the same concepts through vicarious enquiry methods. The authors recommended more active involvement of students in laboratory practical work.

An interesting gloss is place on these findings in a Nigerian study by Ehindero (1980) which argues that the lack of formal operational thought in students might be due to a similar lack in teachers, compounded by expository styles of teaching. A sample of pre-service secondary science teachers were grouped into formal and concrete operators and observed. Judgements were made on how well concrete and formal operational sub-groups realized their teaching intentions in lessons involving concrete and formal concepts. The study found no significant difference between the groups with respect to the teaching of concrete concepts but found significant difference in favour of formal operational student teachers on the teaching of formal concepts.

Looking across 14 countries Kelly (1980) used scales derived from student responses to describe the science learning environments of 14 year-old students. He found that the best science achievement occurred in countries which combine exploratory and authoritarian teaching styles. Within countries, exploratory styles were again associated with high science achievement although the relationship was less strong. These tentative findings, the author cautions, need confirmation in an experimental study since there is a question over the reliability of the reported styles.

Despite these apparently promising insights William and Buseri (1988) paint an all too familiar picture of contemporary science teaching. They analysed 54 science lessons in Nigeria using the Science Teaching Observation Schedule (Egglestone *et al* 1975). It was found that an expository style dominated. An 18 category explanation appraisal scheduled was developed—and instrument for the analysis of teaching effectiveness in the expository mode. Lessons were analysed in two clusters: the fast peddlers and the slow peddlers. The first peddler lessons displayed high incidence of what were judged ineffective attributes such as discontinuities in argument and vagueness in explanation, and were considered to be less coherent and less effective at exposition. The lessons analysed had previously been shown, using the Science Teaching Observation Schedule, to reflect a homogeneous style. All lessons were held to be low on explanations and high on assertion. In the view of the authors, the study confirms

> *"... the accepted picture of science teaching in Nigeria as being highly expository, teacher dominated, short on explanation but high assertion and totally lacking in planned opportunity for students to exercise initiative".*

Other examples of studies of teaching and learning are easy to find. For example, Aminah Ayob (1990) examined the use of group work in science teaching in Malaysia. She found that although group work is widely advocated and is often practised, there is little careful consideration of its purposes, and active management of classrooms, to ensure its effectiveness. As a result talk within groups was mainly task-oriented and at a low cognitive level and interactions were usually between two students, not amongst the groups as a whole. Those who took the most active roles were higher achieving.

Conflicts between the need to ensure that adequate content is mastered on the one hand and that problem solving skills are developed on the other recur. Razali's (1986) Malaysian study has argued that chemistry teachers feel that mastery of knowledge in chemistry was the most important aspect influencing students to continue to study chemistry; in contrast college instructors viewed the acquisition of traits such as study skills and strategies for learning as the most important factor. Adi's (1986) survey of Indonesian teachers, administrators and teacher educators regarding the in-service needs of science teachers report that while teachers and teacher-educators perceived 'mastery of subject area content' as most important, administrators perceived 'use and management of laboratory teaching for teaching-learning process' as the most important.

Mehl and Lockhead's (1987) report on a study designed to investigate the learning problems of disadvantaged South Africans suggests that selective attention to particular concepts that are poorly understood is a teaching strategy that can pay dividends. The study was motivate by concern about the large numbers of students who were poorly equipped to meet the academic requirements of first-year university course in science related disciplines. An analysis of interviews yielded a list of deficient cognitive capabilities. Techniques were developed to compensate for these deficiencies; the strategy required for the use of a specific concept was developed as the concept was taught. The new approach was trailed on a controlled experimental group of first year university physics students. Results for the use of the concepts showed a 30 per cent improvement in favour of the experimental group. The study concluded that there seemed to be three effective approaches to teaching scientific thinking: (i) teaching thinking free of specific content; (ii) integrating thinking skills with content by providing thinking strategies to give more meaningful access to the content of a discipline; (iii) determining the requisite thought processes for understanding using concepts and laws, and then making these explicit in the development of relevant curriculum materials. All seemed to have some merits.

Two other studies, chosen fairly randomly, given the flavour of the extensive literature that reports on teaching experiments. Chiang (1986) studied effects on achievement and growth of scientific ability of Taiwanese eighth grade students who were taught physics using an individualized instruction (II) format as opposed to those taught using conventional instruction (CI), Data were gathered using an IQ test, reasoning ability test, a physics aptitude test, mid-term and final achievement tests, and a follow-up test on the growth of scientific ability. Result indicated that II was superior to CI on mid-term and final achievement measures and in the growth of scientific ability. Marebah (1987) compared the effects of a co-operative learning method called Teams-Games-Tournaments (TGT), and Traditional Teacher-centred method (TTC) on science achievement, attitudes and social interaction in random sample of classes in intermediate schools in Riyadh. It was found that TGT was more effective than TTC in enhancing science achievement and that this was independent of ability grouping.

The problems with drawing conclusions from the literature are obvious. Without knowing a great deal more than is usually reported it is difficult to know how much confidence to have in the findings. Further what may be the case in one school system/school/classroom or with one teacher and group of students is not necessarily replicable in other circumstances. Which is not to say that nothing can be learned from the examples above, but rather to urge caution, and the constant need for validation of findings for the circumstances under which it is hoped to apply them.

5. Practical Activity in Science Education

One of the most comprehensive international reviews of the role of practical activity in science education is that by Headed and Za'rour (1986). The extent to which practical activity was been seen as an integral part of most new science programmes in developing countries is clear from the reports of the 9th and 10th International Clearing House on Science and Mathematics Curriculum Development (Lockard, 1975, 1977). Headed and Za'rour reached a number of conclusions amongst the most prominent of which are that practical activities in science are important, especially at primary level, and with less able students, and that they have a specific and limited role to play in the achievement of the broad objectives of science education found in most curricula. They argue that practical activities need to be selected and restricted to those areas which cannot be treated by more cost effective methods; that activities do not generally require highly sophisticated equipment and extensive laboratory facilities; that there are some teaching strategies that can substitute in part for some of the practical activity currently undertaken (narration of experimental activities with discussion of the reasoning involved; case histories; simulations). Not all these observations are uncontentious. Thus there is evidence (Lewin 1981) that less able students in Malysia do not find practical activity nearly so attractive as more able students and that it fails to motivate them. This in itself does not demonstrate that particular types of practical work could not be helpful in this respect, it does seem to suggest that the experience of practical work less able students have is not of a kind the stimulates them. Nevertheless, many of Za'rour and Haddads suggestions are well made.

In countries which have severe resource shortages practical activity in a conventional laboratory environment is generally unsustainable. For example, Mhlanga's (1984) study of 12 secondary schools in Malawi found that because of the acute shortage of laboratory equipment about half of the practical work is carried out by teacher and the other half by students in groups; classes are too large to see what is happening in teacher demonstrations and the groups are too big to allow everyone to have an opportunity to handle the apparatus. And this is in a system with one of the lowest transitionary rates from primary into secondary schools in Africa where total enrolment is a small proportion of the cohort. Where resources are more generously provided under-utilization is not uncommon. It is not difficult to find upper secondary laboratories in use for a minority of the school day, for reasons divided between the availability of consumable material, the serviceability of equipment, and the willingness and capability of teachers to organise practical work. And to compound the difficulties much of what constitutes practical work is reduced in practice to demonstration, or large group experiments with very limited participation by most students, directed towards the completion of laboratory accounts in standardized form which require very limited intellectual input.

It is self-evident that practical activities have high coasts compared to classroom based teaching both in terms of equipment and time. These costs are both capital (building and equipment costs may be many times the cost of ordinary classrooms) and recurrent (for consumable items and the maintenance of equipment). It is also obvious that the effectiveness of practical activity will depend greatly on the educational outcomes to which it is directed as well as the manner in which it is conducted. If assessment do not test the skills which are likely to developed (and most national examining does not test practical skills directly or extensively) this does not mean that nothing is achieved. On the other hand little may be achieved if practical work is reduced to the ritualistic following of instructions to replicate well established results. Under these circumstances much of the value of practical activity may be lost if its purpose collapses into simply verifying expected outcomes. Students may learn to play the game of getting the right answer for the experiment rather than appreciate anything about the designed of tests of hypotheses and the sources of error that need to be understood and eliminated before test results can be confidently accepted.

On aspect of practical activity to which much attention has been directed is the various forms of low cost provision of materials and source books of ideas for improvisation, often using science centres to promote this approach (Krasilchik, 1979),

Low, 1980, Maddock, 1982, Swift, 1983). These have been developed and tried in many countries with some measures of success. However it is still the exception rather than the rule to find large proportions of the equipment used produced by improvisation. The reasons for this are related to teacher motivation and access to suitable advice. They are also linked to problems of financing that often make it difficult to find even small amounts of non-salary funds at the school level. Where this is so and teachers' salaries are low it is difficult to stimulate much improvization if the costs fall on individual teachers. Other low cost options, like the Minilabs available in Sri Lanka, provide lower cost options than fully found laboratories, which enable a considerable amount of practical science to be taught.

6. Cultural Contests

The cultural contexts for science education differ substantially and there has been a considerable amount of work on how science and scientific ideas are perceived in different cultures. Much of the earlier work is summarized by Wilson (1981). Many studies on different aspects of culture are reviewed covering economic, social, political, religious and philosophical differences and their implications for the curriculum. This valuable bibliography accumulates material on variations in the assumptions and practices of science education that are to some degree culturally bounded. There is no intention here to attempt a synthesis of this work and that which was been added to the field since 1981. Some important features are worth outlining, however.

In a seminal paper Horton (1967) has explored the inter-relationships and misunderstandings that exist concerning the relationships between traditional and scientific belief systems in African societies. This thought provoking piece argues that the differences between African religious thinking and 'Western' theoretical reasoning are often not nearly so great as they appear to some who mistake a language distant from their own as no language at all. Horton identifies key differences in reasoning which he locates around the concepts of closed and openness. These he elaborates in terms of :

'(i) *differences connected with perception of alternatives, i.e.:*

- magical *versus* non-magical attitude to words;

- ideas bound to occasions *versus* ideas bound to ideas;
- unreflective *versus* reflective thinking;
- mixed *versus* segregated motives, and

(ii) differences linked to the interpretation of threats to an established body of knowledge *i.e.:*

- protective *versus* destructive attitude towards; established theory;
- divination *versus diagnosis;*
- existence *versus* non-existence of experimental method;
- confession *versus* non-confession of ignorance;
- coincidence, chance and probability;
- protective/destructive attitude to category systems;
- passage of time as bad or good."

These differences he argues are characteristic of different cultural perspectives that inform different ways of viewing the world. Their existence is of obvious significance to science teaching, since much curriculum development is predicated on the assumptions of a Western rationalist perspective on the various dimensions. To the extent that this is not held by teachers and students, or at least not held consistently, there are likely to be misunderstandings, different interpretations of the same pieces of data, and difficulties in internalising concepts that contradict widely held belief systems. Horton's work suggests these problems are not confined to traditional belief systems but may be exacerbated by them.

Another very readable investigation of culture and schooling is provided by Musgrave (1982) though this is not specific to science. This explores culture and thinking, the social basis for rationality, the relationships between education and the social order and the implications on the curriculum. It demonstrates again how different belief systems can have profound implications on how curricula are received and experienced by students who do not share the same world view as that assumed in curriculum materials. Thus giving just one example Musgrave argues that *gemeinschaft* societies (based on blood ties and sentiment) are very different to *gesellschaft* societies (based on contract and calculation). In the former apparently 'irrational' beliefs can flourish since the mechanisms to undermine them are weak; in the latter reason has more powerful tools to explore the natural world.

Adu-Ampona (1975) has explored the difficulties of bringing Western science to African children whose traditional background places emphasis on myth and superstition, and encourages unquestioning belief in the statements of people in authority. Sawyerr (1979) deepens this discussion in a study of the role of traditional beliefs in the teaching and learning of science in Sierra Leone. He suggests that traditional African world views, on such matters as causality and animism, strongly interfere with the learning of science and are widely diffused amongst secondary school pupils in Sierra Leone. Mundangepfupfu (1986) has examined the influence of magico-traditional scientific beliefs on science education in an attempt to reconcile their existence with rational thinking. She argues that students can learn science without rejecting magic-traditional beliefs, because science is understood through an evidential belief system whereas traditional magic is understood through a non-evidential belief system. Ogunniyi (1987) has shown that literate and non-literate Nigerians often hold both scientific and traditional notions of the world and cosmos simultaneously. Holding both views was evident regardless of the status of the respondent, though persons who had taken a course in the history and philosophy of science were shown to have a preference for the scientific cosmology. Kay (1975) in his study of curriculum innovation in Kenya, notes that new curricula encourage attitudes of individual initiative and personal decision-making which are strongly at variance with the collectivism and consultation that is fundamental to Kenyan children's cultural heritage. He argues that very little attention has been paid to this 'hidden conflict' by those responsible for 'modernising' Kenya's curriculum. Another aspect of learning conditions that Maddock (1975) draws attention to where there may be cross cultural differences relates to the distance seen to exist between school knowledge and that in the community. High school students in Papua New Guinea predicted scores for uneducated villagers which were significantly lower than the scores actually obtained by the villagers. The students also thought that village people were ignorant and could not be expected to show a scientific approach to things. In later work Maddock (1981, 1983) argues that science curriculum reform in developing countries must taking a much more fundamental account of the cultural bases of the societies which they are intended to serve. The adaptation of curricula originating in another country is unlikely to be satisfactory if the cultural and linguistic gap between the to societies is too great. The starting point must be the pre-existent knowledge, practices and belief patterns of the society itself.

Another aspect of teaching and learning that has a cross cultural dimension and has received a lot of attention relates to language issues. This has cross curricula and medium of instruction dimensions that run beyond the scope of this review and also a concern with language in science teaching. For example, Gardner (1976) investigated non-technical vocabulary difficulties among high school students in three regions of the Philippines using word lists arranged alphabetically and by difficulty-level to establish to what extent misunderstood words hampered communication in science. Johnstone undertook similar work in Papua New Guinea (1981) and Isa and Maskill (1982) researched differences in science word meanings in Scotland and Malaysia where Scottish Integrated Science had been adapted. Prophet (1990) attributes observed discrepancy between curriculum-in-action and curriculum-as-planned to second language learning problems and cultural context in Botswana.

> *"The most striking aspect of the science lessons observed in the schools was the passive nature of the pupils. The majority of work involved 'teacher talk' using either a lecture technique, or a simple question and answer routine that demanded only basic recall from the pupils, often as single words or simple sentences".*

Strevins (1976) surveyed the language problems encountered by science educators and by learners when the language of instruction is not the mother tongue, and describes a convergence of interest between (i) science teachers who teach in a foreign language, and (ii) foreign language teachers who teach learners whose principle aims include the learning of science. He distinguishes between linguistic dissonance which originate from the system of language, and socio-linguistic dissonance (which originate from language as a social institution). Keats, Keats and Rafael (1976) investigated the importance of language in the acquisition of the concept of weight with two groups of 5-year old Malysian children, one group being bilingual in Malay and English, the other in Chinese and English. The results support Piaget's contention that language plays only a minor role in the acquisition of cognitive structures. The National University of Lesotho (1980) held a workshop convened to analyse language problems faced in schools where pupils whose mother tongue is Sesotho are learning in English. The report provides a summary of the issues facing both teachers and pupils of science and mathematics in the context of English as a second language. Razak (1989) has explored language issues in science education concentrating particularly on textbooks and reading problems. This illustrates another strand of concern. His study attributes science learning problems to widespread reading difficulties which are compounded by inadequacies in textbook design, structure, vocabulary and editorial procedures.

Finally we note that gender, as opposed to sex, is cultural determined. Thus any discussion of cultural contexts should consider gender issues cross culturally. The disadvantages girls experience in science education, though fairly universal in their incidence, may not have the same causes in different societies. An interesting study from Botswana by Duncan [1989] reports on the influence of gender stereoptypes of science performance among adolescents at the junior school level. Botswana is in fact one of few countries in the developing world where female participation rates are higher than male ones. Her nation-wide survey of mid-secondary students in 27 schools supports her claim that the school learning process not only encourages gender differences in performance, but also operates different characteristics as it impinges on girls and boys. School science appears gender-typed by both boys and girls as a 'male' subject. This impinges on students' attitudes towards the subject and as a result on their performance. Girls who favour divided family roles and have a feminine self-image are more inclined to see science as a male activity. Girls who see science and/or school science as male area of activity generally have less positive attitudes to science and perform poorly. The study found that gender typing was considerably more salient in the achievement process for girls than for boys. The study found no significant differences in the extent to which boys and girls in Botswana gender-type occupations. Only 6 (less than 1 per cent) of girls in the sample aspired to technical occupations (outside medicine) whereas 18 per cent of boys aspire to jobs requiring academic science knowledge. Two processes were claimed to influence occupational aspirations: socio-economic factors which influence job status; and gender which supports distinction in job aspirations. Duncun maintains that the gender dimension is more fundamental than class dimension and takes the view that male and female cultures should be viewed as separate cultures, representing distinctive group identities, adaptive patterns and world views. The implications that Duncan draws from the study are that changes in science teaching practice are needed to favour more participation of girls particularly in practical activities in mixed classes, more relevance of curriculum of family life is necessary and more encouragement has to be provided girls to take up non-traditional roles if their participation is to be improved.

7. Implications for Planners

It is probably more difficult to generalise about teaching and learning in science education than about almost any other aspect. There is no best way of teaching science, suitable for a multitude of different purposes with students from radically different cultural and linguistic backgrounds. There remain many areas where there are strong differences of opinion amongst educationalists concerning which methods are most likely to result in which outcomes. And always there is the problem that what may work with a specific combination of circumstances may not be generalisable at the system level across many institutions with all their idiosyncrasies.

Nevertheless some implications can be drawn which planners need to address from this review.

- Whatever the variation between cultures the evidence there is seems to suggest that cognitive development patterns are broadly similar. To the extent that this is true they place real constraints on the rate at which students can be expected to master the basic ideas of science and progress to more complex abstract learning. The fact that some children acquire these earlier than others challenges curriculum developers to design pathways to understand science that are sufficiently flexible to allow all children to progress at a rate appropriate to their level of cognitive development. It is the planners' job to ensure that this is feasible and all science students are not locked into programmes that contain too many ideas inaccessible to the majority at their stage of development.

- It is a compelling pedagogic stance to proceed from the mental schema of the child to build science ideas from the explanations and understandings that are already present, and to treat apparent errors as possible misconceptions that have to be understood and resolved, rather than mistakes that simply require rectification. To do this is time consuming, especially if it is followed up at the individual student level by teachers. The planners' problem is to consider how feasible this is and how much strategic support for curriculum development and research on students' learning can be used to improve quality and achievement.
- Innovations in teaching and learning can make a difference. Encouraging some experimention, and channelling resources towards it, can offer motivational benefits to groups of teachers as well as achievement gains for students. Practically, this will always be an activity for a minority of teachers. But they, and the school structures (time for subject group meetings), the professional associations and informal networks that disseminate new practices can be support at low cost.
- The role of practical work needs careful examination. If it cannot be provided in conventional form to the majority of students alternatives should be considered. This is difficult teaching and learning problem for

science teachers to address, particularly those without an imaginative approach to their teaching. It will always be difficult to attribute learning gains to the presence or absence of practical activity, especially where the quality of that practical activity is not evaluated. Pedagogically the case is strong, but far too little effort has been invested in linking learning outcomes to the kind of practical activity that is realistically possible.

- The problems of teaching and learning in science education are clearly bound to the cultural contexts in which science education takes place. Thus, although the development aspects of cognition seem to have widespread relevance to planning teaching and learning it is dangerous to assume that research on these in one country is directly transferable to another. The conceptions and misconceptions that students bring to the study of science will also vary from place to place. What constitutes effective teaching methods will depend on the learning outcomes which are desired—it may be that the new methods detailed above are better for certain students, under certain circumstances given appropriate assessment of learning outcomes. But the didactic approaches that seem most common also have their merits, not least that they are the once many teachers are demonstrably happiest to employ, and it is clearly not the case that such methods can or should be abandoned indiscriminately.

7

Teacher Education

This chapter reviews research on teacher education and training and provides insight into the experience and qualifications of science teachers. It continues with consideration of science teacher training and its cultural context. The final two sections discuss issues in pre-service and in-service education.

The five main questions addressed in this chapter are :

1. What can be learned from recent reviews of teacher education?
2. What are main the characteristics of science teachers in developing countries?
3. How do cultural differences impinage on science teacher education?
4. What issues are raised by experience with pre-service teacher training?
5. What issues are raised by experience with in-service support for science teaching?

1. Reviews of Teacher Education Research

Over the past 15 years a great deal of research effort has been devoted to consideration of whether the training of teachers makes any difference to teachers' performance or to pupils' achievement. Teachers are the most expensive element in the recurrent budget for school systems. It is therefore important to try to reassure policy-makers that money spent on improving the quality of teachers is money well spent.

In the late 1960s and early 1970s influential reports such as the Plowden (1967) and Coleman (1966) reports and IEA studies raised some doubt about the value of teacher training in developed countries. Surveys commissioned by the World Bank echoed similar concerns for the developing countries apparently showing that teacher certification and academic achievement were unlikely to be important determination of student achievement (Alexander and Simmons, 1975). An updated study five years later conceded that teachers qualifications were only important at upper secondary in some subject areas (Simmons and Alexander 1980). These findings promoted a flurry of research activity (Husen, Saha and Noonan, 1978; Avalos and Haddad, 1981) which appeared to come to opposite conclusion to the World Bank. For instance, the Husen review found that teacher credentials were particularly important for subject areas requiring specialized skills and knowledge, such as mathematics and science. Heyneman and Loxley (1982) re-examined the International Association of Education Achievement data on the relative importance of school and home influences upon science achievement in high and low income countries. This re-analysis revealed that the effects of school and teacher quality on science achievement in developing nations were greater than previously demonstrated and that home background was relatively less important. Otewa (1983) investigated the contribution of professional qualifications to the teaching of Biology in 10 government and 10 Harambee schools representing 44 per cent of the secondary schools in one district of Kenya. The study used survey questionnaires administered to curriculum developers, head teachers, biology teachers, laboratory assistants and students in form four. Findings from the survey indicate that the more professionally qualified the teacher in a given school the better performance of students in that school and the less difficulty the teacher has with the curriculum material. However, since all the teachers in the Harambee schools were untrained the differences observed could be due to school effects. Guthrie's review of studies on the effects of teacher education (Guthrie, 1982) criticized the research methods used in the World Bank studies but notes that it did stimulate a more careful analysis of teacher training than might otherwise have taken place. Husen *et al* (1978) regarded the question of the value of training as having already been answered by the cumulative body of research but :

> *"... the question that remains unanswered is how, and because of what qualities and in what contexts do teachers make a difference".*

The latest IEA data (IEA 1991) suggest that more post secondary education, more preparation for science education, greater experience, subject specialization, membership of a professional association, and reading science journals are all associated with teachers who can promote effective learning.

The most recent review of teacher education in developing countries notes that it is only recently that research has concerned itself with the deeper question of how the training process makes a difference to teacher effectiveness (Dove, 1986). She posits that the reason there have been few studies is because of difficulties with research methods. For instance, with regard to social factors influencing teaching effectiveness it is possible that what counts as authoritarianism in one context may not be so classified in another (Dove, 1986). Avalos and Haddad (1981) call for more research on the differences in social contexts within which the teacher operates and for teacher effectiveness research which makes fewer assumptions about the nature of the relationship between various variables, and which makes more use of case study research methods. Sharpes (1988) argues for a multidimensional approach to research on teacher education which stress the importance of economic, political and social factors in understanding the relationship between teacher education and national development. In an earlier paper he highlights the special problems of training science teachers in some societies where the spirit of scientific enquiry is at variance with the politics of social control (Sharpes, 1986).

Other see part of the problem as residing in the previous educational experience of those who become science teachers. In their review of scientific and technological education in developing countries Husen and Postlethwaite (1985) contend that the discipline-centred, inward looking curricula offered at university level in many countries have an alienating effect on individuals with respect to the contribution they can make a national development. This has serious implications for potential science teachers who take such courses. They identify some attempts to include history of science and the role of science in national development in science curricula at tertiary level to address this problem. Trends in curriculum development at school level imply a stronger role for teachers in the promotion of scientific literacy and environment education than in the past. This in turn has implications for the way teachers are trained and the kind of science they study at higher levels.

The paucity of available research on teacher education is noted by Dove (1986) in her review of teacher education in developing countries. This is particularly critical in science. The bibliography to her review contains 362 entries, only three which are directly related to the training of science teachers. This is a particular cause for concern given the widespread dissemination of new views of science education related to deeper understanding of cognitive development and the interpretations and mental maps that students bring to science learning. This new view (Staver, 1989) is filtering through the science education community and influencing future directions amongst the professional community of curriculum designers. Without adequate infusion into the training of teachers and sensitive adaptation and development within the constraints of national systems there is a danger that the potential benefit will be lost as half understood, or misunderstood, catchwords. Curricular implications will remain in curriculum developers' rhetoric, but not teachers' practice.

2. Experience and Qualification of Science Teachers

The Second International Science Study (SISS) conducted by the International Association for the Evaluation of Educational Achievement (IEA) is providing a wealth of data on science teaching in developing countries which has implications for the selection and training of science teachers. *Table 3* is derived from data in the Second International Science Study of science achievement in 23 countries (Postlethwaite *et al* 1991). The data refer to those teachers who were teaching at lower secondary level where most students were aged 14 : 0 to 14 : 11 years at the time of sampling (IEA population 2). Only data on China, Ghana, Nigeria, Papua New Guinea, the Philippines, Singapore, Thailand, and Zimbabwe are shown in Table 3.

Most countries apart from China (45 per cent), Singapore (38 per cent) and the Philippines (10 per cent) have a majority of male science teachers, reaching over 90 per cent in Ghana. Science teachers are most frequently between 30 and 40 years old, with between three and five years post secondary education with up to four years of that specifically focused on science. Teaching loads are about 14 hours per week, with about 80 per cent of that time devoted to science teaching. Most of the teachers surveyed had only about two days in-service training per year. In most cases teachers claim to spend as much time on lesson preparation and marking as they do on teaching.

While over 50 per cent of science lessons tend to be taught in the laboratory there is wide variation in the time allocated to practical work, especially in those countries were lack of science equipment is reported. Length of teaching experience is greatest in Papua New Guinea (14.8 years) and least in Ghana (6.3 years). Science teachers in this sample have between 0.8 and 3.9 years of post secondary science education on average.

There are a number of studies which provide further information on the qualifications of science teachers. To cite just two, Jain (1977) presents and account of the qualifications of biology teachers in middle and secondary schools in India. Middle school teachers are expected to hold a first degree and a one-year education qualification; however only 10 per cent actually have such qualifications. A total of 75 per cent of secondary biology teachers are either graduates or have post-graduate qualifications. Wilson (1990), using IEA data for the upper secondary level (Population 3) notes that in 1983 the 'average' science teacher in National High Schools is expatriate, male, between 30 and 45 years old, with 10 years or more experience and tertiary qualification. These teachers spent 94 per cent of their time teaching science.

Most belonged to (foreign) science teacher associations. They teach classes of about 25 students and set about 5 hours homework each week (the schools are residential).

Table 3 base data on science education in eight developing countries taken from the Second International Science Study (SISS)

Country	*China*	*Thailand*	*Singapore*	*Papua N. Guinea*	*Ghana*	*Zimbabwe*	*Nigeria*	*Philippines*
Mean level of students achievement on SISS test [5]	60.0	56.7	56.4	55.3	46.7	42.8	42.2	39.7
Number of science teachers surveyed	607	96	225	94	70	256	261	241
Percentage male science teachers	45%	50%	38%	75%	93%	73%	79%	10%
Salary (%GNP/cap)	n.a.	192	156	986	18	n.a.	n.a.	198
Average age in years	47	28	35	40	30	31	33	33
Years post-secondary education	1.5	4	3.6	3.4	4.2	3.4	4.8	4.8
Years post-secondary science educ.	n.a.	2.5	2.8	1.6	3.3	1.8	3.9	0.8
Years teaching experience	n.a.	6.5	10.7	14.8	6.3	7.2	9.5	9.8
Days per year in service	n.a.	2.2	1.9	3.9	1.2	2.0	1.5	4.1
Hours total teaching per week	n.a.	15.3	17.7	18.2	17.2	19.2	13..7	20.5
Hours science teaching per weak	n.a.	13.9	14.0	12.8	14.7	17.1	11.4	16.3
Percentage science of all teaching	n.a.	91%	79%	71%	86%	89%	83%	79%
Hours/week spent prep. & marking	15.0	15.7	21.8	14.8	17.3	18.3	13.4	13.4
Percentage science taught in science laboratory	n.a.	60%	52%	78%	69%	66%	55%	46%
Percentage time devoted to practical work	17%	49%	32%	38%	29%	n.a.	32%	46%
Percentage perceiving a lack of equipment to be a problem	46%	28%	8%	39%	67%	35%	52%	56%

The most popular teaching method used by these teachers are reported as question and answer sessions and small group practical work, the latter occupies about one third of total class time, and assessment is largely by means of multiple-choice items. Thus there are wide variations between countries in teacher characteristics and, it must not be forgotten, within countries between schools and regions.

We should also note that the indications from the IEA study are that there are generally more males amongst science teachers. However this is from a very small sample of countries and needs to be interpreted in terms of the proportion of males in the teaching force as a whole. Circumstantial evidence suggests that more often than not science teachers are disproportionately male, especially in the physical sciences. This follows from much smaller proportions of girls studying these subjects to high levels. It has been the experience of a number of developing countries that as economic development has taken place and created more job opportunities teaching has become a more female profession. Nevertheless, it remains a problem in encouraging greater female participation in science that female role models are often in short supply.

3. Teacher Training and Cultural Interfaces

As we have seen there is a large body of research that draws attention to the cultural interface between teachers in the culture in which they work. This raises issues of special significance for science education teacher training science education is arguably culturally alien to the communities in many developing countries. Some significant dimension to these problems are identified by the authors cited below and this extends the discussion of cultural contexts.

The first group of studies address the problems that arise from conflict between rational scientific belief systems and traditional ones, and where teachers are expected to adopt teaching styles dissonant with their traditional roles. Whittle (1977) contends that traditional tribal education in Africa was primarily for the preservation of society. But reforms in science education have meant that teachers have had to learn how to foster children's interest in science, and how to conduct an enquiry-based experimental approach, which is at variance with their own dominant role in the classroom that teachers, and the children, instinctively expect from their tradition and upbringing. This situation poses a major challenge to science education in Africa, he argues, which requires some radical re-thinking of the cultural and environmental aspects of science teaching. Similarly Sawyerr (1985) describes how the new science curricula in Sierra Leone required new teacher roles and instructional approaches which were not sympathetic to existing traditions. Cole (1975), also working in West Africa, has pointed to the failure of many government initiated development programmes to improve the health and social conditions of their citizens. He attributes this to the antagonism of the people, arising from conflict between traditional and 'scientific' culture. He argues that it is essential to bridge this gap by teaching science in a way that accepts, rather than seeks to discredit, traditional culture. And a recent study of Nigerian secondary students by Jegeda and Okebukola (1991) found evidence that science instruction which deliberately involves the discussion of socio-cultural views about science concepts engendered more positive attitudes towards the study of science.

Rather than attempting to radically change traditional teaching styles Guthrie (1983) argued for being more realistic about using existing teaching methods in a more creative way. His study in Papua New Guinea on teaching styles, though not specifically concerned with science, found evidence from interviews with secondary school inspectors that a formalistic teaching style (highly organized with emphasis on rote learning and rigid teaching methods) dominated at secondary level. He argues that there may be very sound cultural reasons for this preferred teaching style and, if so, the style anticipated in new curriculum materials should match the empirical reality of teacher behaviour, rather than the aspirations of curriculum developers and teacher trainers oriented towards external value systems. In a paper reviewing science education developments internationally Lewin (1990) argues for further exploration of teaching and learning with respect to curriculum development, in particular a re-examination of the appropriateness of guided discovery approaches in the teaching of science, and an improved understanding of the conceptual development of children. The claims that approaches to teaching and teacher education in developing countries are more widely influenced by historical practices than by grounded research on teacher capabilities and needs. An implication may be that radically new approaches should not be introduced without very carefully consideration of the consequences of their misuse in terms of continued adherence to traditional teaching methods.

There are political and religious dimension to the problems of science teacher preparation that merit consideration. McDonald and Rogan (1985) describe the implementation of an innovatory science education project in the Chiskei region of South Africa at a time in history when the education department was held in disrepute by the majority of students of teachers. The project raises the political as well as cultural dimensions of change. In this case:

> *"Teachers found themselves in a difficult situation, caught between the demands of their pupils for political change, SEP's advocacy of educational change and the government's resistance to political change and suspicion of having its authority diluted by outside educational change agents."*

From a different perspective Sharpes (1986) has considered the training of science teachers in some Islamic societies. He argues that the spirit of scientific enquiry is at variance with the politics of social control in some Islamic countries. He suggests that the angostic rationalism of Western science presents a threat to Islamic belief. In such countries education and science must therefore be protected and rigorously controlled through religious doctrine leading to possible contradictions as seen from Western science educators perspectives. In his review of the preparation of science teachers who will become agents of social and economic change. He discusses the implications of this for the pre-service and in-service training of science teachers and how these need to change to overcome embedded resistance to transformation. Brophy and Dudley (1983) explore how the shift in emphasis from academic science to scientific literacy has met resistance from parents and teachers, partly as a result of perceived dilution of the academic curriculum to strengthen its vocational elements. The paper discusses attempts to overcome these problems in Malaysia and the Seychelles.

Yet another aspect of culture which impinges on teacher preparation is highlighted by Krishna (1988). He draws attention to the historical development of India's textbook culture which ties the teacher to a prescribed textbook. He defines the term textbook culture as, (i) teaching in all subjects based on the textbook prescribed by the state authorities; (ii) the teacher having no freedom to choose what to teach; (iii) resources other than the prescribed textbook not being available; (iv) student assessment being based only on material in the textbook. Dominant expectations of the role learning materials play in science education may therefore also be in opposition to innovations that seek to place the learners understanding and needs at the centre of the lesson planning.

From this discussion it is clear that issues on the interface between orthodoxies of science education and how to teach science, whether of a conventional or innovatory character, need to be absorbed in the teacher training process. Schools are generally associated with the modern sector in development countries and science has perhaps the greatest potential of all school subjects to alienate students from there culture. If teachers are to be effective it will be their job to bridge the gap between value systems and interpret science ideas in a meaningful way to those with other value systems. This is difficult when consciousness of the problem is high, it will be unlikely to happen if training does not address the issues. This is not a new observation, the number of times that it has been made suggests it is still a problem that has not been solved. Thus Dyasi (1977), as long as 1977, discussed the competencies needed by science teachers, particularly for the implementation of innovative curriculum projects associated with the Science Education Programme for Africa. He argued that the science teacher should be concerned with the relationship between the culture of science and the culture of the child, and teacher education should therefore help him or her to develop skills of operation in these cross-cultural encounters.

4. Pre-service Teacher Education

There has been considerable criticism of college pre-service training programmes in many countries, e.g. Stewart (1978). Amongst the most common concerns are curriculum overload, inappropriate pedagogical models, irrelevance, and cost. In discussing the trends in science education in Africa over the last 20 years (Ogunniyi, 1986) notes that rapid expansion has led to sharp increase in student population which have resulted in crash course for the training of science teachers. At the same time new school curricula imported and/or adapted from overseas have been making extensive demands on the skills of science teachers. Among the problems he identifies relevant to teacher education are:

- the poor preparation of teachers who teach the new programmes;
- the lack of motivation among teachers;
- the rapid rate of teacher transfer;
- the shortage of qualified science teachers.

He argues that the new science curricula demand teachers who are capable of using instructional procedures that are supportive of the new emphasis on 'science-for-all'. This implies less discipline-centred per-service training courses and less emphasis on university level qualifications. In Ogunniyi's opinion it would be better to prepare students for teaching using more realistic and relevant science courses closely matched to the abilities of students and the demands of the school science curriculum, than to staff the schools with drop-outs or those who failed the more traditional science courses offered by universities.

Kamariah (1985) also argues for closer collaboration between science educators and science teachers and more emphasis on increasing the relevance of training to teachers' need. He compared needs expressed by Malaysian secondary teachers and by trainers and found discrepancies were helpful in understanding problems that currently arise in the training system.

In the same vein Ojo (1985) offers a critique from the perspective of college lecturer which calls for a change in the organizational structure of academic departments in universities and colleges in the direction of greater integration of instructional activity in the training of science teachers to reflect a much wider interpretation of science. Ojo is extremely critical of what he terms the parochial compartmentalization of teaching in many institutions and calls for less restrictive entry requirements and more emphasis on course systems based on schools of study rather than subject systems based on faculty or departmental training.

The debate on the balance between academic and pedagogic knowledge is extended by Guthrie (1983) who reports that secondary school inspectors in Papua New Guinea rated diploma trained secondary teachers high in instructional and classroom management skills but low on subject knowledge; whereas degree holders were rated high on subject knowledge but low on professional attitude. He reports much less attrition from the diploma course which supplies the bulk of secondary teachers, and argues for a modularized diploma course which could later be upgraded to degree level (not specific to science). Bunker and Palmer (1984) note a trend towards moving teachers away from single subject training courses to more specialist training where science teachers can specialise in more than one science subject.

Teachers not only have to have personal knowledge of subject matter but also they need to know how to represent that knowledge for others. Wilson *et al* (1987) based on research in the USA, argue that research on teacher knowledge has been operationally defined. These researchers are concerned with how subject matter is transformed from the knowledge of the teacher into the content of instruction. They call this the missing paradigm in research on teaching. Hashweh (1985) examined the influence of subject matter knowledge on pedagogical reasoning and found that knowledgeable teachers were more likely to reject textbook explanations which did not match their own understanding and were also more likely to direct student misconceptions.

Practical experience during pre-service training is very limited in some countries. In China, Lewin (1987b) identifies teacher training, professional support, incentives and motivation of teachers among key issues in science education if school level science is to meet the challenges presented by national policy. The study concludes that more balanced training courses and less rigid disciplines compartmentalization of subject matter are desirable. Training is currently heavily content orientated and not much more than 5 per cent of time is allocated to training in pedagogical skill. Teaching practice is too brief and not supervised closely enough to ensure classroom skills are developed which are in improvement on these already employed.

In an apparently contrary view Preece (1988) concludes that traditional concern of science teachers with the content of the curriculum, rather than with teaching methods, is probably justified in view of the small effect reported of differences in teaching style on learning achievement. The positions are not necessarily contradictory since they must be interpreted in context. Where subject achievement of teacher trainees is low, upgrading must be a priority, especially if science teaching materials require a lot of interpretation by teachers. Where subject knowledge is adequate training in teaching methods and supported induction into teaching strategies and effective classroom management assume greater importance. In countries where entrants into science teacher training have low scores on school leaving examinations (say more than half a standard deviation below the mean) understanding science will be a problem for prospective teachers. Where teaching is an unpopular choice of profession such entry scores are not uncommon.

Context is therefore important to strategies for teaching education some strategies for which are reviewed by Fraser-Abder (1988) who summarises research reported in over 300 papers on teacher education in general 17 Caribbean countries. Yoloye (1985) writing in a Nigerian context, focuses attention on three particular problems faced by teacher educators in the training of teachers of integrated science:

- the problem of organising individualized instruction in large classes;
- the problem of selecting appropriate practical work which will bring about an understanding of the underlying unity of science;
- the selection of appropriate evaluation strategies.

The author calls for a more unified approach in the training of teachers of address these problems. Some possible new directions for teacher unidentified by an APEID meeting in 1982 which reviewed science education activities with a view to developing competence and creativity amongst teachers of science. Among the issues discussed was competency-based science teacher education in Thailand (APEID, 1982). Another meeting held three years later (UNESCO 1985) discussed the concept of 'open-competence' and identified the competencies and attitudes needed by science teachers and science teacher educators to cope with changes in science education. The report suggests strategies for designing and developing science teacher education programmes at the pre-service, in-service and continuing education levels, with focus on developing open competence. In a familiar refrain Singh (1986), in commenting on science education in Asia and the Pacific, reports that:

> *"... the pre-service training of science teachers does not always match the demands of new curricula in terms of the needed teacher competencies"*

His call for much stronger links between curriculum developers and teacher trainers echoes that of other and the suggests that the successful implementation of 'science-for-all' curricula will have little success without such links.

It is all too common to find that per-service teacher education systems are the most conservative elements of the school system when it comes to curriculum reform. There are many examples of the introduction of integrated science courses that have not been accompanied by concomitant changes in teacher education. If they are there is often a time lag of many years. Part of the reason lies in the stability and organization of teacher training staff who typically have themselves been single subject trained at degree level and have no career incentives to retrain. Separate subject science allows three heads of department, integrated science has only one. Perhaps most disturbingly, though outside the scope of this review, it is rare to find primary trained teachers in primary teacher training colleges, the more so in science. This cannot be beneficial to the science education system.

Pre-service education of science teachers is an under researched area. Though not a complete backward of neglect as this review shows, there is a shortage, especially at the individual country level, of systematic attempts to trace the products of science teacher education through into the school and evaluate the adequacy of otherwise of their training. It is also generally the case that what research is conducted on teaching and learning science is not located in training institutions as much University departments. The gestation cycle of useful results may therefore be long and understanding of learning problems and curriculum issues may remain the level of casual empiricism in training institutions, not a good basis to adapt pre-service training to meet emerging needs. All this suggests that pre-service training methods do require re-appraisal at the country level. They tend to be expensive in facilities, staff time and opportunity costs. They may not be less effective than in-service and on-service methods, or at the very least a different mix of full-time and part-time study than that which is current. There are many possibilities and many examples of different patterns of organization of training that can be culled for possible alternatives for particular systems. The first step is to obtain a better understanding than is currently demonstrated in the literature of existing patterns, their match with the needs of trainee teachers, and the reasons why teacher training institutions are so rarely centres of curriculum development and new insights into science education.

5. In-service Teacher Education

Like pre-service training in-service teacher education comes in many forms. These vary from short course lasting from less than a day to several days, to longer vacation programmes, to sandwich type arrangements over a year or more where training and teaching in schools are concurrent. In-service training may be on site within schools (sometimes called on-service), or in colleges or teacher's centres. It may be part of regular teacher support. More frequently it has a temporary existence associated with the introduction of new curricula. There are several attractions to in-service activity:

- It may be the only way to reach serving teachers with information and training in support of new courses. Serving teachers will always constitute the bulk of the teaching cadre, since new entrants will be a small proportion of the total each year.

- It is likely to be cheaper in most cases than full-time training if it takes place with minimal interruptions to normal teaching regimes.
- It offers the prospect of reaching large numbers of teachers whose initial training may have been many years previously.
- It can be often be arranged at the local level using facilities that already exist.

An example of the use of in-service training to train new teachers Chivore (1986) examined strategies used to attempt to solve problems of the secondary teacher in Zimbabwe following independence. Rapid educational expression created an unprecedented demand for teachers. As a result, a 4-year teacher training course was introduced comprising of 2 years resident in college and 2 years full-time teaching under supervision. The course used distance teaching methods. Students chose one major subject such as science or two minor subjects and were required to take other courses such as socialist ideology. This system had considerable cost advantages over the previous 3 year pre-service college model and was able to train large number of teachers in a relatively short period. There appears to be no independent evaluation of the quality of the graduates it has produced however.

In-service courses are commonly used to support the introduced of new curricula. Brophy and Dalgety (1980) described the implication of a new science curriculum in Guyana. An in-service distance programme for teachers accompanied the innovation and was evaluated by questionnaire survey. This showed that there was an apparent gap between the intentions of the curriculum developers and actual classroom practices. What were intended as laboratory projects and student-centred activities in reality became teacher-centred, textbook oriented approaches. In another example. McDonald and Rogan (1985) report on an in-service strategy employed by the science education project in introducing its materials and methods into black South African schools. The paper discusses the in-service tactics used in the Ciskei region of South Africa. Teacher security is recognized as of paramount importance, and the importance of gradually increasing teacher freedom. The Science Education Project sought to provide security by starting from highly structured content and lesson plans and gradually relaxing the structure as teachers became more secure in there knowledge of content. Contrary to orthodox practice the aims of the in-service programmes were formulated *after* teacher involvement in the innovation. It was found that teachers lacked the content knowledge required to assist in the formulation of in-service aims. The importance of long-term commitment to in-service education is recognized as well as the need to ensure increasing teacher participation. The approach taken has been to encourage teacher's support through a zonal system of 'centres of excellence' from which gradual diffusion can take place. These centres provide a leadership role for above average teachers. The authors stress the importance of support from school administration and inspectors for an innovation.

Sustained support comes cross as critical to many in-service initiatives. Once the initial need is meet the motivation to continue support sometimes evaporates. 'Exposure' course to new curriculum may become the only training that most teachers receive. Dock (1983) reports on the establishment of science centres, in-service courses, communications with teachers in Zimbabwe as part of the ZIM-SCI project for lower secondary introduced in the early 1980s. This system was apparently very successful initially but its sustainability now seems in question (British Council 1989).

In-service models which depend on cascading information and new teaching methods from key personnel, through regional and district staff, to the school level of in-service work are widespread and have been used in Malaysia and Sri Lanka amongst many other countries. Their attraction is practical, in that this may be the only economic way to multiply training over a short time scale to reach large proportions of the science teacher population. The disadvantages revolve around the adequacy of the training at each level (the trainers may not have much more exposure or experience of the new programmes than the trained), and the risk that whatever the initial messages were, by the time they have filtered down through several levels they may become distorted. Good supporting materials can help reduce these problems were there is time to create these.

Distance education techniques are used widely for in-service support. Though they can be very effective and may be a relatively cheap way of disseminating information and developing skills they may also encounter problems. Thus Guy's (1989) general critique of secondary in-service teacher education in Papua New Guinea discusses the Advanced Diploma in Teaching offered as a means of upgrading teacher knowledge. The diploma provides a mixture of residential and correspondence contact. Progress is affected by clashes between cultural preferences for collectivism and the individualism of distance study. The model has been reviewed in the light of these findings and the distance component has been strengthened through more interactive materials and increased levels of local support for course participants. A survey of pre-service students in Zimbabwe, Chivore (1986) found that there was a difference between the kind of training students expected of colleges and the actual training which the colleges provided. Distance teaching was rated by student-teachers as the least effective of 19 teaching methods suggesting this aspect of programmes has to be carefully designed and supported.

There have been attempts to develop structured methods of identifying training needs amongst science teachers. Zurub and Rubba (1983) report on the development and validation of an inventory designed to identify the needs of science teachers particularly the Arab countries. The instrument, Science Teacher Inventory of Need (STIN), consists of 83 items arranged under seven categories: (i) specifying objectives; (ii) diagnosing and evaluating learners; (iii) planning (iv) delivering; (v) managing; (vi) administering instructional facilities and equipment; (vii) improving science teacher competence. Content and construct validity was determined by a panel of judges and factor analysis, respectively. Al-Mossa (1987) used an Arabic version of this needs assessment instrument together with interviews to identify needs in Saudi Arabia. Analysis suggested a significant relationship between the intensity of professional needs of teachers and the location of their schools (rural/urban), teacher nationality, attendance at in-service programmes, and teacher educational level. Kamariah *et al* (1988) identified the most prominent needs of Jordanian and Malaysian science teachers using STIN. These fell into four categories: delivering science instruction; managing science instruction; administering science instructional facilities and equipment; and improving one's competence as a science teacher. The author's argue that there are similarities in terms of the nature of science education in both countries. Despite espousals of laboratory-based instruction in curriculum materials, teachers in both countries continue to use didactic teaching methods.

Given the diversities of purpose and context in-service support must be very varied in its forms. Some of the delammas are clear, the solutions of them often less so. For example, a common difficultly in organising in-service support is that the clientele is heterogeneous . Teachers participating may include those with much experience and those with little, male and female teachers with characteristically different areas of difficulty, those with good subject knowledge and those with imperfect understanding of the subject. Treating all teachers in such a group similarly risks boring some and exceeding the capabilities of others. A second problem arises when course providers see themselves as information givers, whilst course participants express their needs primarily in terms of the new teaching skills that they need to acquire. Describing new teaching methods is not the same as developing the skills to use them. Whilst much can be achieved by suitable demonstrations of technique and explanations of the ideas behind a teaching method the in-service experience may be ephemeral for many teachers unless it is followed up by supported practise and refinement in the circumstances of real classrooms with real students. It is continuing and timely in-service support that is often the greatest weakness in in-service strategies and it is in relation to this that most imagination needs to be exercised in designing methods that are feasible and cost sustainable. In practice this is likely to involve some institutionalization of staff development activity at the school—or local-level, through professional associations of science teachers, departmental in-service days, peer group support networks or similar arrangements.

6. Implications for Planners

This review shows that the composition of the science teacher cadre varies considerably from country to country in terms of qualification level, years of schooling, sex and age. The significance of this is bound up with other aspects of the development of the education system so on simple consolations can be reached. Science teaching probably does require more systematic training than some other subjects that are closer to the everyday experience of adults, particularly in those countries where science and technology are recent introductions, but even this kind of generalization depends on how science is to be taught and for what purposes.

Given the embryonic state of research on teacher education in developing countries it is appropriate to end this chapter on a more discursive note than the previous ones in considering its implications for planners. These really stem from prior insight and understandings that have yet to be established at a country level for most education systems. What kind of teacher education system is most appropriate and efficient will depend on the responses to the issues raised below.

- There is some evidence that more highly qualified science teachers produce better student achievement in science but clearly there are likely to be interaction effects with school level factors. Given the complexities of measuring both science achievement and teacher competence it is not surprising that some studies do not show strong effects related to training for science teachers. It would be working to conclude from this that training makes no difference for a number of good reasons. First, the effect of training must be related to the quality of that training and few attempts have been made to discriminate between different types of training experience. Second, the mismatches noted throughout this review between the emphasis of assessment systems and those of science curriculum might reasonably be supposed to dilute the training effects that may exist (colleges that trained teachers to simply maximise examination pass rates would justifiably attract criticism from most science education communities). Third, those who have been involved in teacher training, and who can stand at a distance from immediate self-interests, can identify many ways in which systematic training can shorten the learning curve for new teachers which simply working on-the job does not provide. Students are not expected to learn science on their own initiative without support; we should not expect this for science teachers.

- Most of the studies examining teaching methods favour new styles of teaching which make more use of discovery methods, practical work and student-centred learning. Despite this, didactic approaches continue to dominate indicating a preference amongst many teachers for them. Some of the reasons for this reside in familiarity and convenience, some may have cultural origins, some arise from resource constraints, and some reflect lack of changes in the attributes that are assessed which have not changed as rapidly as advice on pedagogy. There is a need for more comprehensive research on the factors which influence teachers to adopt particular teaching strategies and to ascertain how these can be made more effective as well as to introduce gradually new methods.
- Research on cognition seems to point to the need to match more carefully the cognitive demand of science curricula to the capabilities of teachers was well as students. If science teachers have not reached formal operational levels of thinking they are unlikely to be able to teach formal concepts in science other than by rote. This could be another reason for the preferences for exposition. There is some evidence to suggest that many science teachers may attach more importance to the content and concepts of science rather than the processes used in scientific thinking. This reinforces the need for teacher effectiveness research which examines teacher cognitive demand, and the understandings of science that teachers bring to the teaching of science—which can be used in designing more effective teacher

training. This seems almost totally absent in the current literature.

- Because of the special role that science is perceived to have in development, in many developing countries the science teacher is expected to be an agent of social and economic change. Governments keen to vocationalize science curricula require science teachers to implement plans which may be regarded with suspicion and as lacking in relevance by parents and students, and which are outside the direct experience of teachers as relatively successful academic scientists. This requires careful thought about appropriate training and support. So also does the emphasis on scientific enquiry skills in cultures unfamiliar with conflicting expectations of pedagogic role and epistemological validation. Prescriptive textbooks and teachers guides may be an asset for poorly trained teachers and resource starved schools. The challenge is how to encourage initiative and creative approaches to science teaching where circumstances demand detailed guidance for those teachers lacking in confidence and knowledge to go beyond it.

- The pre-service education of science teachers has been the subject of relatively little research and much debate. Whereas curriculum change has been rapid in many school systems much less change seems to have taken place in pre-service training approaches. Much teacher training is subject-based not pedagogically-oriented and moves towards more competency based training that stresses teaching skills and learning needs seem to have been slow to take root. The match between training experience and the day-to-day demands of science teaching could be improved in many systems. Similarly, in-service support appears often to be piecemeal and unlikely to exist as part of a long-term development plan; rather it is concentrated around periods when new curricula are introduced and tends to be one-off in character with limited or non-existent follow up. Yet the new skill teachers are expected to acquire are often complex and demanding and require much longer gestation periods. There is considerable scope to improve these support systems through creative use of new delivery systems like distance education and correspondence courses, which may be cheaper than conventional residential programmes. and stimulate on a much more widespread scale professional self-help groups of science teachers who can pool expertise and provide mutual support and guidance at the school-or local-level.

8

Concluding Remarks

This volume provides an overview of recent work and current issues that are of relevance to the planning of science education. It has a very wide scope and raises questions that need to be addressed national strategic planning as well as those relevant at the curriculum level. From its scope and the varying purposes and conditions under which science education is planned it is clear that singular conclusions are inappropriate. There is on one way to deliver science education effectively throughout the developing world; what may be desirable arises from different national development strategies, different educational starting points, and different desired outcomes. The most effective service this review can perform is to raise the kind of questions that planners need to consider based on the experience reported in the literature. The answers to these questions only begin to have currency in the circumstances of particular systems.

The questions that are most important to address in the process of planning more effective provision in the future are collected here in summary form. They are organized to follow the chapter structure of the review.

1. Context

Current policy is influenced by pedagogical traditions, established infrastructure for science education (facilities, human resources), historical links with curricula patterns in industrialized countries, and emerging trends in the orientation of science education. In most countries there is no *tabula rasa* which allows planning *ab initio* for science education. The room to manoeuvre for new policy must take as its starting point what already exists.

The kind of planning questions that are relevant revolve around dispassionate assessment of key features of current provision which constitute the baseline. This important process is too frequently taken for granted and planning proceeds from the *ought* to be, and not what *is*.

Such assessments should include consideration of:

- the dominant traditions in science education (science for an elite/science for all; curricula borrowing and adaptation/national curriculum development; exploratory child centred pedagogy/didactic pedagogy)?
- flows of students through the science education systems (who studies which science to which level? how have flows been evolving)?
- the quality of the existing stock of teachers and physical infrastructure (science take place over a given period of time).
- the life history of previous attempts to improve access and quality in science education (without this problems may be poorly diagnosed and reasons for ineffective implementation allowed to repeat themselves).
- the merits of increasing the effectiveness of existing practice rather than attempting to replace it with new practice (system maintenance and efficient support and supervision, rather than may be more effective, though less glamourous, in extending access and improving quality).

2. National Policy

National policy question that need to be addressed have several dimensions. First, there has to be a considered view taken of the role that science and technology are to play in the development process in general. Central to this is the extent to which national self-sufficiency is aimed for in science and technology as opposed to mutual inter-dependence. The kind of science education provision that may lead to invention and original invention across many fields may not be the same as that which can service needs to adapt and borrow purposefully science and technology developed elsewhere. Policy with respect to this will be partly politically determined, but it is also constrained by the realities of national development circumstances (e.g. small countries cannot generate sufficient concentrations of investment to support world-class science in many fields).

Second, whatever the strategic judgement, planners have to consider how best science education provision can meet the needs identified. Almost certainly there will be more than one option in configuring provision, each with its own costs and benefits and each with its own organizational and pedagogical implications. What are the criteria that should be used to chose from?

Third, technological changes and economic realignments create new conditions for science education and the development of science curricula. Tomorrow's opportunities need anticipation today—the micro-electronics revolution is transforming the skill mix in the workforce in those countries most able to take advantage of it; science education can offer support for the development of capabilities in technological problem solving, design, creative maintenance of imported machinery. It will only do so if planned change takes place in science education provision to reflect new needs.

Fourth, in those countries suffering from austerity the planning problems for science eduaction are acute and hard choices may have to be made. This needs to explore whether different approaches to education and training in science would make better use of scarce resources and the pool of talent that exists within the population. The kind of choices to be considered will include greater attention to equitable and efficient selection of students to study science, exploring the possibilities of concentrating scarce resources in particular institutions, establishing whether there are more efficient ways of developing science based skills through training related to employment, ensuring that the needs for non-specialists to acquire science based literacy and numeracy are not over-looked.

3. Aims and Objectives

The policy debate naturally leads on to questions of purpose and ends in view. More specifically the science education community has to articulate its educational goals with those of broader development policy. A series of questions need to be put:

- Science for who—which students should benefit to what level? should the bulk of science education be deliberately terminal in nature or preparatory for study at higher levels?
- What kind of science—should science education stress knowledge of science, the development of scientific process skills, or some mixture of the two?
- How can the differing needs and capabilities of students be reflected in flexible learning objectives that may not be the same for all students?
- To what extent should science education be broadened to incorporate technological learning, environmental awareness and the social implications of science?

4. Factors Affecting Achievement

The analysis of the literature on achievement provides the basis for many hypotheses but it cannot result in unambiguous specification of the most influential factors in enhancing achievement. The reasons at one level are obvious. Achievement is not uni-dimensional and it is not, until educational purposes have been clearly defined, that meaningful achievement can be delineated. The kind of achievement that is valued will be different in different systems, and might reasonably be expected to vary for different groups of students with different occupational futures.

In general terms some school inputs seem likely to be more effective than other in enhancing school achievement, but it is clear -that these are not universal prescriptions since the conditions under which effects are demonstrated vary so widely.

The best that can be concluded is that planners should indeed seek evidence of the relative cost-effectives of different types of investment, as indicated by data validated for the system which is planned. There are likely to be variations in sensitivity of outputs to inputs which provide a guide to policy but these have to be seen in terms of agreed positions on purpose and the assessment of outcomes. Thus, textbook provision may be a very good investment in many countries but is not sufficient in itself to overcome many of the teaching and learning problems that are apparent. Science laboratories are expensive facilities that may not be fully justified by some patterns of use. More especially practical activity will have limited impact on measures of achievement unless achievement be expected to contribute to. These are curricula questions as well as investment issues. The under-achievement of girls, and other disadvantaged groups, should be a continued cause for concern both on equity and efficiency grounds. Science the reasons for this are predominantly social not cognitive they are in principle open to change if priority is attached to problems of this kind.

5. Implementation and Organizational Issues

The literature on the implementation of educational innovations is extensive and heavily influenced by the experience of industrialized countries. It produces many insights into the processes of planned change, all of which have to be interpreted into specific organizational contexts to be useful. Perhaps the most important question for planners is to require them to express their assumptions concerning the conditions necessary to achieve the changes desired and critically examine these. A suggested agenda would involve answering questions like:

- Why is change needed?
- Does the diagnosis stand up to analysis?
- What assumptions are made about willingness to adopt new methods?
- What benefits and costs are involved for different participants?
- How is the innovation to be explained and supported?

- What current beliefs are held about the problems which the innovation is designed to overcome and what is the evidence that these beliefs are valid?
- What alternative options are there to achieve the same ends?
- What plans are there for the after-care of changes that are to be introduced?
- Under what conditions will such after-care be sustainable?

The organization of science education provision has been the subject of much debate. The most recent trends at secondary level are to treat science as a whole in the lower secondary schools with separate subject teaching remaining fairly common at higher levels. Organizational decisions both reflect and impinage on pedagogical ones. Thus, there are practical constraints on how much time can be allocated, how many teachers are available, and what kind of teaching styles can be adopted. However key decisions—integration of the sciences, the balance between physical and biological science, the inter-relationships with other subjects, and the conditions under which science is to be taught—all require educational rationalies that stand up to scrutiny and represent some level of consensus amongst those what the responsibility of organising the teaching of science.

Relevant planning question, when organizational change is completed, will include:

- What are the resource implications of changing cirriculum patterns?
- How best can use be made of the existing stock of trained science teachers?
- What curricula patterns will facilitate this?
- How can the facilities for practical science be effectively utilized at tolerable cost?
- How should be science be time-tabled to allow the sequential development of the subject over the secondary school cycle for all students?

Tracking and streaming policy in science education has implications for costs and internal efficiency. The evidence suggests that early selection does not have very substantial impact on achievement—especially when gains for the selected group are balanced against possible deterioration amongst those not selected for special treatment. It is a matter for conjecture whether these findings are cross-culturally transferable. At higher academic levels some forms of streaming and tracking are inevitable for several reasons including the increased difficulty of the science to be learned, the preferences of students to study science, the difficulties of resourcing science adequately. What form this should take has generally no appropriate prescription and must be examined at the country and school level. Key questions for planners include:

- On what basis should science education resources be concentrated on selected groups?
- What range of units costs are justified in teaching science in selective institutions?
- How will selection be accomplished reliably, efficiently and equitably?
- How will the quality of science education for those not selected to study science to high levels be protected?

6. Examinations and Assessment

Analysis of public examination papers in many countries suggests that the full range of outcomes specified in science curriculum materials is rarely assessed. In particular, there is evidence that assessment over emphasizes the recall of information and this continues to account for most of the items used. This is likely to discourage teaching directed towards higher level cognitive outcomes, and those in the affective and psychomotor domain. These difficulties seem to arise from a number of factors including the familiarity with recall based examining, the needs to stress reliability, discrimination and objectivity in assessment for selection rather than curriculum validity, and limited co-ordination between examination bodies and those responsible for defining curriculum goals.

Examining systems are low cost levers for introducing changes into teaching and learning. Cost of improving their quality and relevance are likely to be much lower than many other interventions which will effect teachers' classroom practice.

At least five strategies may offer some promise in improving matters. These are:

(i) Curriculum sensitive item writing where technical criteria for item selection is balanced with curriculum goals. External examinations can then be more effective in reinforcing curriculum goals.

(ii) Greater provision of diagnostic information such that examination performance analysis at the individual item level can be fed back to schools to indicate on what types of items students are performing badly. This can be used as the basis for designing intervention programmes (in-service courses, enrichment materials, etc.) targeted at areas of special need.

(iii) More school-based examinations to extend the range of types of performance assessed but only where the antecedent conditions exist for this to be feasible. The additional demands on teacher time and competence should not be underestimated.

(iv) Regional examination groups which allow regional variations in assessment of reflect variations in educational experience again only where antecedent conditions suggest this is feasible.

(v) Systems for monitoring standards. Norm-referenced national examinations provide little information of changes in standards of achievement in science. A more criterion-referenced approach to assessment could meet this need.

7. Teaching and Learning

Our review shows how complex the issues relating to how best to teach science are and how patchy existing understanding is of how students learn science. There is no best way to teach since aims and contexts vary so widely. The identification of effective teaching methods requires investigation of the developmental psychological aspects of concept acquisition, understanding of the ideas that students bring with them to science education which represent starting points for learning, and analysis of the structure and organization of learning material so that it can be presented and developed coherently. These are tasks for professional curriculum developers that cannot easily be short circulated since language and culture are likely to play a significant part in these understandings. Research needs to be based on the populations to whom science is to be taught and not simply extrapolated from findings elsewhere. Some implications can be drawn from this review which planners need to address.

Whatever the variation between cultures the evidence there is seems to suggest that cognitive development patterns are broadly similar. If true this place real constraints on the rate at which students can be expected to master the basic ideas of science and progress to more complex abstract learning. The fact that some children acquire these earlier than others challenges curriculum developers and planners to allow flexibility in the learning process to reflect this and ensure that students are not locked into programmes that contain too many ideas inaccessible to the majority at their stage of development.

It is a compelling pedagogic stance to proceed from the mental scheme of the child to build science ideas from the explanations and understandings that are already present. To do this is time consuming. The planners' problem is to consider how feasible this is and how much strategic support for curriculum development and research on students' learning can be used to improve quality and achievement.

The role of practical work needs careful examination. If it cannot be provided in conventional form to the majority of students alternatives should be considered. Padagogically the case for practical activity is strong, but far too little effort has been invested in linking learning outcomes to the kind of practical activity that is realistically possible.

The didactic approaches that seem most common have their merits, not least that they are the ones many teachers are demonstrably happiest to employ, and it is clearly not the case that such methods can or should be abandoned indiscriminately.

8. Teacher Education

Though doubts have been expressed about the effectiveness of investment in teacher training there is no convincing evidence that it is unnecessary. Students are not expected to learn science on their own initiative without support; it would seem paradoxical were this to the expected for science teachers. For science teaching in developing countries where the educational level of teachers is often not many years greater than those who are being taught, training would seem essential. The more so if the nature of science education is to be changed. Teacher education has often been an afterthought in innovatory projects, the features of which have been slower to take root in pre-service training than most other parts of education systems.

What training is required, through which delivery mechanism is partly dependent on existing conditions (how many teacher are trained, what is their background and level of achievement in science?), and partly a strategic issue (how much is practice expected to change with the introduction of a new curriculum?). These are under-researched questions in most developing countries. The debates about training methods will therefore continue. The needs in this area for research are therefore extensive and some pressing issues suggest themselves:

- What can be said, in particular systems, of the relative advantages of traditional pre-service and systematic in-service training of teachers?
- How much is known about the cognitive capabilities of entrants to the teaching profession—this knowledge is needed to begin to identify misconceptions and misunderstands of science amongst trainee teachers.
- How can the quality of teacher training institutions be improved?
- To what extent are problems diagnosed as soluble through improved training actually a function of school organization, leadership, and reward systems?
- How can in-service support be restructured away from *ad hoc* programmes for specific purposes that have little enduring effects?

9. Some Final Remarks

This review has taken a broad sweep across a large number of complex issues. It would be surprising if it had been able to reach simple conclusion particularly when the task was cast in terms of so many varied contexts which can only be grouped together by the fragile set of assumptions that classifies countries as developing. This should put be allowed to detract from the significance of the issues that are raised. The original purpose was to develop a series of frameworks to provoke debate of the issues raised as a primer for attempts to examine them more closely at individual country levels. It is for those with planning responsibilities to reflect on how the various insights, assertions and arguments stand up to application and interpretation in relation to the problems which confront them.

The key strategic role that science education can play in the development process should be clear from the development of the early chapters of this review. It is now perhaps more important than ever to try to gain some real purchase on the problems and issues identified, both on a practical and on a theoretical level, if the next generation of investment in improving the teaching and learning of science is to capitalise on the experience that has been accumulated over the last thirty years.

Bibliography

Adams, S.; Chen, D. 1981. *The process of educational innovation.* London: Kogan Page; Paris: UNESCO/IIEP.

Adamu, A.U. 1988. *Science schooling and manpower production in Nigeria: a study of Kano State science secondary schools.* D. Phil. dissertation, University of Sussex.

Adaye, A. 1982. *Personalisation of national objectives of Ethiopia into educational objectives.* Bonn: Deutsche Gessellschaft fur Technische Zusammenarbeit (GTZ); Nairobi: African Curriculum Evaluation. (African Studies in Curriculum Development and Evaluation, No. 60).

Adev, P. 1979. *Science curriculum and cognitive development in the Caribbean.* Ph.D. thesis, Chelsea College, University of London.

Adi, D.S. 1986. *The perceived in-service training needs of science teachers in public senior secondary schools in Bandung Municipality, Indonesia.* Ph. D. thesis, University of Iowa.

Adu-Ampoma, S.M. 1975. Myth and superstition: the African child's background, *Science Teacher* 18 (3-4): 21.

Ahmed, R. 1979, The environment as an integrating factor in science education. *Integrated Science Education, Worldwide (ICASE)* 53:7. (International Council of Associations of Science Education).

Al-Mossa, I.A. 1987. *A needs assessment of Saudi intermediate school teachers of science; a basis for in-service and pre-service programmes.* Doctorial dissertation, Kanasas State University.

Alabi, R.O. 1980. The science education programme for Africa. In: Bude, U. (ed.), *Science for self-reliance: 20 years of science education in Africa.* Report of the S.E.P.A. Review Conference, Gabarone, Botswana, Bonn: D.S.E.

Alexander L.; Simmons, J. 1975. *The determinants of school achievement in developing countries: the educational production function.* Washington D.C.: The World Bank. (Staff Working Paper No. 201).

APEID. 1982. *Towards a better science education, Asian Programme of Education Innovation for Development (APEID)*. Bangkok: UNESCO regional Office for Education in Asia and the Pacific.

Archenold, W.F.; Driver, R.H. Orton, A; Wood-Robinson, C. (eds.). 1980. *Cognitive development research in science and mathematics*. Leeds: Centre for Studies in Science Education, University of Leeds.

Arriagada, A. 1983. *Determinants of sixth grade student achievement in Peru*. Unpublished document. Washington D.C.: Education Department, The World Bank.

Ausubel, D.P. 1968. *Educational psychology; a cognitive view*, New York: Holt, Rinehart and Winston.

Avalos, B.; Headed, W. 1981. *A review of teacher effectiveness research in Africa, India, Latin America, Middle East, Malaysia. Philippines, and Thailand: synthesis of results*. Ottawa: International Development Research Centre (IDRC).

Baez, A. 1976. *Innovation in science education world-wide*. Paris: The UNESCO Press.

Bajah, S., 1975. Preparation of the secondary school teacher of the physical sciences for the African environment, *West African Journal of Education*, 19 (1), 85:96.

Bajah, S. 1985. A Nigerian case study of perceptions in science. *Prospects* 15 (4), 577:582.

Bajah, S.; Lewin, K. 1990. *Evaluation of environmental and agricultural science in action in Zimbabwe*. Report for Deutsche Stuffing fur International Entwicklung, Bonn.

Bala, J.; Gow, L. 1988. In-Service teacher education: a search for efficiency, *South Pacific Journal of Teacher Education* 16 (1) 87:100.

Barros, S. De Souza; Elia, M. 1990. Assessment of attainment in physics in Brazil. In: Layton, D. (ed.) *Innovations in science and technology education, Vol. 3* Paris: UNESCO.

Beacher, T.; Maclure, S. 1978. *The politics of curriculum change*. London: Hutchinson.

Biraimash, K. 1982. Different knowledge for different folks: knowledge distribution in a Togolese school. In: Altbach, P.G. *et al* (eds.), *Comparative Education*. New York: Macmillan.

Board of Education. 1943. *White paper on educational reconstruction*. London: H.M.S.O. (Cmnd. 6458).

Bolam, R. 1978. The management of educational change: towards a conceptual framework. In: Harris, A.; Lawn, M.; and Prescott, W.

Curriculum innovation. Milton Keynes (United Kingdom): Open University Press.

Bowles S.; Gintis H. 1976. *Shooling in capitalist America: educational reform and the contradictions of economic life*. New York: Basis Books.

British Council. 1989. *Partners in development; a review of science and mathematics education, 1965-89*. London.

British Council. 1990. *Education for capability: report to the World Bank*. London.

Brophy, M.; Dalgety, F. 1981. Curriculum diffusion and adoption: a West Indian experience, *Education for Development* 6 (4), 53:62.

Brophy, M.; Dudley, B. 1983, Science education in developing countries: a changing role. *Education for Development*. 8 (1), 29:37.

Bruner, J.S. 1961. The act of discovery, *Harvard Education Review* 31 (1), 21:32.

Bunker, C.; Palmer, W. 1984. *The implementation of a program for the improvement of academic knowledge of new teachers of science*. A paper presented to the Association for Science Education, Exeter (United Kingdom), June.

Cahill, B. 1984. Science education in Asia and the Pacific. *Bulletin of the UNESCO Regional Office for Education in Asia and the Pacific* 25, 1:498.

Carr, M. 1976. *Economically appropriate technology for developing countries: and annotated bibliography*. London: Intermediate Technology Development Group.

Chelliah, T. 1981. Training of teachers with science or humanities background for environmental education: a Malaysian case study. *Environmental Education and Information* 1 (2), 95:107.

Chiang, S. 1986. *Individualised instruction of junior high school physics in Southern Taiwan*. Doctorial dissertation, University of Indiana.

Chin, R.; Benne, K. 1968. General strategies for effecting change in human systems In: Bennis, W.: Benne Chin, R. (eds.) *The planning of change*. New York: Holt, Rhinehart and Winston.

Chisman, D.G.: Wilson, B.J. 1989. *Partners in development. A review of science and mathematics education*. London: British Council.

Chivore, B. 1986. Teacher education in post-independent Zimbabwe: problems and possible solutions. *Journal of education for teaching* 12 (3), 205:232.

Cobern, W.W. 1987. *A across-cultural, nature of science investigation: a comparative analysis of NOSS profiles on Nigerian and American pre-*

service, secondary science teachers. Paper presented at the 60th Annual Meeting of the National Association for Research in Science Teaching, Washington D.C. April.

Chen, D. (ed.). 1977. *New trends in integrated science teaching*, Vol. 4.

Paris: The UNESCO Press.

Cole, M. 1975. Science teaching and science curriculum development in a supposedly non-scientific culture. West *African Journal of Education* 19 (2), 313: 322.

Coleman, J.; Campbell, E.; Hobson, C.; McPartland, J.; Mood, A.; Weinfall, F.; York, R. 1966. *Equality of educational opportunity*. Washington D.C.: Government Printing Office.

Collison, G. 1976. A new dimension in science curriculum development in Africa. *Journal of the Ghana Association of Science Teachers* 16 (1), 9:8.

Comber, L.; Keeves, J.P. 1973. *Science education in nineteen countries: an empirical study*. New York: John Wiley and Sons. (International Studies in Evaluation, I).

Commonwealth Secretariat. 1985. *Interrelating science, mathematics and technology education: a basis of general education for all*. London.

Cooper, C. 1980. *Policy interventions for technological innovation in developing countries*. Washington D.C.: The World Bank. (Staff Working Paper No. 441.

Cooper, C.; Hoffman, K. 1981. *Transactions in technology and implications for developing countries*. Mimeographed. Brighton: Science Policy Research Unit, University of Sussex.

Cox, M.V.; Bryant, D.C., Agnihotri, R.K. 1982. A cross-cultural study of spatial ability in children. *Educational Psychologist* 2 (1), 37:46.

Crossley, M.; Smith, P.; Bray, M. 1985. INSET: Prospects and practices in developing countries. *Journal of Education for Teaching* 11 (2), 120:232.

Dalin, P. 1978. *The limits to educational change*. London: MacMillan.

Dasen, P.R. 1975. Concrete operational development in three cultures. *Journal of cross-cultural psychology* 6 (2), 151:172.

Davies, L. 1986. Women, educational management and the Third World: a comparative framework for analysis. *International Journal of Educational Development*. 6 (1).

Dekkers, J.A.: Allen, L.R. 1977. *Science cognitive and activity preferences and their relationship to present practices in science instruction in secondary schools in Penang. Malaysia*. Penang: Universities Sains.

Deutrom, B.; Wilson, M. 1986. Science for all in Papua New Guinea. *Science Education* 70 (4), 389:399

Dock, A. 1983. *The ZIM-SCI project: Zimbabwe secondary schools science project*. Progress Report No. 2. Harare: Ministry of Education and Culture.

Dore. R. 1976. *The diploma disease*. London: Unwin Education.

Dore, R. 1984. Technological self-reliance: sturdy ideal or self-serving rhetoric? In: Fransman, M.; King K. *Technological capability in the Third World*. London: Macmillan.

Dove, L.A. 1986. *Teacher and teacher education in developing countries: issues in planning, management and training*. London: Croom-Helm.

Driver R. 1983. *The pupil as scientist*. Milton Keynes (United Kingdom): Open University Press.

Driver, R.; Erickson, G. 1983. Theories-in-action: some theoretical and empiricial issues in the study of conceptual frameworks in science studies. *Science Education*, Vol. 10, 37:60.

Driver, R.; Oldham, V. 1986. A constructivist approach to curriculum development in science studies. *Science Education*, Vol. 13, 105:122.

Duncan, W. 1985. *Engendering school learning*. Stockholm: Institute of International Education, University of Stocklom. (Studies in Comparative and International Education, No. 16).

Duncan, W.A. 1989. *Engendering school learning: science attitudes and achievement among girls and boys in Botswana*. Stockhlom: Institute of International Education, University of Stockholm.

Dyasi, H.M. 1977. Three groups of skills essential for science teachers. *Cambridge Journal of Education* 7 (3), 173:179.

Dyasi, H.M. 1980. Some environmental education activities in Africa. *Journal of Environmental Education*, 12 (2), 24:28.

Egglestone, J. *et. al.* 1975. *A science teachers observation schedule*. London: School Council. (Research Studies).

Ehindero, O. 1980. Relationships between actualising concrete and formal science teaching intentions and the levels of cognitive development among some prospective teachers in Nigeria. *Science Education* 64 (2), 185:193.

Eiseman, T.O. 1979. The implantation of science in Nigeria and Kenya. *Minerva* 17 (4), 504:26.

Ellis, N. 1969. The occupation of science, *Technology and Societies*. Vol 5, 33:39.

Entwistle, N.J.; Wilson, J.D. 1977. *Degrees of excellence: the academic achievement game*. London: Hodder and Stoughton.

Eshiwani, G. 1983. *A study of women's access to higher education in Kenya with a special reference to mathematics and science education*. Nairobi: Kenyatta University.

Eshiwani, G. 1988. *Participation of girls in science and technology education in Kenya*. Ann Arbor: Michigan State University. (Working Paper 1968).

FASE. 1982. Report of the first international conference of the Council of Associations of Science Education. Harare: Forum of African Science Educators.

Fenshem, P.J. 1984. A second chance for school systems and a new vision for the population outside of school. *Bulletin of the UNESCO Regional Office for Education in Asia and the Pacific* No. 25. 437:468.

Fletcher, R. 1973. Purpose, scope and structure of public examination councils in the Third World. In: Commonwealth Secretariat. *Public Examinations*. Report of the Commonwealth Planning Seminar, Accra, March 1973. (Education in the Commonwealth, No. 8.)

Fransman, M.; King, K. *Technological capability in the Third World*. London: Macmillan.

Fresher-Abder, P. 1988. *Summary of science education research in the Caribbean, 1970-1987*. A paper presented at the annual meting of the National Association for Research in Science Teaching (61st. meeting, Lake of the Ozarkas, Missouri, April 10-13, 1988).

Freeman, C.; Clark, J.; Soete, L. 1982. *Unemployment and technical innovation : a study of long waves and economic development*, London: Frances Pinter.

Fullan, M. 1982. *The meaning of educational change*. New York: Teachers College Press.

Fullan, M.; Pomfret, A. 1977. Research on curriculum and instruction implementation. *Review of Educational Research* 47 (1), 335:397.

Fuller, B. 1987. What school factors raise achievement in the Third World. *Review of educational research*, 7 (3), 255:292.

Fuller, B.; Heyneman, S.P. 1989. Third World school quality; current collapse, future potential. *Educational Researcher*, 18 (20, 12:19.

Gardner, P. 1976. *Project WISP (Words in science-Philippines)*. Melbourne: Monash University.

Gilbert, J.K.; Watts, D.M. 1983. Concepts, misconceptions and alternative conceptions; changing perspectives in science education studies. *Science Education* 10, 61:98.

Gimeno, J.B.; Ibáñez, R.M. 1981. *The education of primary and secondary school teachers: an international comparative study*. Paris: The UNESCO Press.

Goonatilake, S. 1982. *Crippled minds*, London: Zed Press.

Goonatilake, S. 1989. Inventions and the developing countries. *Impact of Science on Society*, No. 147, 223:231.

Goswami, D. 1984. Science for all: the strategies involved and problems encountered in reaching the mass—the Indian experience. *Bulletin of the UNESCO Regional Office for Education in Asia and the Pacific*, No. 25, 426:36.

Gross, N.; Giacquinta, J.B.; Bernstein, M. 1971. *Implementing organisational innovations; a sociological analysis of planned change*. London: Harper and Row.

Gunstone, R.F. 1985. Science education; secondary school programmes. In: Husen, T. and Postlethwaite, T.N., *International encyclopaedia of education: research and studies*. Oxford: Pergamon Press.

Guthrie, G. 1982. Reviews of teacher training and teacher performance in developing countries; Beeby revisited. *International Review of Education*, 28 (3).

Guthrie, G. 1983. *An evaluation of the secondary teacher training system.*, Boroko (Papua New Guinea): National Research Institute. (ERU Report 44)

Guy, R. 1989. *Present initiatives and emerging trends in in-service teacher education in Papua New Guinea*. Paper presented to Extraordinary Faculty Seminar, 'Teachers for the 90s' at the University of Papua New Guinea, 1—4 September.

Haddad, W.; Za'rour, G, 1986, *Role and educational effects of practical activities in science education*. Washington. D.C.: The World Bank. (Education and Training Series, Discussion Paper No. 51).

Haggis S.; Adey, P. 1979. Review of integrated science worldwide. *Studies in Science Education* 6, 69:91.

Halsey, A.H. 1977, Towards meritocracy? The case of Britain. In: Karabel, J.; Halsey, A.H. (eds.). *Power and ideology in education*. New York: Oxford University Press.

Hamilson, M.A. 1982. Jamaican students. Attitude to science as it relates to achievement in external examinations. *Science Education* 66 (2), 155:169.

Hanushek, E.A. 1986. The economics of schooling: production and efficiency in public schools. *Journal of Economic Literature* 14, 351:388.

Harlen, W. 1990. Recent developments in primary and lower secondary school science. In: Layton, D. (ed.). *Innovations in Science and Technology Education*, Vol. 1, Paris: UNESCO.

Hashweh, M.Z. 1985. *An exploratory study of teacher knowledge and teaching: the effects of science teachers knowledge of subject matter and their conceptions of learning on their teaching*. Ph.D. dissertation, Stanford University.

Havelock, R.G. 1969. *Planning for innovation through dissemination and the utilisation of knowledge*. Ann Arbor, Michigan: Centre for Research on the Utalization of Scientific Knowledge, University of Michigan.

Havelock, R.G. 1973. *The change agent's guide to innovation*. Englewood Cliffs, New Jersey: Educational Technology Publications.

Havelock, R.G.; Huberman, A.M., 1977. *Solving educational problems: the theory and reality of innovation in developing countries*, Paris: UNESCO/International Bureau of Education (Studies and Surveys in Comparative Education).

Head, J. 1985. *The personal response to science*. Cambridge: Cambridge University Press. (Cambridge Science Education Series).

Heyneman S.; Jamison, D.; Montenegro, X. 1983. Textbooks in the Philippines: evaluation of the pedagogical impact of a nationwide investment. *Educational Evaluation and Policy Analysis*-6, 139-150.

Heyneman, S. 1987. Uses of examinations in developing countries: selection, research and education sector management. *International Journal of Educational Development* 7(4), 251:264.

Heyneman, S.; Loxley, W. 1982. Influences on academic achievement across high and low income countries: a re-analysis of IEA data. *Sociology of Education*, 25 (1), 13:21.

Heyneman, S.; Loxley, W. 1983. The effect of primary school quality on academic achievement across 29 high and low income countries. *American Journal of Sociology*, 88, 1162:1194.

Hirst, P. 1978. *Implementing innovatory projects*. (Paper commissioned by the World Bank for the diversified secondary curriculum project). Washington D.C.: The World Bank.

Hirst, P.H.; Peters, R.S., 1970. *The logic of Education*. London: Routledge and Kegan Paul.

Hobday, M. 1985. The impact of micro-electronics on developing countries: the case of Brazillian telecommunications. *Development and Change*, 16 (2).

Hornett, B. 1978. *Non-western science: adoption and implementation with particular reference to developing Anglophone countries, 1960-1978.* M.Ed. dissertation for Chelsea College, University of London.

Horton, R. 1967. African traditional thought and western science. *Africa* Vol. XXXVII.

Howes, M. 1979. Appropriate technology: a critical evaluation of the concepts and the movement. *Development and change* 10 (1).

Hoyle, E. 1970. Planned organisational change in education. *Research in Education,* Vol. 3.

Huberman, A.M. 1973. *Understanding change in the education; an introduction.* Paris: UNESCO/International Bureau of Education. (Experiments and Innovations in Education, No. 4).

Huberman, A.M.; Miles, M.B. 1984. *Innovation up close: how school improvement works.* London: Plenum Press.

Hudson, L. 1963. Personality and scientific attitude. *Nature,* Vol. 198, 913:914.

Hudson, L. 1967. The stereotypical scientist. *Nature,* Vol. 213, 228:9.

Hurst, P. 1978. *Implementing innovatory projects.* London: British Council.

Husen, T.; Postlethwaite, T.; (eds.). 1985. *The international encyclopedia of Education, Vol. 8. Oxford:* Pergamon Press.

Husen, T.; Saha, L.J.; Noonan, R. 1978. *Teacher training and student achievement in less developed countries.* Washington D.C.: The World Bank. (Staff Working Paper No. 310).

IEA. 1991 and 1992. (International Association for the Evaluation of Educational Achievement). *Second international science education project.* Oxford: Pergamon Press. [See individual entries in this bibliography under Rosier; Keeves. (Volume 1): Postlethwaite; Wiley, (Volume 2): Keeves. (Volume 3)].

ILO. 1981. *The paper qualification syndrome and the unemployment of school leavers: a comparative sub-regional study of four West African and four East African countries.* Geneva: International Labour Organization. (Two volumes).

Ingle, R.; Turner, A. 1981. Science curricula as cultural misfits. *European Journal of Science Education* 3 (4), 357:371.

Inkeles, A.; Smith, D.H. 1974. *Becoming modern: individual change in six developing countries.* London: Heinemann Educational Books.

Isa, A.M.; Maskill, R. 1982. A comparison of science word meaning in the classrooms of two different countries: Scottish Integrated

Science in Scotland and Malysia. *British Journal of Educational Psychology*, 52 (2), 188:198.

Jain, S. 1977. Biology teachers in Indian schools and their training. *Journal of Biological Education*, 11 (2), 91:94.

Jegede, O. 1982. An evaluation of the Nigerian integrated science project (NISP) after a decade of use in the classroom. *International Review of Education* 28 (3), 321:336.

Jencks, C.S. *et al.* 1972. *Inequality: a reassessment of the effects of family and schooling in America.* New York: Basic Books.

Jenkins, E.W. 1979. *From Armstrong to Nuffield.* London : John Murray.

Jequier, N. 1979. *Appropriate technology directory.* Paris: O.E.C.D.

Jevons, F. 1973. *Science observed.* London: George Allen and Unwin.

Johnstone, C.T. 1981. A minor replication of project SWNG. *Papua New Guinea Journal of Education*, 17 (1), 111: 114

Kamara, A. 1983. The training of science teacher educators in Africa. In: Harlen, W. (ed.), *New trends in primary school science education.* Paris: UNESCO, pp. 175-184.

Kamariah, H.; Rubba, A.; Tomera, A.; Zurub, A. 1988. Jordanian and Malaysian science teacher's prominent perceived professional needs: a comparison. *Journal of Research in Science Teaching*, 25 (7), 573: 588.

Kaplinsky, R. 1984. Trade in Technology—Who, What, Where and When? In: Fransman, M.; King, K. *Technological capability in the Third World.* London: Macmillan.

Katz, D.; Kahn, R.L. 1964. *The Social Psychology of Organisations.* New York: John Wiley and Sons.

Kay, S. 1975. Curriculum innovation and traditional cultur study of Kenya. *Comparative Education*, 11, 183:191.

Keats, D.; Keats, J.; Rafael, W. 1976. Concept acquisition in Malaysian bilingual children. *Journal of Cross-cultural Psychology*, 7 (1), 87:99.

Keeves, J.P. 1992. *Changes in science education and achievement, 1970-1984.* Oxford; Pargamon Press (Forthcoming). (Second International Science Project, Volume 3).

Kellaghan, T.; Greaney, V. 1989. *Discussion paper for 'Seminar on using examinations and standardised testing to improve educational quality'*, held in Lusaka, Zambia, 28 November—1 December 1988. (Organized by the 'Economic Development Institute' of the World Bank and 'Higher Education for Development Co-operation', Ireland).

Kelly, A, 1980. Exploration and authority in science learning environments—an international study. *European Journal of Science Education*, 2(2), 161:174.

Kelly, A. 1981. *The missing half: girls and science education*. Manchester: Manchester University Press.

Klopfer, L.E. 1985. Scientific literacy. In: Husen, T. and Postlethwaite, T.N. (eds.). *The International Encyclopedia of Education. Vol.* 8. Oxford: Pergamon Press, 4478:4479.

Knamiller, G. 1981. Environmental education and the North-South dialogue. *Comparative Education*, 17 (1), 87:94.

Knamiller, G. 1984. Linking school biology and community In developing countries. *Journal of Biological Education* 18 (1), 77:81.

Koech, M.K. 1984. Curriculum evaluation of heuristic methods in developing countries: a case study from East Africa. *Journal of Abstract in International Education*, 13 (2), 43:49.

Krasilchik, M. 1979. Biology teaching in Brazil: a case for curricular transformation. *Journal of Biological Education*, 13 (4), 311:314.

Krishna, K. 1988. Origins of India's textbook culture. In: *Comparative Education Review*, 32 (4), 452:464.

Kuhn, T. 1970. *The structure of scientific revolutions*. Chicago: The University of Chicago Press.

Kumar, A.; Khandelwal, D.P.; George, S. 1987. Science education in India. *Science Education* 71 (2), 189:200.

Kutnick, P.; Jules, V. 1988. Antecedents affecting science achievement scores in classrooms in Trinidad and Tobago. *International Journal of Educational Development*. 8 (4).

Lacey, C. 1970, *Hightown Grammar: the schools as a social system*. Manchester: Manchester University Press.

Layton, D. (ed.) 1986. Innovator's dilemmas: recontextualising science and technology education. In; Layton, D. (ed.). *Innovations in science and technology education*, Vol. I. Paris: UNESCO.

Loyton, D. (ed.): 1988. *Innovations in science and technology education*. Vol. II. Paris: UNESCO.

Layton, D. (ed.) 1990. *Innovations in science and technology education*, Volume III. Paris: UNESCO.

Leach, F. 1991. *Counterpart relationships in technical co-operation projects: a Sudanese study*. D. Phil Thesis for the University of Sussex.

Lewin, K. 1947. *Resolving social conflicts*, London: Harper and Row.

Lewin, K.M. 1980. *Science education in Malaysia and Sri Lanka: an evaluation of curriculum development in the last decade.* Brighton: Institute of Development Studies, University of Sussex. (*Development Research Digest,* No. 4).

Lewin, K.M., 1981. *Science education in Malysia and Sri Lanka: Curriculum development and course evaluation.* D.Phil thesis for the University of Sussex.

Lewin, K.M. 1985. Quality in question : A New Agenda for Curriculum reform in Developing Countries. *Comparative Education* 21 (2), 117:133.

Lewin, K.M. 1987a. *Education in Austerity: Options for Planners,* Paris: UNESCO/International Institute for Educational Planning. (Fundamentals of Educational Planning, No. 36).

Lewin, K.M. 1987b. Science education in China : Transformation and Change in the 1990s. *Comparative Education Review,* 31 (3), 419:441.

Lewin, K.M. 1989. Planning for scientific and technological development. In: Husen, T. and Postlethwaite, T.N. (eds.), *The International encyclopaedia of education. Supplementary Volume-One,* Oxford, Pergamon Press.

Lewin, K.M. 1990. International perspective on the development of science education : food for thought. *Studies in Science Education* 18, 1-23.

Lewin, K.M.; Little, A.W. 1982. *Examination reform and educational change in Sri Lanka 1972-82: modernization or dependent underdevelopment?* Brighton: Institute of Development Studies, University of Sussex. (Discussion Paper No. 180) [Revised version reprinted in: Watson, K. (ed.). *Dependence and interdependence in education,* London: Croom Helm.]

Lewin, K.M.; Little, A.W., Colclough, C. 1982. Adjustment to the 1980s: taking stock of educational expenditure. In: International Development Research Centre, *Financing educational development.* Ottawa (IDRC 205e).

Lewin, K.M.; Stuart, J.S. 1991. *Educational innovations in developing countries; case studies of changemakers.* London: MacMillan.

Lewin, K.M.; Wang, Lu. 1990. University entrance in China: a quite revolution. In: Broadfoot, P.; Murphy, R.; Torrance, H. *Changing educational assessment; international perspective and trends.* London: Routledge. (First presented at the British Comparative and International Education Society, Bristol (United Kingdom), September, 1988).

Lewin, K.M. Wang, Lu. 1991. Access to University in the People's Republic of China; a Longitudinal analysis of the structure and content of the university entrance examinations, 1984-88. *International Journal of Educational Development,* 11 (3), 231 : 244.

Likert, R. 1966. *The Human Organisation.,* New York: McGraw Hill.

Lillis, K; Lowe, J. 1987. The rise and fall of the school science project in East Africa. *Compare,* 17 (2), 167:180.

Lillis, K. 1981. *Expatriates and the process of secondary curriculum innovation in Kenya.* D.Phil thesis for the University of Sussex.

Lin, B.; Crawley, F.E. 1987. Classroom climate and science related attitudes of junior high school students in Taiwan. *Journal of Research in Science Teaching,* 24 (6), 579 : 551.

Linn, M.C. 1987. Establishing a research base for science education: challenges, trends and recommendations. *Journal of Research in Science Teaching,* 24 (3), 191 : 216.

Little, A. W. 1975. The rise of the heritocracy. *I.D.S. Bulletin,* 7 (3), 21:25.

Little, A.W., 1978. *The occupational and educational expectations of students in developed and developing countries.* Brighton: Institute of Development Studies University of Sussex. (Research Report, No. 4).

Little, A.W. 1990. *Understanding culture; a precondition for effective learning.* Paris: UNESCO. (Conference paper, World Conference on Education for All, Jomtien, Thailand).

Lockard. D.J. 1975. *9th international clearing house on science and mathmatics curriculum development.* College Park (Maryland): University of Maryland Centre of Science Teaching.

Lockard, D.J. 1977. *10th international clearing house on science and mathematics curriculum development.* College Park (Maryland): University of Maryland Centre for Science Teaching.

Lockheed, M.; Vail, S.; Fuller B., 1986. How textbooks affect achievement in developing countries: evidence from Thailand. *Journal of Educational Evaluation and Policy Analysis,* 8, 379:392.

Lockheed. M.; Vespoor, A. *et al.* 1990. *Improving education in developing countries; A review of policy options.* Washington D.C. The World Bank.

Lockheed, M.E.; Fonancier, J.; Bianchi, L.J. 1989. *Effective primary level science teaching in the Philippines,* Washington D.C.: Population and Human Resources Division, The World Bank (Working Papers, No. 208).

Lowe, N. 1980. *Directory of low cost science teaching centres.,* London: British Council.

Lutterodt, S. 1979. Evaluation in a developing context: constraints on the evaluation of an integrated science course in Ghana. *International Review of Education*, 25 (1), 90:95.

Maddock, M. 1975. The culture gap. What is formal schooling with its science education component doing to Papua New Guinean society? *Australian Science Teachers' Journal*, 21 (1), 93:97.

Maddock, M. 1981. Science education: an anthropological viewpoint. *Studies in Science Education*, 8, pp. 1-26.

Maddock, M. 1982. *Some trends in the evolution of science curriculum centres in Asia*. Bangkok. UNESCO Regional Office for Education in Asia and the Pecific. (Occasional Paper No. 12).

Maddock, M. 1983. Two decades of school science education in Papua New Guinea. *Science Education*, 67 (5), 561:573.

Manyuchi, E.P. 1981. *An investigation of the relationships between* Ph. D. Thesis for the University of London.

Mathews, J.C. 1985. *Examinations: a commentary*. London: George Allen and Unwin.

Maundu, J. 1988. Family background and student achievement. *Kenyan Journal of Education of Education*, 4 (1), 53:87.

Maybury, R. 1975. *Technical assistance and innovation in science education*. New York: John Wiley and Sons.

Mayo, E. 1945. *The social problems of industrial civilization*. Boston, Harvard University Press.

Mazrui, A. A. 1975. The African university as a multinational corporation: problems of penetration and dependency. *Harvard Educational Review*, 45 (2) 191:210.

McDonald, M.; Rogan, J. 1985. The in-service component of an innovation: a case study in an African setting. *Journal of Curriculum Studies* 17 (1), 63:85.

McDonald, M.; Rogan, J. 1988. Innovation in South African science education: science teaching observed. *Science Education* 72 (2) 225:236.

Measurement Services Unit. *School certificate examination reports, 1984-1990*, Waigani (Papua New Guinea): Department of Education.

Medawar, P. 1969. *The art of the soluble*. London: Penguin.

Mehl, M.; Lohhead, J. 1987. *Teaching thinking in subject-specific contents to disadvantaged South African communities*. (A paper presented to the 3rd international conference on thinking, Honolulu).

Merebah, S.A.A. 1987. *Co-operative learning in science: a comparative study in Saudi Arabia,* Doctorial dissertation for Kanasas State University.

Mhlanga, A. 1984. *Problems of teaching MCE physical science practical in secondary schools in Malawi.* Bonn: Deutsche Gesellschaft fur Technisch Zusammenarbeit (GTZ); Nairobi: African Curriculum Organisation. (African Studies in Curriculum Development and Evaluation, No. 158).

Mamari, G.R.V. 1977. Attempts to link school with work: the Tanzanian experience. *Prospects,* 7 (3), 379:388.

Morales, J.; Pinellsiles, A. 1977. *The determinate factors and costs of schooling in Bolivia.* La Paz: Universidad Catolica Boliviana. (Working Paper No. 77).

Mulopo, M. M.; Fowler, H.S. 1987. The effect of traditional and discovery instructional approaches on learning outcomes for learners of different intellectual development : a study of chemistry students in Zambia. *Journal of Research in Science Teaching,* 24 (3), 217:227.

Mundangepfupfu, R.M. 1986. *The distinction of magico-traditional from scientific beliefs in the teaching of science in Africa,* Doctorial dissertation for the University of Toronto.

Musgrave, F. 1982. *Education and anthropology; others cultures and the teacher,* New York: John Wiley and sons.

Mutsune, M.K. 1983. *An investigation into the relationship between theory and practical biology at 'A' level in Kenyan secondary schools..* Bonn: Deutsche Gesellschaft für Technische Zusammenarbeit (GTZ)/ Nairobi: African Curriculum Organisation. (African Studies in Curriculum Development and Evaluation, No. 100).

National University of Lesotho. 1980. *Language in mathematics and science lessons. Parts 1:2, Workshop Report.* Roma : Department of Science Education, National University of Lesotho.

Nichter, R. 1984. International science education : A study of UNESCO science education improvement projects in selected Anglophone countries in Africa; projects problems. *Science Education,* 68 (4), 381: 396.

Nwakoby, F.U. 1988. *The educational change process in Nigeria; an evaluation of the junior secondary school innovation in Anambra State.* D. Phil. thesis for the University of Sussex.

Nyiti, R.M. 1976. The development of conservation in the Meru children to Tanzania. *Child Development,* 47, 1122: 1129.

OECD. 1973. *Case studies of educational innovation; III. At the school Level.* Paris: Centre for Educational Research and Innovation, O.E.C.D.

OECD. 1983. *Assessing the impacts of technology on society;* Paris: O.E.C.D.

Ogawa, M. 1986. Towards a new rationale for science education in a non-western society. *European Journal of Science Education,* 8 (2), 113:119.

Ogunniyi, M.B. 1986. Two decades of science education in Africa. *Science Education,* 70 (2), p. 122.

Ogunniyi, M.B. 1987. Conceptions of traditional cosmological ideas among literate and non-literate Nigerians. *Journal of Research in Science Teaching,* 24 (2), 107:117.

Ogunniyi, M.B. 1988. Adapting western science to traditional African culture. *International Journal of Science Education,* 10 (1), 1:10.

Ojo, D.F. 1985. Towards a new approach to the training of science teachers at intermediate level, *Journal of Teacher Education* (University of Ife. Nigeria), 1 (2), 178:190.

Okebukola, P.A. 1987. Students' performance in practical chemistry : a study of some related factors. *Journal of Research in Science Teaching,* 24 (2), 119:126.

Okpala, N.P.: Onocha, C.O. 1988. The relative effects of two instructional methods on students' perceived difficulties in learning physics concepts, *Kenya Journal of Education,* 4 (10), 147:161.

Oladele, J.O. 1985. Curriculum for teacher education : the contribution of the Nigerian Educational Research Council (NERC). In: Mgbodile, T.; Ayodele, S.; Akube, A.; Obioma, G. *Issues in teacher education and science curriculum in Nigeria.* Lagos: Curriculum Organisation of Nigeria. (Nonograph Series No. 2).

Osborne, R.; Freyberg, P. 1985. *Children's Science.* London : Heinemann Educational .

Osunde. E.; Ellis, P. 1986. Teacher education in Nigeria : an evolving academic system. *International Education* 15 (2), 63:68.

Otaala, B.; Ohuche, R. (eds.) 1980. *Concept development in African children,* Monrovia: African Educational Resources, Olewa, J.O. 1983. *The factors affecting the teaching of biology in both government and Harambee secondary schools in Kenya,* Bonn: Deutsche Gesellschaft für Technische Zusammenarbeit (GTZ); Nairobi: African Curriculum Organisation. (African Studies in Curriculum Development and Evaluation, No. 80).

Oxenham J, (ed). 1984. *Education versus qualification.* London: Unwin Education.

Papagiannis, G.J.; Klees, S.J.; Bickel, R.N. 1982. Toward a political economy of educational innovation, *Reviews of Educational Research,* 52 (2) 45:290.

Pavitt, K. (ed.) 1980. *Technical innovation and British economic performance,* London, MacMillan.

Pennycuick, D, 1990, Factors influencing the introduction of continuous assessment systems in developing countries. In: Layton, D. (ed.), *Innovations in science and technology education, Vol. III,* Paris: UNESCO.

Peterson, A. 1981. Concept learning project in science and mathematics of South-east Asian children. *Journal of Science and Mathematics Education in South-east Asia,* 4 (1):20.

Phenix, P.H. 1964. *The realms of meaning,* New York : McGraw Hill.

Pidgeon, D.A. 1970. *Expectation and pupil performance.* Slough (United Kingdom): National Foundation for Educational Research.

Plowden Report. 1967, *Children and their primary schools.* London: H.M.S.O.

Postlethwaite, T.N.; Wiley, D.E. (eds.) 1992. *Science achievement in twenty-three countries : second international science study,* Volume 2. Oxford: Pergamon Press.

Pottinger, F.M. 1982. The Pacific experience and its implications for science education in the 80's. *Educational Perspectives,* 21 (2), 24:28.

Preece, P.F.W. 1988. A decade of research in science education. *School Science Review,* March, 1988, 579:586.

Prophet, R. 1990. Rhetoric and reality in science curriculum development in Botswana. *International Journal of Science Education,* 12 (1), 13:23.

Rains. G. 1984. Determinants and consequences of idigenous technology activity. In: Fransman, M.; King, K. *Technological capability in the Third World.* London: Macmillan.

Ravetz, J.R. 1971. *Scientific knowledge and its social problems.* Oxford: Oxford University Press.

Razali, S.N. 1986. *Comparison of perceptions of the importance of high school chemistry among various instructors and students in the United States and Malaysia,* Doctorial dissertation for the University of Iowa.

Reay, J. (ed.) *New tends in trends in integrated science teaching.* Vol. 2. Pasris : UNESCO.

Richmond, P.E. (ed). 1974. *New trends in integrated science teaching.* Vol. 3, Paris : UNESCO.

Richmond, P.E. (ed.) 1970. *New trends in integrated science teaching*. Vol. 1, Paris: UNESCO.

Roemer, M. 1981. Dependence and industrialisation strategies. *World Development*, 9 (5).

Roethlisberger, F.J.; Diskson, W.J. 1939. *Management and the worker*. Boston: Harvard University Press.

Rogers, E.M.; Shoemaker, E.F. 1971. *Communication of innovations : as cross cultural approach*, New York: Free Press.

Rosenthal, R.; Jocobson, L. 1968. *Study pygmalion in the classroom*, New York: Holt, Rhinehart and Winston.

Rosier, M.J.; Keeves, J.P. 1991. *Science education and curricula in twenty-three countries*. Second International Science Study, Vol. 1, Oxford: Pergamon Press.

Ross, A.R. 1990. *School certificate examinations in Papua New Guinea*. Unpublished manuscript prepared for the University of Sussex.

Ross, A.R. 1977. *The remedial treatment of problems of depth perception in diagrams : a Nigerian study*, M.Sc. dissertation for the University of East Anglia.

Ross, A.R. 1981. An analysis of the grade Ten examination, 1980. *Papua New Guinea Journal of Education* 17 (2), 210:215.

Rostow, W. 1960. *The stages of economic growth : A non-communist manifesto*, Cambridge: Cambridge University Press.

Rowntree, D. 1974. *Educational technology in curriculum development*. New York: Harper and Row.

Rutter, M.; Maughan, B.; Mortimore P.; Ouston J. 1973. *Fifteen thousand hours: secondary schools and their effects on children*, London: Open Books.

Savane, L. 1973. Problems of scientific and technological development in black Africa. *Impact of science on Society*, 23 (2).

Sawyerr, E.S. 1979. The role of traditional beliefs in the teaching and learning of science in Sierra Leone. *Science Teacher* 22 (3/4), 3:42.

Sawyerr, E.S. 1985. The science curriculum and the secondary student in Sierra Lone. *Science Education*, 69 (2), 147:153.

Schiefelbein, E., Simmons, J. 1981. *The determinants of school achievement; a review of research from developing countries*, Ottawa: International Development Research Centre.

Schumacher, E.F. 1973, *Small is beautiful* London: Blond and Briggs.

Seers, D. 1983. *The political economy of nationalism*. Oxford: Oxford University Press.

Seng, C. 1980. Recent trends and issues in school physics education in South East Asia. *Journal of Science and Mathematics Education in South-East Asia*, 3 (2), 20:28.

Sharpes, D. (ed). 1988. *International perspectives on teacher education*, London: Routledge.

Sharpes, D.K. 1986. Teacher training and higher education in selected Islamic centres, *Journal of Education for Teachers*, 12 (3).

Shayer, M.; Adey, P. 1981. *Towards a science of Science teaching; cognitive development and curriculum demand*. London: Heinemann Education.

Shea, J. 1985. Studies of cognitive development in Papua New Guinea. *International Journal of Psychology*, 20, 33:61.

Sibanda, I, 1990. The assessment of science practical work in Zimbabwe. In: Layton, D. *Innovations in science and technology education*. Vol. III, Paris: UNESCO.

Singh, R.R. 1986. *Education in Asia and the Pecific: retrospect: prospects.* Bangkok: UNESCO Regional Office for Education in Asia and the Pacific.

Skinner, B.F. 1948. *Walden Two*. New York: MacMillan.

Slater, D. 1985. The management of change: the theory and the practice. In: Huges, M.; Ribbins, P.; Thomas, H. *Managing education: The system and the institution*. New York: Holt, Rhinehart and Winston.

Slimming, D. 1979. The introduction of integrated science teaching into Swaziland. *Journal of the Association of science Teachers in Ghana* Vol. XIX, p.1.

SLOG. 1987. *Why do students learn; a six country study of student motivation*. Brighton: Institute of Development Studies, University of Sussex. (Research Report 17).

Smith, L.; Sheath, P. 1971. *Anatomy of educational innovation; organisational analysis of an elementary school*. New York: John Wiley and Sons.

Somerset, H. 1982. *Examination reform: the Kenya experience*. (Report prepared for the World Bank, Washington D.C.)

Somerset, H. 1988. Examinations as an instrument to improve Pedagogy. In: Heyneman, S.; Fagerlind I. (eds.) *University examinations and standardised testing; principles, experience and policy options*. Washington D.C.: The World Bank (Technical Paper No. 78).

Staver, J.R. 1989. A summary of research in science education : 1987. *Science Education* Vol. 73 (3).

Stewart, F. 1979. *International technology transfer : Issues and policy options.* Washington D.C.: The World Bank. (Staff Working Paper No. 344).

Stewart, I, 1978. Problems of teacher education in developing countries, with special reference to Papua New Guinea : some current strategies, *British Journal of Teacher Education,* 4 (3), 187:202.

Strevins, P. 1976. Problems of learning and teaching science through a foreign language. *Studies in Science Education,* 3, 55:68.

Swetz, F.; Meerah. T. 1982. The reform of physics teaching in Malaysian schools : a case study of curriculum adaptation, *Science Education,* 66 (2), 171:180.

Swift, D. 1983. *Physics for rural development : a source book for teachers and extension workers in developing countries,* New York: John Wiley and Sons.

Thias, H.; Carnoy, M. 1973. *Cost benefit analysis in education: A case study of Kenya,* Baltimore: Johns Hopkins Press.

Thijs, G. (ed.) 1982. *Science education in Southern Africa : Pre-entry science courses and science teachers' upgrading programs.* Report of the Inter-university Workshop, Maseru, Lesotho, 2-5 December.

Tiberghien A. 1986. Difficulties in concept formation. In: Layton, D. (ed.) *Innovations in science and technology education,* Paris: UNESCO.

Tuppen, C. 1981. *Schools and student differences; grade ten examination and assessment results.* Waigani: Educational Research Unit, University of Papua New Guinea. (Report No. 39).

Ukaegbu, C. 1982. Educational experiences of Nigerian scientists and engineers : Problems of technological skill formation for national self-reliance. *Comparative Education,* 21 (2) 172:182.

UNESCO Regional Office for Asia and the Pacific. 1985. *Training of science teachers and teacher educators.* Report of Technical Working Group, Quezon City: Philippines, July 17-27, 1984.

UNESCO Science Education Division, 1986. *The place of science and technology in school curricula : A global survey.* Paris: UNESCO.

UNESCO. 1976. *Trends and problems in science and technology education in Asia.* Report of the Regional Meeting, Singapore.

UNESCO. 1982. *Conference of Ministers of Education and those responsible for economic planning in African Member States; Hasrare, 28 June—3 July 1982,* Paris. (Various documents).

UNESCO. 1986. *The place of science and technology in school curricula : A global survey.* Paris: Division of Science Technical and Environmental Education.

United Nations. 1979. *Report of the United Nations Conference on Science and Technology for Development*, Vienna, 20-31 August.

University of Papua New Guinea. 1990. *Evaluation of bachelor of education in-service science [BEDIS] Program*. mimeo to Chairman of the Educational Research and Publications Committee, 25 October, 1990.

Vulliamy, G. 1988. Adapting secondary school science for rural development : some lessons from Papua New Guinea. *Compare* 18 (1), 79:92.

Wallberg. H.J. 1991. Improving school science in advanced and developing countries, *Review of Educational Research*, 61, 25:69.

Warf, J. 1978. Reflections on science education in the pan-Malay world. *Science Education*, 62 (2), 257:262.

Watson, K. 1980, Influences and constraints on curriculum development in the Third World. *Canadian and International Education*, 9 (2), 28:42.

Watson, K.; William, P. 1984. Comparative studies and international awareness in teacher education: the need for reappraisal, *Journal of Education for Teaching*, 10 (3), 249:255.

Webb, G.; Brissett, B. 1986. The mental maps of Jamaican school children: a case study. *Caribbean Journal of Education*, 13 (3), 181:204.

Whitfield, R.C. 1979, Educational research and science teaching, *School Science Review*, 60, 411:430.

Whittle, P.A. 1977. *Science teacher education for new secondary school curricula in Anglophone Africa*. M. Phil. thesis for Chelsea College, University of London.

Williams I.; Buseri, J. 1988. Expository teaching styles of Nigerian science teachers. Part 2: The explanation appraisal schedule. *Research in Science Teaching in Education*, 6 (2) 107:115.

Williams, I. W. 1979. *The implementation of curricula adapted from Scottish integrated science*. Jerusalem: Isarael Science Teacher Centre, Hebrew University.

Williams, I.W. 1977. *The Swaziland integrated science project: An evaluation*. Mbabane: Government of Swaziland/London: Ministry of Overseas Development.

Wilson, B. 1981. *Cultural contexts of science and mathematics education : A bibliographic guide*. Leeds: Centre for Studies in Science Education, University of Leeds.

Wilson, M. 1978. *Science teachers in Papua New Guinea high schools, 1977.* Waigani: Teaching Methods and Materials Centre, University of Papua New Guinea. (Research Report No. 33).

Wilson, M. 1992. *The second international science study (Papua New Guinea: Population 3).* Boroko, Papua New Guinea: Educational Research Division, PNG Education Department. (Forthcoming).

Wilson, S.; Shulman, L.; Richert, A. 1987. 150 different ways of knowing: representations of knowledge in teaching. In: Calderhead, J. (Ed.) *Exploring teachers' thinking.* London: Cassell Education. Wong, K.; Yeoh, O.C. 1987. Science process skills and cognitive preference styles, Singapore. *Journal of Education* 8 (1), 55:62.

World Bank. 1988. *Education in Sub-Saharan Africa.* Washington D.C.

World Bank/British Council. 1989. *Educating for capability : The role of science and technology education.* London: British Council. Vol. 2, October 1989. (Report to the World Bank).

Yoloye, E.A.; Bajah S.T. 1980. Survey of a preliminary evaluation of ASPS/SEPA activities in Africa, In: Bude, U. *Science for self-reliance.* Bonn: D.S.E.

Yoloye, T.W. 1985. A unified training programme for integrated science, In: Mgbodile, T.; Ayodele, S.; Akube, A.; Obioma, G. *Issues in teacher education and science curriculum in Nigeria.*

Lagos: Curriculum Organization of Nigeria. (Nonograph Series No. 2).

Ziman, J. 1980. *Teaching and learning about science and society.* Cambridge: Cambridge. University Press.

Zurub, A; Rubba, P. 1983. Development and validation of an inventory to assess science teacher needs in developing countries. *Journal of Research in Science Teaching,* 20 (9), 876:873.

SCIENCE KITS IN DEVELOPING COUNTRIES :

AN APPRAISAL OF POTENTIAL

1
Introduction

"Such plows of the rich can do more damage than their swords."
— *Ivan Illich*

1. Scope, Rationale and Organisation of Review

This reports reviews the use of science kits in developing countries, and is primarily targeted at those responsible for educational planning and the provision of science education for both teachers and students at primary, secondary and teacher training levels. Although science kits are the main focus of the review, low cost production strategies for science equipment are also discussed. For this brief review it has not been possible to undertake field studies of science kit production and use. The review is therefore a compilation based on earlier reviews and reports, and from postal communications with science educators in developing countries. The review focuses primarily on English-Speaking developing countries in Africa, Asia and Oceania. This does not imply that there has been no activity in other parts of the developing world such as Latin America, Francophone Africa and the Middle East. Indeed, Brazil was one of the first countries to develop and market science kits. More recently German agencies such as Goethe institute and the Deutsche Gesellschaft für Technishe Zusammenarbiet (GTZ) have conducted seminars in Bolivia, Colombia, Ecuador and Nicaragua aimed at training teachers to assemble their own science kits. However, it has proved impossible to access detailed information on these activities through correspondence with science education organisations in these countries.

The expanding world of learners in Asia Africa, South America and the limited or even declining resources available for science education make it imperative to determine the efficacy of various measures to improve its quality. Our particular concern here is with high-risk forays in to the field of science kit production and/or provision. Recent estimates for constructing fully equipped general science laboratories range from $57,800 in Korea to about $107,800 in Botswana (Caillods; Göttlemann, 1991). Over the period 1984 to 1990 Papua New Guinea has spent almost three quarters of a million US dollars on the provision of imported science kits to abut 130 secondary schools, representing an expenditure of about $6,000 per school. The provision of such facilities may be a luxury no longer affordable in many countries and may in any case be unnecessary in the light of recent changes to science curricula and the implications for the way science is taught and for the nature of the materials used to teach it.

The 1970s witnessed a flurry of activity on the use of science kits in developing countries probably reflecting the attempts of countries without much tradition for teaching science with apparatus to adapt or develop their own science curricula. The German Foundation for International Development, the Goethe Institute and the Commonwealth Secretariat have conducted regular workshops and seminars in many developing countries aimed at developing skill in teachers in the production and use of equipment from low-cost materials. For instance, in 1975 the Common wealth secretariat, acting on the recommendations of Member states, initiated a programme of investigation and assistance in the fields of low-cost production of school science equipment. Three Regional Seminar-Workshops were organised in Bahamas, Tanzania and Papua New Guinea. In the late 1970s the British Council compiled a Directory of educational equipment production centres (British Council, 1979) which include 15 countries in production of science kits. These reviews provide a useful backdrop on which to re-examine some of the future plans and prospects discussed at that time in the light of current developments, almost 20 years later, in order to identify successful and unsuccessful strategies.

Chapter 1 considers thee context of science education in developing countries, current trends in curriculum development, the nature of practical work in science, the role of teacher and the implications for science equipment. Following this introduction the body of the review is organised as follows. *Chapter 2:* Rationale for science kits; *Chapter 3:* Availability; *Chapter 4:* Contents, *Chapter 5:* Manufacturer Uses; *Chapter 6:* Distribution, replenishment, storage and repair; *Chapter 7: Uses Chapter 8.* Teacher training; *Chapter 9:* Costs; *Chapter 10:* Appraisal and conclusion.

Each chapter concludes with a discussion of implications. The Appendices provide a full list of sources of information; a summary of activities in over 50 developing countries and list of abbreviations.

2. Context of Science and Technology Education

The economic background, especially in Sub-Saharan Africa, is not encouraging. Taking, at random, recent projections from swaziland reveals a common if not universal story of the prospects for educational investments. According to a mid-1980s analysis:

> "Fiscal growth of 3.4 per cent will be insufficient for the future needs of the educational sector. But as projected government revenue is expected to increase by only 1.7 per cent, and spending by 2.2 per cent, education will be fortunate if it receive an annual increase of 3.4 per cent required to maintain the current level of services. Qualitative improvements that require higher unit costs, such as reduction in the student-teacher ratio employment of higher grade teachers, and additional input into production of teaching materials and curriculum resources are unlikely."
>
> — *Sargeant, 1986.*

Countries in such dire economic straits are unlikely to be able to finance educational development and quality from available resources. They may find it necessary to request donor assistance. If they do so in the area of science education, equipment and science kits are likely to be an issue.

Economic constraint is not the only problem facing developing countries. There are topographic constraints which can prevent schools functioning effectively; heavy rains can demolish schools and landslides can completely isolates already remote schools from sources of support. There are also social constraints as people apply traditional method to solve local disputes as in case of Papua New Guinea where tribal fights and compensation demands frequently close down or even destroy schools and teachers houses. In these circumstances it may be difficult to justify giving much priority to the provision of science teaching materials, But on a more optimistic note, there are many countries in which conditions are not so extreme, where there are high proportions of effective schools and opportunities, where given enough thought and commitment, a modest increase in investment could bring about large gains in quality of science education.

Zymelman (1990) in his review of science education in Sub-Saharan Africa calls for a full assessment of science education and its impact as a prerequisite for a full assessment of science education and its impact as a prerequisite for the rational allocation of resources for science teaching. He points out the needs to consider the type of science education needed to improve the economy and pedagogical and financial implications of this He presents some revealing science indicators for the region. For example, the Sub-Saharan Africa (SSA) share of world total of science publications is 0.4 per cent but it has 8.5 per cent of the world population; relatively low enrolment rate in science courses at secondary levels means the chances of spotting scientific talent in the general population may be 7-8 times lower than in Europe and less than half that in Latin America . Zymelman notes a general deficiency in quality and quantity of laboratories, equipment and books. He notes that lecturing takes up 50 per cent of the teachers' time and where there is practical it takes up less than 20 per cent of the time allocated for science. The low ratio of science inspectors to teachers (less than 1:300) probably means that there is little professional support for science teaching. A very vicious circle is in operation:

> "...there is not sufficient demand for scientists and engineers because the rate of technological change is low, but this rate is low because there are not enough scientists and engineers."
>
> *Zymelman, p. 61.*

Apart from the implications for science education deficit in technological manpower his obvious implications for capacity producing its own science equipment.

There has been an historical tendency for donors to be attracted by the more vocational and equipment-intensive elements in secondary education which seem more relevant to the pursuit of development based on science and technology (World Bank/British Council, 1989). But many developing countries are now attempting to meet the need of two different group of students—those who continue with a formal study of science as well as vast majority who do not... As Wallberg (1991) has noted, there are different needs of *science-for- continuation* and *science-for-all*. For the later group *"the emphasis must be on the development of science,and of laboratories and equipment that can be furnished locally"* (p.72). He is critical in the lack of foresight exhibited in tendency of donors to treat science equipment as a form of food aid' for the basic cycle of education. Instead, he calls for as implication of syllabi to involve selection of experiments which use materials from market place and from local equipment suppliers. Efforts should also be made to encourage local production in cases where the number of schools and demands for equipments warrants this, but local production should be market-led and not the responsibility of the ministry. *For science-for-continuation* that there is a strong case for donors to assist in supply of more specialised equipment, and to give encouragement and professional support to key schools committed to pursuit of excellence in science.

3. Changes in Curriculum

In recognition of the important role of science and technology in economic development, many countries have attempted to introduce policies on science and technology and to reform their science curricula. Recent reports (IEA, 1991) discuss these developments. Reforms have led to changing emphasis in subject matters and teaching methods which have implications for the nature, supply and use of science teaching materials. We have already the *science-for-all* and *science for-continuation* needs and their implications for materials. It is important now to identify further trends in science curriculum development in order to appreciate the role expected of practical science activities and, by extension, the possible role of science kits.

There has been a trend towards greater emphasis on *technology* either as part of science curricula or as a separate course of study. There has been a shift on emphasis from the rote learning to enquiry activities and centred approaches. There have been attempts to integrate subjects matter from biology, chemistry, physics, geology, technology, health and science rather than knowledge, that is process rather than content. Yoloye (1986) expresses concern about the relevance of educational content to national development needs in Africa. As Lewin (1991) notes, broader definitions of science education have emerged to embrace concepts in health education, nutrition, earth science and environmental studies. In his state-of-the-art review of science education in developing countries he identifies the following as emergent trend:

> "Teaching scientific skills and cognitive processes related to scientific problem solving and reducing emphasis on the recall of information will remain the curriculum orthodoxy."
>
> — *Lewin, 1991: 10.*

All these approaches set great store on 'hands-on' experience with familiar materials and much experience is regarded as particularly important for children from non-technological environment (Haddad, 1986)

The *ethnoscience movement* (Campos, 1989) also prevent new ideas and methodologies for science education with the aim of placing it in harmony with the socio-cultural context. As Cole (1975) points out cultural objects from a group of materials that could be investigated and manipulated in the process of finding out things—how they work and how they interact with other body and forces. These cultural objects can provide links between what is familiar in the students ' environment and scientific concepts. In the Caribbean context, Goerge and Glasgow (1989) discuss 'street science' themes such as child rearing practices, food and nutrition, pregnancy, birth and post natal care, temperature change in physical environment and household practices. Sometimes street science and conventional science reinforce one another and there is a need to promote awareness that will allow intelligent appraisal of street and conventional science. Constructivists approaches also stress the centrality of the leaner and his/her perceptions as a starting point for science teaching (*e.g.* Driver, 1983). So in addition to new emphases in content there are new theories about the way student construct meaning from their experience which have implications for the nature of practical work, for the provision and use of equipment and for the role of the science teacher.

4. The Role of the Science Teacher

The rhetoric embedded in statements of curriculum aims and goals imply a change role for science teachers with respect to the organisation of teaching content, co-ordination of learning activities and there participation with students in learning process. The teacher is now expected to take on the role of participation with students in the learning process. The teacher is now expected to take on the role of facilitator rather than imparter of scientific knowledge. However there is considerable disparity between programmed expectation and reality. The aims as stated are not the same as the aims that are attempted; what actually happens is in the hands of teachers and students. While there have been outward changes in curriculum orientation, science teaching in the majority of the classroom in developing countries is still characterised by student passiveness, teacher centeredness, examination orientation and lip services to a few practical activities. For instance Guyana Brophy and Dalgety (1981) report that what were intended to be a student-centered, laboratory-based activities were in practice teacher-centered and textbook oriented. In Jordan and Malaysia, Kamariah *et al* (1988) report that despite espousal of laboratory-based instruction in curriculum materials, teachers in both countries continue to use didactic teaching methods . A country monograph (WA KUK LEE 1992 on Korea reports that existing laboratories facilities are not been use sufficiently, with most science lessons being provided as classroom lectures. There are many other similar reports (Caillods, Gottlemann, 1991 mimeo). The curriculum reforms has largely not been internalized by those responsible for the delivery of science education. Many projects seem to have evaded the real issues and consequences of reform—its long term effect on teachers, students and society.

Schmidt (1986) discusses some of the psychological barriers which can prevent teachers employing the new methodologies and making more use of practical work. In his opinion based on extensive experience in workshops on the production of low-cost equipment the problem goes deeper than the mere availability of materials, which is often use as an excuse for ignoring practical work. It concern the use of materials by teachers with a preference for frontal-style delivery. Inexperienced teachers fear the responsibility for breakage of expensive-looking apparatus, fear the possibility of management problems and unsettled classes in practical work and fear looking foolish when the experiment goes awry. Reluctance to use equipment in tertiary institution has also been noted. For instance, Pullan (1991) report on a vast quantity of neglected and rapidly deteriorating physics equipment in a science teacher training institute in Africa.

There are other constraints to the frequent and efficient use of science equipment in the classroom. Among these are the requirement for storage space; effective procedures for sharing equipment among many teachers with each teacher responsible for the care of equipment and for tidying up after use; there are daunting bureaucratic procedures involved in procuring imported apparatus and in replenishing existing stock. Catalogues of scientific equipment are sometimes of little assistance. For instance, the bewildering variety of resistance wire and the technical terms use in classification must make ordering this item from catalogues a harrowing experience for many teachers.

Schmidt (1951) reminds us the term 'low-cost' is properly associated with the idea of appropriate technology which places value on the incorporation of local resources, user-friendliness and economic viability. Unfortunately, as he points out, the term, can also be associated with 'low value' and 'low prestige', a point also made by Tobon (1988). Even students teachers trained to improvise equipment at college expect to find the 'real thing' when they go to schools. Efforts to promote the use of low-cost materials are often resisted by administrators and teachers who see it as an attempt to provide a watered down science education and to impede development along western lines—so that such initiatives fail to receive support necessary. It should be noted however, that many of the industrialized nations have themselves become involved in a major implication of science at the basic science for-all level (World Bank/British Council, 1989). In Scotland, the primary science development project

(McLeod, 1985) has found that cardboard and plastic were more appropriate than wood and metal for the construction of materials. On the question of quality Tobon (1988) ask: " What is the quality of education given when expensive equipment is kept locked away and never used by students? Do we obtain good quality education when teachers make a few demonstration using expensive and sophisticated equipment?"

5. The Role and Impact of Practical Work

Analysis differ in their opinions about the purpose of laboratory work because of their different views of learning theory. Kreitler and Kreitler (1974) argue that laboratory experiences help students establish the accuracy of their beliefs as well as providing them with direct experience than concepts. Others argue that laboratory work provides a training ground in problem- solving. However early research in the developed world (Yager *et al* 1969) suggests that laboratory activity does not fulfil the various functions expected of it, except perhaps for the development of manipulated skill. But better manipulative skill hardly seems a sufficient return for the resources committed in laboratories

Students often have no clear purpose in the laboratory and perceive laboratory sessions as isolated events (Tasker, 1981). According to white (1988) laboratory work may not achieve the aims expected formate precisely because the laboratories themselves are inappropriate. One weakness of laboratories is their very 'laboratoriness'. They seem divorced from the materials and experiences that student encounter in their daily lives. If a substantial proportions of laboratory investigations used common materials instead of things never encountered elsewhere it might be possible for them to achieve the various functions expected of them. As white (1988; 190) reminds us: *"acids can be found in fruits and bases in household cleaners as well as in glass jars"*. Eshiet (1988) discuses the use of waste of agricultural products commonly found in developing countries to supply bases for chemistry lessons. There are many other examples illustrating the use of every materials in science teaching.

The evidence for the impact of practical activity on science achievement is inconsistent, as review by Bredderman (1983) and others have shown. A recent Philippines study (Lockheed *et al*, 1989) showed small positive benefits of laboratory work, but other strategies such as small group teaching and frequent testing had larger effect. But it is not always clear from many of the studies how practical activity is provided, e.g. through fully equipped laboratories or through the use of science kits or through field exertions. Gallagher (1987: 351) reviews several studies on the impact of practical activity and concludes that *"Laboratory work is an accepted part of science instruction. Given its important place in the education of youth, it is surprising that we know so little about its functioning and effects"*. A recent study in Malaysia (Sharifah Maimunoh, 1991) found that although generally teachers were adept at organizing practical work, they were less competent in using the practical work as a learning experience, *e.g* by organizing discussion around practical work.

Wellberg (1991) points out that practical science in schools is often perfunctory and follows a recipe approach. It often wastes time particularly when poorly managed. A great deal of practical work is in reality aimed at proving or verifying facts already taught in theory work. A mid-1980s seminar of science educators held in India reports that:

> "The current practise of students carrying out experiments that are mere verifications of things they have already been told in theory classes is purposeless—they know what they are supposed to produce and experimentation thus becomes a thoughtless pursuit of trying to produce the expected result by data fudging, back calculation or wrong interpretation of one's observations."
>
> — *Eklavia, 1985:6.*

Despite the apartment lack of a firm basis for any positive impact of practical work, there is little enthusiasm for dropping practical work. In fact, more and more countries are beginning to recognise its importance, atleast as judged by the rhetoric of curriculum statements. It is the aims content and implementation of practical work in science that have to be reviewed, including the need to redesign science rooms and science equipments to incorporate more of the materials from nature laboratory so that students have more opportunity to explore the properties of everyday materials and the scientific principles embedded in everyday phenomena.

υ. Implications for Science Equipments

A positive outcome of the many conferences and workshops on science equipments is that there is now no dearth of ideas for low-cost materials and experiments. These can be found in publications of UNESCO, the Commonwealth secretariat, the German foundation for international development, and many others (see Bibliography) . Schmidt (1986) illustrates the potential of even the humblest of resource: *"With only a candle and only few other common materials, one can carry out atleast 25 illustrative experiments which stimulate scientific thinking concerning oxidation, reduction,heat and environmental protection "*.

The idea of making use of what is freely available using human and natural resources is not new. In 1762 Rosseau in his book *Emile,* called for education based on textbooks and academic imparting of knowledge. Schmidt (1991) notes that in the reconstruction period after World War II teachers in central European schools were forced through circumstances to draw on their experience to construct appropriate teaching aids from locally available materials.

But there is often a political and social need for imported foreign materials to enhance the status of school. Highly publicized presentation ceremonies in which the education minister receives supplies of science equipment from foreign donors, or present sophisticated equipment to schools, probably earn the minister more kudos than a commitment to linger term stratgies such as local equipment production projects. Science education has traditionally been associated with great expense and possession of impressive arrays of imported science equipment constitutes a status symbol for many schools.

But even if laboratories were properly used many student need to exposure to conventional science apparatus? In Papua New Guinea education in science, and of those less than half are admitted to science (Goerge, 1990). In the united only about 20 per cent of students advance to the fifth and sixth forms where they would be prepare for university education (Murray Thomas 1990). And yet as Warren and Lowe (1975) remind us, most of the equipment used (where it is available) is of the type more relevant to those who continue, *e.g.* much of the expensive equipment used for quantitative work in chemistry and physics. But there is evidence for greater awareness that it may not be necessary for students to conduct laboratory style investigations; that the environment provide a natural laboratory to facilitate much less costly investigations

Thomas; Kobayashi (1987) remind us that educational technology itself carries certain educational values as a new technologies become predominant they change the consciousness of society and the shape of the culture. In the case of imported science equipment in developing countries these value may not be shared by both those who have to use the equipment. Many of the design features of the equipment used in school science laboratories have remained unchanged since the early part of these century. These help to reinforce the stereotyped image so common in books and films of middle aged white, male scientists in white coats intent on taking reading and measurement in laboratories filled with strange equipment. Images of Einstein and other eminent scientists helped to promote this stereotyped view of both scientists and laboratory.

There seems little doubt that materials of greatest value are those to be found in immediate environment because there are within everyone's experience because they are less expensive than traditional science Laboratory-ware and have the potential of being more 'user-friendly'. More effective use of local materials would kept the cost of science provision to a minimum. But the term 'low cost' has little meaning unless specifically related to local conditions and these vary widely from one developing country to next. As Warren and Lowe, 1975 point out, the real need is for client-states who know the local problems to identify these for themselves. Later section of these review draw attention to conditions and problems of individual countries at these have been reported in the literature.

2

Rationale for Science Kits

The economic constraints facing developing have led to increased emphasis on low cost equipment in science education. Recent trends in curriculum development provide sound educational reasons why low-cost equipment is appropriate. In these chapter we list some of these trends and examine how they might influence decisions to introduced science kits. Among the issues considered in these chapter are the nature of science kits, their most commonly expressed advantages and disadvantages, the research basis for these claims and nature of decision making with respect to science kit provision.

1. Nature of Science Kits

A concise definition of the term 'science kit' is difficult but nevertheless essential for this review. The *Glossary on Educational Technology* (Osborne 1973) defines a kit as a collection of institutional materials, giving information on a subject and assembled, perhaps in a folder for distribution. It is clear that this defamation is inadequate for the kind of materials normally included in science kits, which might include hardware items such as laboratory glassware, chemicals, instruments, in addition to printed materials. Even the cursory review of the literature reveals the enormous in what are termed science kits-from a collection of item of science equipment and notes dealing with a single topic such as weather or heat, to more general collections of equipment covering an entire grade or even curriculum, to mini-laboratories designed for schools without laboratories, to pocket size kits of very simple experimental equipment with accompanying text. Some science kits are composed of sub-kits, *e.g.* optics, electronics; some are designed for student use, other are for teacher demonstration purposes, still others are for both teacher and student. Science kits have also been developed for a wider market than school teachers and students. In Brazil ' The Scientists project comprises a series of locally produced kits, each with a biography of scientist, and instructions and materials for carrying out experiment related to that scientist's work the kits appeared in the market were widely sold on newspaper stands and in shops (Krasilchuik, 1979). Some kits are entirely locally produced, others are imported; others consist of centrally produced, prototypes of equipment with a set of tools for teacher assembly. *The key feature seems to be that a science kit comprises a pre-selected collections of items designed to illustrate particular scientific principles, usually linked to published curriculum material, sometime containing tools for assembly and general box in such a way as to serve as a store cupboard for items in classroom or home.*

2. Advantages and Disadvantages

Both economic and educational advantages have been claimed for science kits seems to lie in the fact that pre-selection is preferable for those teachers unable or unwilling to make their own selections from the more traditional science equipment catalogues, storage is simple and convenient and kits are usually linked to existing curriculum material. They also offer the attraction of providing science equipment to schools in conveniently sized and easily distributed packages.

There is increasing recognition of the educational merits of including low-cost production of school equipment in science kits. In his opening address to a meeting on low-cost production of school equipment in Manzini, Swaziland, 1979, the minister of education, Senator Dlamini, said:

> "I am glad to note that your concern is with low-cost equipment. My reason is not only that our budget will not extend to buying and making expensive items. I also believe that highly sophisticated equipment is unnecessary, undesirable and irrelevant to our schools. Our way of life is traditionally a simple one . We want to preserve that tradition... Classroom filled with

elaborate equipment would contrast too strongly with our -pupil's homes."

Swaziland, 1979:3

In a similar vein, Warren, reporting from Bangladesh in the 1970s sees a need of technology to improve the living conditions of the majority of the poor, and therefore a need to make science education attractive by providing practical experiences using cheap and familiar materials. The need for greater relevance in practical work has been noted by many writers. For instance, King (1985) notes that context-free approaches to practical work can mitigate against student understanding of science and technology in relation to state of development of their own country; Yoloye (1986) expresses concern about the relevance of educational content to national development needs in Africa. He calls for greater relevance in terms of needs, characteristics and resources.

Educational advantage will only be achieved if science kits are developed as part of an overall strategy to improve science education. A regional seminar on science equipment in Asia (UNESCO, 1973) reports that the main consideration in developing a philosophy of school science equipment is the pedagogical output which needs to go hand in hand with objectives and national goals. There is a need to consider course requirements together with the pedagogical output expected from such courses and the potential of equipment to enhance learning, and to implement strategies aimed at *maximising interaction between equipment and the course.*

The Hoshangabad Science Teaching Project (HSTP) in India (Eklavya, 1985) has taken such a holistic approach to science in education and centred it around a functional science kit. The kit is designed for the active involvement of the child, their integration of learning with the environment, the development of problem solving skills, observational skills, and manual dexterity as well as promotion of enjoyment in science. Furthermore, the kit is constantly evolving towards increasing the element of local content.

In the science equipment literature there is increasing emphasis on the notion of user-friendliness both in terms of student and teacher. Perhaps this is a sin-off from the 'science-for all' movement, where there have been attempts to reflect more of everyday reality in science lessons, rather than to alienate teachers and students with conventional science apparatus. It is well known that there are psychological barriers which prevent teachers using equipment in science lessons. As Schmidt (1986) has observed, inexperienced teachers fear the responsibility for breakage of expensive-looking apparatus, fear the possibility of management problems and unsettled classes in practical work and fear looking foolish when the experiment goes away. Many science educators believe that these problems can be overcome by helping student-teachers and teachers develop their own low-cost equipment from simple materials. Such strategies promote user-friendliness by developing a sense of ownership and environment-relatedness which is missing from expensive and alien imported equipment.

Thus, apart from economic reasons there appear to be sound pedagogical reasons for promoting the use of low-cost equipment to :

- provide simplified and more relevant science learning experiences;
- promote the use of technology to improve living conditions;
- make science education more attractive and enjoyable;
- overcome psychological barriers to using equipment.

There are additional reasons more specific to low-cost science kits; they can :

- make it easier to store and order equipment;
- support a hands-on approach and child-centered teaching;
- maximise the interaction between equipment and course;
- overcome the lack of laboratory facilities in remote schools;
- improve the management of science lessons;
- ease equipment shortages caused by rapid expansion.

But there is a danger that centrally produced science kits could easily become stereotyped to reflect a particular image of science, and that imported ready-made kits would constitute another form of curriculum imperialism. Ahmed (1977) is generally critical of the kit approach because it provides a form of packaged science which allows only the demonstration of simple and idealised phenomena, thus frustrating the exploration of real-life situations. The lack of scope for creativity has been noted in Sri Lanka which has opted for a mini-laboratory approach using a wide range of conventional apparatus. On the other hand, the Hoshangabad project in India provides science kits high in local content which are continually evolving to meet the need's of users; the Zim-Sci approach in Zimbabwe allows considerable flexibility by limiting science kits to basis simple multi-purpose equipment.

3. Research Basis

It is important to note that the advantages discussed above are advanced by proponents of science kits and are not necessarily based on research or evaluation findings. They have emerged from conferences and seminars aimed at sharing the experience of science educators from different countries. While many commentators have expounded the merits of science kits and low-cost equipment there appear to be have been few pertinent research studies.

What little research has taken place has generally involved studies of existing patterns of provision and use of science equipment. For instance, in India there were initial attempts to study the equipment for teaching science that was being manufactured by industry with an exploration of how its quality could be improved. This was followed by design and development work which eventually led, against a backdrop of curriculum reform, to the production of compact science kits.

Other research studies have concentrated on the availability and use of existing equipment in school. Udwin and Manjoro (1987) claim that the Zim-Sci project in Zimbabwe has researched the development of low-cost science kits high in local content based a survey of conditions in rural day secondary schools. In Kenya, a questionnaire was designed to probe the apparatus market. This three part instrument collected general school information, availability of funds for purchase of equipment, and science teacher comments on a proposed equipment price list. There have also been inspectors' reports on science teaching and equipment provision in many countries.

There are difficulties in conducting a survey of science equipment needs. A survey of secondary schools in the Caribbean found that many science teachers were not familiar enough with the equipment, especially physics equipment, to know whether the school had supplies or not. Also, in Zimbabwe it was found that few teachers were able to make suggestions as to what should be included in kits. In Papua New Guinea equipment lists are prepared by the Curriculum Unit of the Department of Education, and are periodically reviewed by the Syllabus Advisory Committee. Although science teachers are represented on such committees they are generally drawn from the better resourced schools which have a reputation for providing quality science education. Such committees may be divorced from the realities facing many school and merely rubber stamp equipment lists drawn up by curriculum specialists. There are also problems with the rapid turnover of teaching staff and the general scarcity of qualified laboratory technicians to participate effectively in such surveys.

Kits have also been developed indirectly as a result of general surveys on the difficulties faced by science teachers, most of which indicate a perception that science teaching is hampered by lack of equipment, especially at primary level. In Papua New Guinea the Three Phase Primary Science (TPPS) course attempted to tackle the problem of equipment shortage by providing each TPPS school with a kit of simple materials supplied by UNICEF in a locally-made lockable wooden cabinet with further equipment for the kit supplied by the District Education Office and the teacher.

There have been general research reports and reviews which are critical of conventional approaches to practical work in science. Wallberg (1991) points out that practical science in school is often perfunctory and follows a *recipe approach*. It often wastes time particularly when poorly managed. A great deal of practical work is in reality aimed at proving or verifying facts already taught in theory work. There have also been called for a re-examination of the *discovery approach* in science teaching. As Layton (1973: 175) has noted:

> "Only on the basis of the most superficial analysis of the nature of scientific activity could it be said that such methods (discovery) enable children to think and work in ways characteristic of a successful practitioner of science."

All they do is rediscover or verify accepted laws and relationships; students are locked in a predetermined step-by-step procedure and do not experience the real scientific method. The whole notion of experiment design and hypothesis formulation is missing from most activities in science lessons. Obviously, science kits designed to follow a recipe approach would be quite different from those requiring student to initiate their own enquiries.

In summary it can be said that there have probably been a number of surveys of science equipment needs and science teacher perceptions about practical work, but there are problems in ensuring validity of instrument design and in maximising teacher participation in such surveys. Studies on the impact of science kits on teaching appear to be rare. Most of the research evidence in support of science kits comes indirectly from the implications of various studies and reviews on the nature of practical work in science and from the implications of trends in curriculum reform.

4. Decision-making

Policy decisions on science education are often taken by non-scientist administrators. For instance, in Papua New Guinea the majority of senior decision-makers in the Education Department come from the rank of primary teachers who would have taught in the 1960s before many of the country's curriculum reforms were introduced. They have a limited science background, and so depend on the quality of advice provided by their science education advisors. Often there is no national policy on science to guide decision-making. Lewin (1991) has noted the importance of a national science policy in determining the framework for effective science education. As a commentator in Sierra Leone reports:

> "Society's perception of science is that it is just another subject like history or literature and that its content can be adequately taught by the lecture method. The processes and to some extent the methods of science are not perceived as part of science...because of this limited perception of science administration and policy-makers do not readily give the teaching of science the importance it deserves."
>
> *O'Brien, 1987.*

There is considerable dependence on the quality of advice offered by science curriculum specialists and teacher educators. But the evidence suggests that these groups rarely work together as a team; often the structure of Education Departments mitigates against co-operative ventures between divisions. Much of science education planning may be *ad-hoc* and spear-headed by well-meaning expatriate advisers holding a variety of views on the nature of both science and science education. It is true that there have been many nation and international seminars, conferences and papers on science education equipment, but these have to be translated into action at a local level, and the recommendations may not be compatible with those of groups with vested interests to protect. In addition, the rapid turnover of curriculum staff may result in a finished product with little internal coherence with the aims and objectives of curriculum materials already approved years before. Teachers need guidance on where equipment is to be procured, how it is to be stored, used and managed.

In the absence of clear policy and effective decision-making at higher levels, many teachers' colleges have attempted, with varying degrees of success, to develop their own strategies for improving the quality of science education, such as the development of improvisation skills in graduates in order to alleviate the equipment problem. However, so much depends on the goodwill of teachers to sustain these efforts. The implications for in-service training are obvious. But in-service needs are often determined by supervisory staff such as inspectors, few of whom are science trained and who may have only a vague idea of what to consider as good practice in science teaching.

There is a need to widen the base for decision-making regarding science kits to include more active involvement of those often excluded (e.g. female teachers; parents). Hawes and Stephens (1990) point to the SETI project in Nepal which shows that increased participation in education of those in remote areas can have generous 'spill-over' effects for rural development. The Hoshangabad Science Teaching Project in India has decentralized decision-making at its core . It has been developed through the participation of scientists, teacher educators, teachers, voluntary agencies and interested members of the community. Through the co-ordinated activities of various local committees, decision-making involves senior administrators, representatives from specialist science groups, textbook developers, district education officers, lecturers, headteachers, teachers and members of local government district committees.

The development of low-cost science kits is likely to appeal to administrators who are anxious to fulfil the needs of expansion and to reduce the costs of providing quality in science education. Proposals for the local production of equipment can be very appealing when there is some assurance that the locally-made product will be less costly that the imported commodity. For instance, the Science Equipment Production Unit (SEPU) in Kenya estimated an 80 per cent saving on the local production of a 3-d kinetics kit. In Burma, local production was estimated in 1972 to have halved the cost of science equipment. Local production certainly has political appeal in that it can encourage self-reliance, independence and promotes local industry.

5. Implications

Science kits have many attractive features which could improve the quality of science education as well as reduce costs. But there are many psychological barriers to the use of the equipment which have to be overcome. There is a need for carefully designed observational studies of the way teachers use science equipment as well as surveys of what equipment is actually available. There may be a need to review the nature of the practical experiences prescribed in teachers' guides and worksheets in order to determine how these could be made more relevant, using less costly equipment. Planners, developers and users need to have a clear rationale of what science kits are intended to achieve. If science kit provision is to be part of an overall quality enhancement strategy planners need to consider questions such as:

- Are science kits consistent with national policy on science education?
- Have research findings been studied in the light of local conditions?
- Is there consensus in the science education community on the use of kits?
- What evaluation design is required to study the impact of science kits?

3
Availability

This chapter is concerned with the current availability of science kits in developing countries. Question of interest are :

- When were science kits introduced?
- Which countries are using or have made use of science kits?
- Are the kits intended for all schools/level of education?

1. Historical Development

In 1964 the Rangoon Arts and Science University (RASU) in Burma started to make science equipment for education and production began in 1965. The RASU was one of the first centres of local production in the region. There were spin-off effects in the Asian region which stimulated local production efforts in India, Pakistan and Bangladesh. The curriculum reforms of the 1970s and efforts to promote primary science received considerable international aid agency support in terms of one-off supplies of kits, *e.g.* the UNICEF kits provided at primary level in Papua New Guinea and the ODA kits supplied to Ghana. In Africa, curriculum development projects such as the Science Education Programme for Africa (SEPA) resulted in new demands for equipment which eventually led to the local production of low-cost equipment and science kits. In 1968 Kenya established the Industrial Arts Department within Kenya Science Teachers College and set up an equipment production unit. Workshop construction started in February, 1970 and production started in September the same year. In 1970, the Federal Ministry of Education in Nigeria established a Science Equipment Centre in Lagos with UNDP/UNESCO support until 1976 and there are now branches in three others states. In Ethiopia, local production at the Educational Materials and Distribution Agency (EMPDA) started in 1977. Curriculum reform effort continued in many countries in the 1980s but expansion in emerging countries such as Zimbabwe, and post-war reconstruction efforts in Viet Nam made it imperative for countries to search for low-cost production or procurement strategies.

2. Global Provision

While a great deal of information about the global provision of science kits is available for the 1970s and early 1980s, developments since then are rarely reported in the literature. Annual yearbooks have been of little help in obtaining information on the availability of science kits. For instance the International Yearbook of Educational and Instructional Technology 1986/7 (Osborne, 1986) includes few references to science kits. Indeed, the terms 'kit' and 'low-cost' do not appear in its index of principal key words. It is difficult to obtain information from in-country sources unless equipment development is an aid -supported activity for which regular reports are prepared. Country reports prepared for international seminars provide the main source of information for this review, as well as correspondence with international specialists in the field of low-cost production and science kit development. Towse *et al* (1991) report that they are currently attempting to prepare a Directory of Science Education Resources in Anglophone Africa.

In 1980, UNESCO listed 21 developing countries which had established school science equipment and low-cost production and development units. However, it is by no means certain these are still viable, and no doubt there are new ones to add to the list. The Directory of Educational Equipment Production Centres (British Council, 1979) is based on a questionnaire survey of all British Council offices (Except Europe and USA). The 1979 Directory lists 28 countries with some activity: 12 countries producing prototypes only; 16 with prototype and production; 15 producing kits; 25 producing individual items. Information from this source is summarized in the following table and additional updates provided where this has been possible. Appendices 1 and 2 provide further details of developments.

Country	Provision of science kits
Bangladesh	1979 Directory: Bangladesh Educational Equipment Development Bureau produces prototypes and some products and single items: *Update:* non-formal groups make tool kits for use in school; currently ADB project includes support for the production of science kits.
Bolivia	1980s: Chemistry kits designed with DSE support; hand experiment source books.
Botswana	Teaching Aids Production Unit with potential for mass production; late seventies progress report notes a lack of machinery and staff for further large scale production and recommends local production by private enterprise or by Builders and Carpenters Brigades. *Update:* Botswana Science Kit based on Zim-Sci is currently being used.
Caribbean region	1982: many examples of teacher developed kits but no local production; plans for regional centre.
Ecuador	1980s: Integrated science kits developed with DSE aid.
Ethiopia	1979 Directory: Education Equipment Production and Training Centre produces prototypes of individual items, runs laboratory assistant courses and provides repair service.
	Update: has production centre (EMPDA); in period 1977-86 has produced over 4,000 kits; a contract to produce 6,000 kits in 1987-89 has been signed between EMPDA and the World Bank.

Ghana	ODA supplied some kits for secondary; new proposal (1991) for involvement of student teachers in the production of their own kits.
Hong Kong	1979 Directory: Simpson has developed Simplex Kits using components available locally. *Update:* Simplex kits no longer produced.
India	1979 Directory: National Council for Educational research and Training has workshop for the production of prototypes and finished products in the form of kits; also has State Institutes of Science Education involved in prototype production; many local manufacturers. *Update:* Hoshangabad Science Teaching Project provides kits for middle-School in the region; Vigyan Ashram develops prototypes of apparatus.
Indonesia	Prototypes of kits have been developed; DSE has helped develop and produce kits for primary science.
Kenya	1979 Directory: Science Equipment Production Unit produces prototypes and finished products as single items and kits for secondary; Teaching Aids Section at Kenya Institute of Education produces prototypes. *Update:* SEPU produces individualized, multi-component kits for student use as well as demonstration kit for teachers; options for single-item supply.
Republic of Korea	Science Equipment Corporation (1975) mass produces equipment and supports curriculum development; has produced kits for primary and individual items for secondary; plans to expand production; has Student Science Centre; small commercial firms; md-1970s proposal for Science Equipment Centre.

Malaysia	1979 Directory: Curriculum Development Centre produces prototype of individual items; production by commercial enterprise. *Update:* now manufacturing most of its secondary school needs.
Republic of Mauritius	Primary science kits provided by MOE (1985)
Nepal	1979 Directory: Janal Educational Materials Corporation products prototypes and finished products; the Science Education Centre of JEMC produced some prototypes in 1974 but there are reports of problems in production. *Update:* ADB project on local production in progress Vacation workshops for teachers.
Nicaragua	Eighties: DSE has helped develop kits for integrated science.
Nigeria	1979 Directory : School Equipment Centre produces prototypes and finished products of individual items; provides training and repair service, Science Education unit in Oyo designs prototype items; Science Equipment workshop in Abraka produces prototypes and finished products in the form of kits *Update:* mobile repair service, in-service; helps teachers categorize equipment.
Oman	1979 Directory: Science Laboratories and Audio Visual Aids Section produces prototypes and finished products of kits and individual items.
Pakistan	1979 Directory: National Equipment Centre produces prototypes and some finished products in kit form and as single items. *Update:* kit for primary science and primary teachers' tool kit covering science, mathematics, social studies and Urdu.

Papua New Guinea	In the 1970s UNICEF provided standard kits for primary science as part of TPPS; electricity kits were assembled by Boys' Reformatory; In mid-1980s PNG imported science kits for secondary - supported by World Bank; now has recurrent reimbursement scheme for equipment provision.
Peru	*1979 Directory* : Lau Chun SAE produces prototypes and finished products as kits and individual items; private enterprise concern.
Philippines	*1979 Directory* : Science Education Centre at the University of the Philippines produces prototypes for private sector production in kit form. *Update:* National Science and Technology Authority has supported various science equipment efforts; one or two equipment firms but output is small; School Science Equipment Development Project supplied some kits but only partially met needs; University of Philippines has produced an elementary school science kit and guide to use.
Singapore	Many commercial enterprises; few import restrictions.
South Africa	*1979 Directory* : H. Sparks-Science Teaching Aids (Durban) develops prototypes and finished products in kit form; run as private enterprise but activities geared to Science Education Project at Fort Hare.
South Pacific	Possibility of regional centre has been discussed.
Sri Lanka	*1979 Directory:* Science Equipment Production Unit produces prototypes and finished products for primary and secondary levels in kit form and as single items. *Update:* now promoting mini-laboratories; focus on rural school.

Swaziland	*1979 Directory:* Science Education Centre produces prototypes and finished products as single items for primary and secondary; reports of lack of direction after departure of foreign expert.
Tanzania	*1979 Directory:* School Equipment Development Unit produces prototype items; expansion expected in 1981.
	Update: development of prefabricated prototype kits; kit sharing schemes; many workshops for teachers.
Thailand	*1979 Directory:* Institute for the Promotion of Science and Technology produces prototype items to support curriculum innovation; a limited range of products in class sets is produces for trial schools; the National Curriculum Development Centre produces prototypes; Suksapha Panich mass produces individual items; proposals for demonstration kit production at teachers' college. *Update:* IPST produces both teacher demonstration and student kits for General Science, Chemistry, Biology, Physics and Physical and Biological Science; kits require no specialised laboratories and can be easily moved from class to class, problems with quality of kit items.
Vietnam	Has Science Education Equipment Project which started in 1981; SEEP has had several phases: (i) the revision of existing equipment and practical activities; (ii) try out of materials in several schools; (iii) the development of prototypes of kits of equipment; (iv) production of biology and chemistry kits; (v) distribution of kits and instructions.
Zimbabwe	1981: Zim-Sci project; kits are assembled from local and imported components; general kits provided for ZJC and 'O' level; plans for 'A' level physics

kits; intends to provide for single item purchase; Harare Generator (seminar, 1991) produced prototype low-cost micro-electronics kit.

It has not been possible to obtain information about the current activities of the older established production centres in India, Kenya, and Nigeria. However, there are disturbing anecdotal reports from Kenya of lack of basic teaching equipment and materials in schools, and that Nigerian production efforts are not meeting the needs of schools. In the face of competition from commercial firms some production centres have switched to other activities such as providing an advisory service, training and carrying out repair and maintenance. Plans to expand some existing teaching aids production centres have floundered in the face of lack of machinery and expertise. There are trends towards the production of improved science kits in teacher training in Ghana, Tanzania and Thailand, and there have been many sponsored seminars in Africa and South America. Earlier plans for regional production centres have remained as plans in the Caribbean and South Pacific. The Hoshangabad Science Teaching Project in India is an example of a local curriculum development project based on the use of student science kits. There may be other similar innovations around the world. At least one new production centre, EMPDA in Ethiopia, has been established since the 1970s and has now reached full production. Bangladesh, Nepal, Vietnam and Zimbabwe have more recently embarked on added projects involving the provision of low-cost equipment and kits. Some countries (Papua New Guinea) import items for the local assembly of science kits whereas others (Zimbabwe) provide a mixture of imported and locally available materials and others (Hoshangabad) continuously evolve the content of kits to reflect greater use so locally available materials.

It is probably true to say that science kits are now more widely available than a decade ago but this does not necessarily imply that there has been increased emphasis on local production or that the kits have been found effective. Notable is the trend towards personalised science kits produced by teachers and student-teachers, and the trend towards increasing the local content of kits.

3. Intended Users

The table presented earlier shows the target levels of various kits. Science kit have been produced for a variety of schools and levels of education but they are less common at upper secondary level where the emphasis appears to be on more conventional science apparatus, although Zimbabwe has plans to develop a kit for 'A' level Physics. Many kits are designed for use in rural schools, e.g. Zim-Sci kits in Zimbabwe. Sri Lanka's mini-laboratory approach is intended for disadvantage rural secondary schools without conventional laboratories. In the Philippines and Tanzania there have been generally unsuccessful attempts to supply only disadvantage schools with provision for kit sharing between the schools. In Papua New Guinea each lower secondary school, regardless of size or development, is provided with uniform kits. Many of the kits (*e.g.* HSTP, in India) require additional items from the immediate school environment and teacher-produced improvised apparatus is encouraged.

4. Implications

While there is a great deal of information about the availability of science kits, much of this is scattered in a variety of documents. There is a need to assist planners by compiling information about science kits for inclusion in yearbooks on educational technology so that worldwide developments can be more readily monitored. There are now many countries which provide science kits, particularly at primary, lower secondary and middle secondary levels. Some science kit projects are well established and others are more recent. Each country has to consider its own conditions and there are several options for provision which could be investigated further by planners. Among the planning issues to be considered are :

- a review of available information on science kits to determine content, production and use;
- the need to plan feasibility studies of various options.

4

Content

> "On the whole it must be said that the stocking of a science kit under given conditions in Africa is perhaps done best if it considers a mixture of science equipment and tools, concentrates on multiple-use items and those that cannot be easily bought or made by the teacher."
>
> — *Schirmer, 1987:174*

The content of science kits should reflect the particular orientation of the science curriculum. Obviously kits designed for primary levels are different from those designed for secondary, and those designed for an environmental or technological orientation are different from more traditional specialized science kits. This section provides some examples of the content of primary and secondary science kits from some of the countries listed in the table presented in chapter 3, in order to identify salient features and the implications for planners and developers. Questions of interest are :

- What kind of items are generally included in science kits?
- What is the balance between different types of resources?
- How specific are science kits for different courses, levels and abilities?
- What printed material is provided to support the use so science kits?
- What is the quality of materials included in science kits?

1. Science Kits for Primary Level

In Papua New Guinea a community schools (primary) science materials check-list 1989 numerated the following items required for a basic science kit :

alcohol burner	forceps	rubber stoppers
bar magnets	hand lenses	rubber tubing
copper sulphate	iron filings	tin snips
copper wire-insulted and uninsulated	lamp	single pulley
	lamp holder	syring
filter funnel	mirror	wire gauze

The check-list also indicated 31 school-made or school-obtainable items, such as empty biros, torch batteries, balloons and drawing pins. A resources book provides ideas for constructing alcohol burners, bicycle pumps, burner stands, candle burners, funnels, lamp-holders, simple magnifier, simple pulley, simple switch, aquarium, water wheel, weighing machine heating pan, tongs, battery holders and a science storage cupboard.

This kit is based on a science kit originally supplied by UNICEF to support a curriculum intended to be taught by teachers without much background in science, and one which would encourage active-enquiry and questioning in pupils. Since the original kits have long since been depleted, teachers would have to order most of replacement items from overseas, via local mail order companies. However, teachers who are prepared to improvise using the resource book could replace many of the imports themselves, provided the materials were locally available. Some of the more remote schools might experience difficulty purchasing items such as balloons and drawing pins.

At primary level in the Republic of Mauritius the Ministry provides a basic science kit to all schools consisting of:

2 dry batteries	1 plastic jug	1 thermometer
elastic bands	2 plastic mugs	1 torch light
1 pair of scissors	4 small mirrors	
1 plastic bucket	1 spirit lamp	

The basic kit is much simpler than the Papua New Guinea example. It is intended for use in environment-based science.

Teachers are encouraged to supplement this basic kit with their own aids from scrap items in the environment such as empty tins, bottles, rocks, levels coral etc.; funnels from plastic bottles, stands from scrap wood. Teachers have little option but to improvise, thus placing considerable reliance on their goodwill.

The primary science kit produced by the National Council for Educational Research and Training (NCERT) in India has 50 items stored in a box, including circuit board, marbles, hand fans, hand lens, magnet, polythene containers, mirrors, spring balance, thermometer, toy, electric motor; the kit comes with a tool kit consisting of triangular file, claw hammer and hand drill. In this kit teachers are expected to produce some of their own equipment.

A United Kingdom based company has supplied primary teaching kits for Tanzania. The kit provides equipment for 38 experiments covering plant growth and soil, magnetism, electricity and basic laboratory techniques. Breakable and consumable items are kept to a minimum. The kit contains items such as a tripod stand, gauze, cotton thread, stand, beakers, funnels, measuring cylinder, test tubes and rack, kitchen roll, cotton wool, spirit burner, compass, rulers; and has optional extras such as a bioviewer microscope. Kit items come in a robust, heavy-duty, insect-proof plastic container. A major criticism of the kit is that most of the items could quite readily have been produced in Tanzania—the kit even includes a packet of salt! Nevertheless it is based on a well-defined and well-illustrated set of experiments and intended for use in rural schools by untrained teachers. It could well serve as a prototype for local production. The concepts covered are considered those essential for a basic understanding of the science concepts needed for rural development. About 5,000 of these kits were supplied to Tanzania in 1986, using World Bank aid. The kit cost in 1991 £85 ($151) and is now popular in schools in the United Kingdom.

2. Lower and Middle Secondary Science Kits

At this level it is possible to distinguish between integrated or general science kits and specialised science kits.

Integrated Science Kits

The Hoshangabad Science Teaching Programme (India) integrated science kit for middle secondary level is made as much as possible from local materials. Each kit is designed for a group of four students and consists of 44 permanent items such as hand lenses, cell holders, microscope, compass, thermometer; perishable items such as microscope slides, torch bulbs, convex lens, steel wire; consumable items such as razor blades, napthalene, candles. In addition there are permanent and consumable items for the class as a whole (stove, chemicals).

The Zim-Sci (Zimbabwe) basic kit for secondary level is very simple and consists of a beaker, an alcohol burner, a funnel, plastic bottles, a stand, a boiling tin, a peg, a box of matches, a spatula/stirrer, measuring scoops, an evaporating dish, plastic cups with lids. The kit was originally designed for use in rural day high schools. The need to extend this kit for the new 'O' level necessitated the importation of several additional items.

In Sri Lanka 'The Mini Laboratory Unit' consists of 82 permanent items such as an ammeter, atomic model set, spring balance, circuit board kit, electronics kit, dissecting set, microscope, tool kit; 55 glassware items such as beakers, burettes, flasks, lenses, mirrors, prisms, thermometers; and 35 perishable items such as corks, clips, test tubes, litmus paper, wire. No chemicals are provided but a steel cupboard for storage is provided. The kit is based on conventional science apparatus. The 'Mini Laboratory Unit' is designed for demonstration purposes but could accommodated a group of 5 students. The Mini-Lab kit is an extension of the Mini Laboratory Unit with additional furniture designed to accommodate up to 20 students.

Specialised Science Kits

The SEPU is Kenya produces separate student and teacher demonstration kits for biology, chemistry and physics at secondary level. There is sufficient flexibility to enable schools to purchase mixed kits of, say, physics and chemistry equipment. About 50 per cent of the SEPU chemistry kit for students consists of items of glassware, bought mainly from local branches of international companies. Many items fulfil more than one function to the extent that SEPU estimates that at least 100 simple experiments can be performed with the set of apparatus contained in the kit.

Papua New Guinea has supplied lower secondary science kits for physics, chemistry, biology and geology. The physics kit contains:

Electrical meters: voltmeter, ammeter, galvanometer (5).

Electricity and magnetism equipment : e.g. 10 magnets, 10 compass needles, 200 crocodile clips, lamp-holders, switches, wire, bulbs, battery holder.

Electro-magnetic equipment : motor bell, cell plates.

Energy change equipment : solar cell, radiometer.

Heat expansion apparatus : e.g. bar and gauge, ball and ring, bimetallic strip, mirrors, lenses, magnifiers.

Light box and optical set.

Mechanics equipment : 20 spring balances, standard masses, pulleys (20).

Power-supply : 2 variable voltage units.

There is an additional kit of assorted items suitable for all four of the sciences. Virtually all of the kit items are imported. The kits contain materials intended for grades 7 to 10 so teachers have to select from the kits for particular lessons, but the kits contain sufficient equipment for class sets of about 40 students working in groups of four. There are now plans to provide grade specific kits.

In addition to these centrally provided kits there are many examples of teacher-made kits. DSE has been particularly active in this field and has conducted many extended seminars for teachers and student-teachers in Africa, South America and Asia. The materials used are simple and locally available and selected to illustrate simple experiments on a variety of topics. There have been in-service workshops (Caribbean, Botswana, Swaziland) which have focused on the specific needs of integrated science, and there is some evidence from the

Caribbean that this has resulted in greater levels of teacher confidence.

3. General Features of Kits

There is a tremendous range in the content of science kits. At primary level there is an emphasis on very simple basic equipment with additional material provided by teachers. Sometimes, tools are included for teacher assembly. Most of the primary kits are designed for teacher rather than student use. At lower and middle secondary level there is a much greater range in content with greater representation of more specialized science equipment. Most of the kits are intended for use by students of all ability levels such as those found in unstreamed science classes, although in some cases there is provision of material or ideas for optional activities for special groups. Virtually all of the centrally produced kits are intended for use by all students in all grades. In many cases the kits come in two versions, one for teacher demonstration and the other for student use.

4. Nature of Materials

Most science kits provide a mixture of permanent, perishable and consumable items. Permanent items such as microscopes, thermometers and electric meters have to be imported unless they can be obtained locally. Provided they are well-made and maintained, permanent items can be expected to last three or four years. Perishable items include items such as torch bulbs and microscope slides. These may or may not be available locally and have to be regularly replaced. Many consumable items such as candles, matches, razor blades can be obtained locally in urban areas, but chemicals would have to be imported. The kinds of items generally assumed not to be locally available might appear surprising, *e.g.* connection wires, matches, magnets and torches. In a throw-away society such as in the West, many of these items may be available from scrap yards or the teacher's attic but this is less likely in developing countries. There are other sources of scrap materials such as hospitals and clinics but this requires time and organisational skills to collect such items. There are many ideas in the improvisation literature on how to construct items such as filter funnels. Many countries assist teachers by categorising science equipment so that they can more easily obtain supplies from various sources.

5. Support Materials

Many of the early kits were simply collections of apparatus with the minimum of guidance on use. When manuals were provided they were not easy for teachers without much background in science to understand. Developers of more recent kits have recognized the need for careful illustration and appropriate use of language. One United Kingdom manufactured kit exported to Tanzania comes with a teachers' guide written in Swahili (Baldwin, 1986); the guide describes various experiments which can be done using the kit and provides clear illustrations of the apparatus required. There are also examples of kits which include worksheets or work cards for students. The Papua New Guina assorted science kit include charts, reference books, slides, rock, safety manual and mineral collections, etc., as well as equipment; it is really a multi-media package to support the other kits. Many kits contain sub-kits on specific topics such as optics and electricity which have their own manuals for experiments. The biology kit in Papua New Guinea contains models of biological structures, slides and notes; the geology kit contains rock and ore specimens. There are examples of other more specific kits such as the South Pacific Regional Environment Programme Coral Reef Kit (1989) and resource book—there are plans to distribute the kits to secondary schools in the region; the Teaching Aids Production Unit (TAPU) in Botswana has produced kits on Wildlife Conservation for the Ministry of Local Government and Lands.

6. Quality

While an effective tender system can help to ensure quality in commercially obtained equipment, lack of quality control is commonly reported as a major constraint to local production. The relatively low levels of skill in technicians is largely responsible. Quality is particularly threatened where teachers or students produce equipment. Early reports from SEPU in Kenya indicated up to 80 per cent loss in production of kits due to poor quality control. UNICEF evaluation of the early NCERT primary science kits showed imperfections such as poorly moulded plastic syringes. Recent reports state that some IPST (Wilailak, 1992) materials are easily broken and not easily repaired. In Zimbabwe teachers complained about equipment that had past its 'use by' date, poorly labelled chemicals, non-functioning microscopes, and the general low prestige of items. Problems due to the rapid depletion of consumables have been noted in many countries.

Most production centres have quality control laboratories where items are regularly tested against their specifications, but despite this, things can go wrong due to the over-complacency of suppliers. NCERT has a team of inspectors who determine specifications for quality controls and the extent to which local commercial enterprise is capable of meeting requirements. Handbooks have been prepared so that teachers and technician can carry out routine tests on instruments provided in kits. The Regional Centre for Education in Science and Mathematics (RECSAM) in Malaysia provides training for the in-country testing and evaluation of prototype items. DSE (1986) has developed guidelines for evaluation of kits including ease of handling, student, teacher and environment fit, safety. Some countries such as the United Kingdom have facilities for the independent evaluation of equipment.

7. Implications

If kits are designed to reflect more local content then it is imperative that teachers are properly prepared for such an approach. It is widely reported that teachers often fail to collect even the simplest of materials for science lessons despite the guidance provided in resource books. There seems to be no incentive for doing so; teachers are in many cases underpaid, irregularly paid and overworked. The personal touch achieved by involving teachers in the production of low-cost equipment can help to promote greater acceptance, particularly when related to simple relevant experiments that can be done with the minimum of preparation time.

Teachers need to be made aware through training of the possibilities of 'junk' material (UNESCO, 1980). However, as Allsop (1991) notes:

> The kind of creative use of improved equipment often seen in the primary classrooms of industrialized countries does not readily transfer to a primary teaching force lacking professional esteem, and to a society where one person's junk is the next person's artefact." (p.37)

There is plenty of junk in throw-away developed societies but it may be scarcer in developing countries. Also, as experience in Bangladesh, the Caribbean and India bears out, the local production or improvization of equipment from junk materials may create new demands for such items with consequent increase in costs (Commonwealth Secretariat, 1982). Often items such as empty bottles are refundable. In many countries there may be a need to survey what relevant junk material is actually available in the immediate environment of a wide variety of schools.

It is important that kits are designed to support a particular approach to science education and are not just *ad hoc* collections of conventional apparatus. For specialized science courses, science kits will probably have to comprise more of the expensive, conventional science apparatus than needed for integrated science. However, a review of the nature of science activities might identify approaches which could use lower-cost alternatives. The durability of non-renewable resources also needs to be considered with constant search for quality improvement. Indeed, there is a need for a systematic approach to quality control at all stages in production and assembly.

There is a need for the kind of flexibility and user-friendliness in design that is probably only possible with local production. The design concept of flexibility should also embrace the need to ensure that science kits are genuinely user-friendly for students and teacher, and for girls and boys. It is indeed important to avoid the kind of gender strereotyping common in many science curriculum materials (Duncan, 1988). There is evidence from the United Kingdom studies of low levels of female participation in practical work with boys 'monopolizing' equipment in group work. In general, care should be taken in the design of illustrated manuals.

Questions for planners include:

- What basic items are needed for a user-friendly, low-cost science kit?

- Which items could confidently be expected to be obtainable locally?
- Which items are currently produced in the country.
- Which items would have to be imported?
- What additional resources are needed, e.g. manuals, tools, etc?

5

Manufacture

An essential requirement for manufacture of science kits is that there must be close integration with all other aspects of science education. There is a concurrent need for teacher training to improve the use and management of science kits and for laboratory technician training to maintain and repair kits. The content of science kits must be determined according to the teaching approach and practical activities advocated in curriculum materials, reviewed if necessary in order to identify lower-cost alternatives. Climatic and school design factors have to be considered in the design of kits. All of this implies major input from science educators. This is more likely to occur if local production is carried out under strict Ministry of Education guidelines. But government agencies are not ideally suited to commercial ventures. The local production of science kits requires the kind of technical skill and commercial know-how usually found in industry and not in government run bureaucracies. Also, public service salaries are unlikely to attract or retain the kind of workforce required. The high production runs required for susceptibility make it extremely difficult to get backing for composite factory production. Even with detailed feasibility studies, initial estimates of returns can be quite misleading. For instance, a proposal for local production in the Western State of Nigeria (Nigeria, 1972) estimated market demand would increase by as much as 300 per cent in five years. These highly optimistic estimates were based on a survey of schools. However, the vagaries of school budgets and local politics are such that there is no guarantee that schools would have sufficient funds to maintain such a demand.

The role of commercial manufacturers has been discussed in many seminars on local production. Some countries have government institutions and entrepreneurial bodies established to promote local industry, others already have an infrastructure for small-scale production of general school equipment, others have branches of international science equipment manufacturers. Thus new centres of production might have to compete with established centres in a limited market. As Whittel, who as involved in the early development of SEPU in Kenya, has noted :

> "a locally based attempt to manufacture will be successful ...only to the extent that it can compete successfully with established commercial manufacturers in the four key area of design, price, quality and early delivery."
>
> *Whittel, 1975:670*

This chapter is concerned with the manufacture of science kits. Area of interest include :

- Responsibility for manufacture
- Production strategies employed
- Raw materials and facilities required
- Nature of workforce

Case studies of various countries involved in manufacture will be presented.

1. Responsibility for Manufacturer

Thailand

The Institute for the Promotion of Teaching Science and Technology (IPST) in Thailand is autonomous within MOE, and entrusted by MOE to produce prototypes of equipment which are simple, made of locally available materials and low-priced. The IPST Chairman is the under Secretary for Education. This Institute designs and makes prototypes and small-scale production runs of apparatus for schools involved in the trailing of IPST curriculum materials. Kits are marketed on a commercial scale by the Business Organization of the Teachers Council which has branches in each province for nationwide distribution at low prices. Schools are required to buy local equipment. The Academic Section of the IPST has design teams for chemistry, physics, biology, physical science, general science; and service teams for evaluation of equipment design, production and distribution. Some of the prototype science kit components are put out to tender for manufacture by Technical Institutes and Small-Scale Industry. Although primarily concerned with supplying the needs of schools involved in trilling IPST materials, other schools may order kits or class sets of apparatus from IPST. Items come from various sources including IPST, local commercial enterprise, imports and expendables. In the mid-1970s about 75 per cent of the components for chemistry and physics kits and 23 per cent of biology kits were locally produced.

India

The National Council for Educational Research and Technology (NCERT) in India operates a government-run production unit but uses local companies to make some of its kits under contract. NCERT's Central Science Workshop (CSW) is a purpose-built building with main workshop, prototype design workshop, dies and sheet metal workshop, optics glass workshop, wood workshop, plastic workshop, etc. The CSW produces specialized science kits from components produced at the workshop and those manufactured by local industry. Kits are supplied to schools *via* the State Ministries of Education. The NCERT employs a team of inspectors responsible for quality control both in the CSW and in supplier factories which are regularly assessed for physical facilities, staffing patterns, availability of raw materials and capability to duplicate science items in large number of schools.

Kenya

The Science Equipment Production Unit (SEPU) in Kenya is equipped for full-scale local production as well as prototype development, but some components and raw materials for kits are imported. The SEPU operates commercially but as a non-profitmaking venture. Its directors are appointed by government bodies. It sells direct to schools and has salesmen to promote marketing.

Ghana

Ghana has embarked on a project aimed at encouraging teachers to build up their own kits from improvised materials. This is a teachers' college initiative and student-teachers are encouraged to produce their own equipment during training. Products are housed in specially designed kit-boxes made at the colleges. The kit becomes the permanent property of the student-teacher on graduation and practising teachers are encouraged to add to the kits using improvisation ideas provided in source books.

Most of the production centres discussed above are subjected to a great deal of government control. There are few examples from the Third World of composite factories specializing in the exclusive production of science equipment on a commercial basis. Instead, most existing production centres makes use of supplies from a variety of local and foreign companies, supplementing these with production runs of their own.

2. Production Strategies

It is important to distinguish between local production and improvisation strategies. Local production is usually a matter of import substitution and is often an attempt to meet the demands of the whole school system. On the other hand, improvization is generally a teacher-centered activity and its encouragement at workshops and in-service courses can provide an important means of stimulating a more experimental approach to science teaching. Improvized items produced at such workshops are intended to enable the teacher to explain a particular scientific principle in his or her own way. The development of high level improvization skills in teachers could obviate the need for the local production of many items, and could also ultimately reduce the need for expensive imports. The problem facing many countries is to decide on which strategy will be more cost-effective.

A varied pattern of production is found. In this chapter we will examine the strategies adopted by two of the most established production centres, those of Kenya and India.

SEPU (Kenya) Production Strategy

Lists were prepared of the most acute apparatus needs of schools, and these needs were matched to the availability of raw materials and the amount of design work required and the difficulty of production. Priorities were decided, and for each item one or more prototypes was produced for costing. Vetting and quality control procedures were introduced. SEPU found it possible to develop quite sophisticated mass production techniques using semi-skilled labour, *e.g.* making pulleys from wood and jigs for bending hooks for hanging masses. It was found possible to cut down costs by using multi-functional components in its kits. For instance the basis of the chemistry kit was a pegboard stand on which it was possible to mount all the components of an experiment set-up. A salesman was appointed to promote sales and arrange demonstrations of SEPU equipment in schools. Considerable cost-saving was possible for schools: for instance the cost of the ray optics kit was about half of the imported price. But according to Whittel (1975): " *over the second 6 months of operation ...the sales from the unit were running at approximately 84 per cent of the locally incurred outgoings, and 55 per cent of total costs.*"

NCERT (India) Production Strategy

Unlike Kenya, India has a well developed industrial base of small-scale industry and engineering capable of producing many of the components required for science kits. CSW adopted the following production strategy :

- studying the equipment for teaching science that is manufactured by industry.
- exploring how its quality could be improved;
- designing, manufacturing and experimental testing of new teaching equipment;
- designing and producing teaching equipment;
- producing new designs for manufacture by industry.

Simpson (1979) has described the problems experienced by the Simplex company in Hong Kong which produced an initial series of 12 self-instructional kits. The production strategy involved procuring kit components from over fifty suppliers and assembling these into self-contained kits. His account highlights the kind of problems which can occur even in a highly sophisticated and industrialised state such as Hong Kong. Among the problems he lists are :

- the difficulty in locating suitable small factories and winning approval to look around;
- the tendency of manufacturers to sell whole units rather than component parts;
- the incompatibility of parts obtained from different suppliers;
- the difficulty of ensuring future supply when small factories change products;
- the lack of interest in small orders;
- the problems of quality control and unskilled labour;
- the difficulties in dealing with a multiplicity of suppliers;
- the need to have all components available before kit assembly;
- the difficulty in generating an economy of scale for kit production.

The Simplex kits are no longer produced. To some extent the problems encountered in Hong Kong are not as likely to occur in less developed countries, mainly because there is generally not the range of suppliers, thus reducing some of the organizational problems. On the other hand existing suppliers are not likely to be able to supply all of the materials needed, there are likely to be problems associated with compatibility, and delays in overseas component supply. For use in the conditions prevalent in many developing countries science kits need to be designed so that they are versatile, self-contained, cheap, lightweight, compact, and sturdy. This is indeed a tall order and is unlikely to be met cost-effectively by a single local production centre, especially in the smaller developing nations. However, with effective management and organization, strategies based on the procurement and assembly of science kit components might prove viable.

UNESCO (1973) has suggested a general system for the design, production and distribution of school science equipment, starting from ideas for equipment contributed by teachers' colleges, schools, curriculum specialists and textbook developers. Suitable ideas are incorporated in prototype design, evaluated in schools and modified where necessary for industrial use. This is followed by the design and evaluation of industrial prototypes before production. *Chart 1* summaries the system.

Key features of this model are the integrated approach to design, and the centrality of the schools in evaluation of these designs. The model closely approximates the production system employed in many of the countries reviewed in this study, although the emphasis on different stages varies. The IPST in Thailand employs teams of science educators to contribute ideas for prototypes. India places more emphasis on quality control, research and development, and at least in the beginning, has a tendency to adapt existing designs. Kenya started from the existing needs of schools, but some ideas for new designs came from the Science Teachers' College. Production centres need not produce all of the components for science kits and industrial prototypes could be developed by a variety of different commercial manufacturers as well as by the production centre itself. In many countries, particularly in the Asian region, there are many small engineering firms which already make suitable components for science kits. For instance, India has many commercial suppliers of its own; the Nigerian 'Yellow Pages' telephone directory (1979) devotes seven pages to advertising scientific and medical equipment. In addition, some countries have long established traditions of small industries and roadside repair workshops. Some items would probably have to be imported from overseas suppliers. Papua New Guinea obtains some of the component parts for its kits as far away as the United Kingdom. In this case follow-up is difficult and there can be considerable delays, necessitating the distribution of partially completed kits. In Papua New Guinea legal expenses were incurred as a result of failure of a United Kingdom company to comply with tendering agreement.

Chart 1. Model of design and evaluation of industrial use

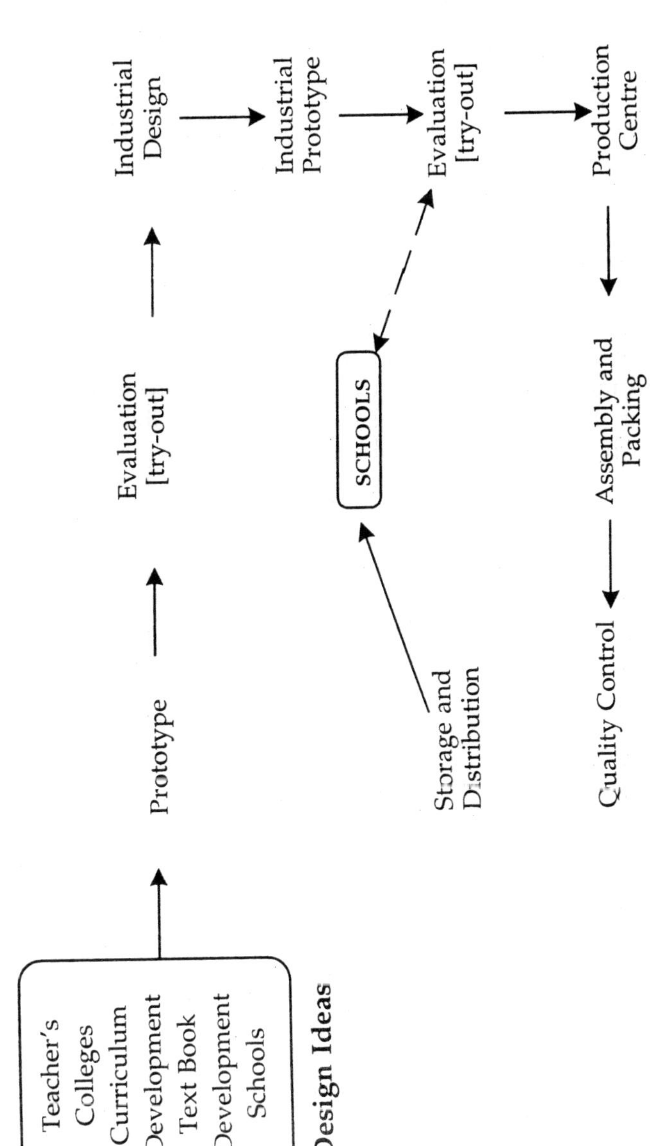

Source: UNESCO 1973.

Many developing countries have branches of international firms but only limited stocks of apparatus are kept and interests are focussed on the supply of equipment for large projects such as new tertiary education institutes, hospitals and research laboratories.

Some United Kingdom companies illustrate what can be achieved by closer-co-operation between schools and commercial enterprise. Many of these companies have an association with education dating back to the early part of the last century. Production efforts today are for science and technology equipment and kits designed to make teaching easier.

The needs of non-specialist science teachers are foremost in design considerations and there are effective links between product development and teaching at all stages. Some commercial firms also assist in the organization of local workshops for teachers, and representatives are on hand at every major convention of science teachers. New demands brought about by the introduction of the national curriculum are being met by co-operation between science equipment production companies and schools. A company in the united Kingdom, working in conjunction with the Ministry of Education and teacher educators in Tanzania, has developed a primary science kit designed to meet the needs of Tanzania's rural primary schools and untrained teachers. Over 5,000 kits have been exported to Tanzania, and later to Nigeria and Ghana. The company has participated in in-service training on the use of the kit in Tanziania. Such close co-operation is to the benefit of both commerce and education. There is a need for suppliers to strengthen their contacts with local curriculum development projects and for greater awareness of needs and local conditions.

3. Raw Materials and Tools

In the late 1970s estimates of the cost of local production were based on an assumed average annual production output of about $200,000 which at that time was considered to be a target for sustainability. Such an output was estimated to require workshop space of a least 2,000 square metres and a staff of 100. While cost estimates are likely to have increased substantially since then, there is scope for cost reduction by strategies such as limiting output to low-cost equipment; limiting the range of experiments illustrated by kits; spreading production between the main production centre and local commercial manufactures; adapting existing production facilities; using suitable spare production facilities in existing industries; making greater use of small-scale industry; extending the market for science kits to include independent learners and distance education. Aid-assisted projects will have to be designed in such a way that the foreign assistance part becomes self-liquidating and the national part becomes self-perpetuating. Thus training and staff-development components will have to be introduced from the beginning.

One estimate (Melton, 1972) of the basic facilities needed for the full factory production of science equipment is shown below:

Hand tools	*Machine tools*	*Raw materials*
chisels, cutters, drills & borers files, hammers measuring aids, planes, pliers, saws, screwdrivers, vices, wrenches and miscellaneous items such as safety goggles and soldering equipment.	band saw, circular saw, drill press, grinder, metal lathe, buffing machine, oxy-acetylene set, planer, wood lathe. materials.	adhesives, electric materials (bulbs, batteries), glass plastics, nuts, bolts, screws, etc., wood, metals, paint

The most costly recurring component is the supply of materials. For instance, in the mid-1970s 60 per cent of NCERT's annual production budget was allocated to the purchase of raw materials. Science kit production requires materials such as plastic, glass, wood, metal and chemicals. The costs and availability of these materials vary considerably from country-to-country.

Plastic has many attractive features in that it is hard-wearing, light-weight and suitable for many of the components of science kits. There are many examples of plastic kits in the developed world. For instance, the Japanese produce mini-science kits of plastic; many British companies produce plastic kits for the construction of working models of a variety of technological products, and to provide problem-solving exercises for students. SEPU in Kenya uses plastic to produce high quality lenses and multi-functional plastic components for chemistry and physics experiments. Plastic moulding is often supplied in kit boxes to conveniently house and display individual kit components. However, there are prohibitive costs involved in the moulding and pressing of plastics and once educational needs have been satisfied the moulds become redundant. It would be more economical to use an existing company that specialises in the production of plastic components rather than to embark on the development of plastic moulding facilities. In many countries there are long established production runs of everyday plastic items such as cups, polystyrene, food containers, etc., which with some modification could serve as containers in science.

Glassware is bulky and fragile and greatly adds to transport and storage costs. Nevertheless, its use is unavoidable in many cases where its transparent quality is essential to the observation of chemical and biological reactions in reagent flasks. There are cheaper alternatives to glass which are suitable for many science activities, *e.g.* natural containers such as gourds and bamboo stems and empty bottles and jars.

Most local production centres have woodworking workshops to prepare wooden prototypes. In some countries there have been attempts to take advantage of the local timber industry by redesigning plastic components in wood, but the quality and attractiveness of the finished product varies. In the United Kingdom teachers are encouraged to use balsa wood to prepare working models from cardboard templates. Storage boxes for many kits are often made from wood. However, wood tends to wrap in humid tropical conditions and is also held in great esteem by hungry termites! Heavy-duty plastic or aluminium containers might be more suitable.

Metal is required for many kit components, especially in physics Workshops require metal working facilities and, to increase attractiveness and durability, there is a further need for buffing and electroplating equipment. For science kits in the tropics there is an important role for light-weight and non-corroding metals such as aluminium.

Chemicals are also supplied in many science kits. Special safety procedures are needed to pack these and many airlines refuse to carry volatile or explosive chemicals. Some production centres import chemicals in bulk and pack them into kit size locally. In many cases chemicals have to be imported and delivery delays can create bottlenecks in final kit assembly. There are possibilities for exploiting the local environment to obtain supplies of chemicals such as acids, bases and indicators (Eshiet, 1988). Although such locally extracted chemicals may not be pure enough for quantitative work they can be used to illustrate many qualitative phenomena and there are also important skills developed in the process of extraction.

Science kits also contain electronic scientific instruments such a voltmeters, pH meters. These would normally have to be imported. There are examples of locally produced versions which are quite satisfactory for activities which do not require high levels of precision.

Finally, science kits can be supplemented using locally available materials and junk material, but there needs to be a comprehensive survey of what is and is not likely to be readily available at minimum cost to the school.

4. Nature of Workforce

The kind of materials used in the production of science kits calls for highly skilled craftsmen, particularly for the early stages requiring the development of production jigs and moulds. Most production centres employ a mixture of professionally trained tradesmen, engineering, accountants, unskilled workers, temporary packers and assemblers and teams of science educators as advisers, evaluators and market researchers. There are also requirements for people with highly developed interpersonal skills to liaise effectively with local companies and science educators.

Labour costs vary. Even in India, where labour is relatively cheap, a labour cost figure equivalent to about 60 per cent of staff costs was included in the price of the initial run of science kits. Skilled labour expects the same terms and conditions as would be found in similar commercial enterprise. Government-run centres cannot compete with profit-orientated private enterprise, and the salaries offered are not likely to attract much interest. For instance, in Thailand the IPST workers may only be paid at national civil service rates. The result is that once they are trained they realise they have a high market value and leave for industry.

In Nigeria, the promotion of intermediate technology is seen as a problem solving approach to meet local technological needs.

Medical, agricultural and kitchen equipment have been produced by small-scale industry and vocational centres. Projects have become self-supporting once initial costs have been met. It seems likely that these groups could also meet the demand for some forms of science equipment, e.g. circuit boards, burners, stands etc. Vigyan Ashram in India uses appropriate technology methods in its production of scientific instruments. For example, students have developed a technique for water prospecting using electrical resistivity measurements. New product designs are being commercialized, *e.g.* its Earth Resistance Meter is 20 per cent of the cost of existing models.

The potential of local craftsmen groups such as the Trade Brigades in Botswana has also been recognized (Giffould, undated). Elliott (1988) reports that many metal working needs in Africa were in fact being met by the technology of the informal sector rather than the formal sector. But although supplies were found to be functional and reasonably priced, standards varied. He also notes problems due to the lack of spare parts and poor management. If there is to be a role for such groups in local production there is a need to ensure better management and quality control, especially where kit components from different sources have to be compatible.

Krishan Sane of Delhi University conducts workshops on the production of chemical instrumentation for senior chemistry students: products include pH meters, calorimeters and conductmeters. The approach has been widely replicated, with evaluation suggesting that quality control can be maintained, and that product costs are of the order of 10 per cent of commercial equivalents for comparable performance (Sane, cited in Woolnough, 1991).

The evidence generally points to failure if mass production is combined with teacher training. According to Whittel (1975): *"the very object of the operation, that of giving students experience of production techniques, rule out high quality products"*. Such an approach is also tied to the school and college vacation periods. Teachers attending a workshop course in Kenya were found to produce equipment at 6 time the catalogue cost and couldn't meet delivery dates. There is scope for the involvement of voctional centres and technical colleges for some aspects of local production (assembly and packing) but they need much higher levels of government support if priority training needs are also to be met.

5. Implications

A varied pattern of provision is evident and combinations of approach are possible, depending on needs and available resource. These are summarized in the following table.

Provision	Requirements	Advantage	Disadvantages
Importing science kits	Needs close co-operation with overseas suppliers; effective distribution strategies	Appropriate where there are low levels of technology; cost saving possible by local assembly	Drain on foreign exchange; more difficult to ensure that tender requirements are met; may result in met; may result in stereotyped kits; replenishment could be difficult
Full-scale local production	Needs large capital outlay; regular supply of raw materials; skilled labour; quality control; needs holistic approach to Planning; need to provide for single-item supply; needs to become self-sustainable	Can cater for local conditions; provides opportunity for continuous evaluation	Small annual demand; can result in more costly versions of imported items; can imported items; can result in low-prestige
Local assembly of science kits	Needs organisational and management skill; needs to identify suppliers; need to ensure compatibility of components; need for bulk supply	Cheaper than full-scale production; can use technical and vocational centres for packing and assembly	Only possible where there are a variety of suppliers and high level organisational skills; relies on entrepreneurial skill

Teacher-produced kits	Needs committed teacher educators specially designed workshops; review of existing training	Can develop sense of ownership; can overcome psychological barriers; greater scope for environment relatedness; can develop improvisation skills; can improve demonstration skills	Lack of follow-up; low quality of materials
The production of a 'shoe-box' kit for emergency situations	Needs support from teacher educators; effective supervision; needs integration of craft and science programs	Provides more of a sense of realism of conditions in schools	Could become an easy option and limit science practical to very basic forms
The production of models and prototypes	Needs workshop and skilled labour; need to supply teachers with tools and manuals; needs knowledge of industrial requirements	Many useful ideas in the literature; can stimulate local production and develop construction skills in teachers	Relies on goodwill of teachers; needs preparation time
The development of 'hand-experiments' with everyday materials	Needs simple hand tools and adequate supply of local materials; needs a review of practical work	Can be carried out by anyone in a short time; can illustrate important science concepts	Impact relies on the quality of experts chosen to lead workshops; and on the extent to which ideas can be disseminated to reach a wider audience.

It is of course, possible to combine many of the above approaches. For instance, student science kits could be locally produced to illustrate hand experiments, and teachers could be trained in improvization skills and provided with tools and materials to construct their own demonstration kits from prototype designs. The approach adopted depends on local conditions.

If local production is considered a viable option then planing needs to be oriented from the beginning to sustaining the co-operation of many different interest groups, especially through long and difficult gestation periods. Where foreign assistance or local development bank assistance is sought, project planning has to actor for self-sustainability when the foreign aid component ceases. State controlled local production enterprises have the advantage that production can be more easily linked to curriculum development, teacher training and textbook development but are less likely to operate on a profitable basis. Private enterprise is more likely to attract the kind of specialist manpower needed but may lose sight of quality and relevance unless effective measures are incorporated in the production system. There is a role for technical colleges and voctional institutions in the production and assembly of components but there needs to be a clear definition of role and responsibilities so that the priority training needs of these institutions can be met. Finally, there is a need for considerable research and development skill and funding provision to enable designers to observe equipment being used in typical classroom situations. Even if production is limited to prototypes for teacher use there are may costs involved which derives the need for follow-up and evaluation, and the need to supply tools, manuals and some raw materials for construction. In summary, the needs are for planning orientated towards:

- identifying items that can be manufactured at low-cost locally;
- sustaining high levels of co-operation between different interest groups;
- ensuring that local production has the capacity to become self-sustainable;
- ensuring that effective means of quality control and evaluation are built in;
- identifying possible cost-saving strategies at each stage in production.

6

Distribution, Replenishment, Storage and Repair

Wallberg (1991) warns about the earlier tendency of donors to treat science equipment as a form of 'food aid'. Indeed there are now many examples of depleted science kits littering the Third World simply because no provision was made for replenishment and repair of kit items. Also many kit production projects have encountered, problems of rapidly deteriorating science kits gathering dust in warehouses due to the fact that transport and fuel are not available to get them to the schools. No matter distribution, replenishment, storage and repair.

This section is concerned with issues such as:

- Distribution of science kits to schools
- Responsibility for distribution
- Problems in distribution
- Equity of distribution
- Storage in schools
- Replenishment
- Repair

1. Distribution

Various distribution systems exist. In Papua New Guinea centrally assembled kits were distributed to the 20 provincial education offices to be collected by individual schools or by the provincial secondary inspectors. Most of the packing was done centrally by a local science equipment company. As some of the kits included volatile chemicals these had to be transported by ship and road rather than by air. Since there was only one kit per school and only 130 high schools this was probably an efficient distribution system but it did rely on the goodwill of school inspectors to use their vehicles for this purpose. Distribution is reported to have been reasonable efficient despite transport difficulties, and there were few losses. Freight and packing costs amounted to about 6 per cent of the kit purchase costs. The distribution of science kits to primary schools would encounter much more serious difficulties due to the isolation of many primary schools. In some remote areas teachers have to leave school mid-week to collect the salaries of their colleagues from the provincial or district education office.

In the early stages of Zim-Sci science kits in Zimbabwe, they were assembled in rented halls before distribution. Transport delays resulted in considerable damage to equipment as it was stockpiled to await distribution. In addition, transport services were poor. Distribution problems were solved by establishing a permanent centre for science kit assembly and distribution. This centre has permanent staff including storeman and packers and operates a card index system. Transport contractors were found who could deliver kits to depots closer to the schools. Inspection found that the stores were considered satisfactory with proper and up to date records. However, lengthy storage in the tropics can incur considerable damage and should be avoided unless suitable facilities are available such as air-conditioned warehouses. Stock control lends itself well to computer systems.

The IPST in Thailand has a permanent equipment stores and distribution team with additional unskilled labour taken on during schools vacations. The team is responsible for labelling kit items, final quality control, and kit assembly. Kits are marketed by the business Organization of the Teachers Council which has branches in each province and schools are required to buy local equipment.

The Hoshangabad Science Teaching Programme (HSTP) in India provides student science kits to 350 schools spread over seven districts in Madhya Pradesh (which has a population of over 50 million). HSTP started as a pilot project in 1972, and now covers an entire district and has plans to expand to 8 more districts in 1986. Hoshangabad science kits are purchased and distributed by *Sangam Kendras* which are units consisting of one or more high schools and the middle schools associated with them. Each *Sangam Kendra* has a Principal responsible for all aspects of the project, and a teacher or assistant teacher with responsibility for kit distribution to participating middle schools, and for maintaining records. Science kits and replenishment items are distributed directly to participating schools during regular meetings of schools involved in the project. Kit distribution is proportional to the size of each school and the teacher is also responsible for overseeing kit maintenance.

The main problems with distribution are in the transport and warehousing aspects. Prolonged storage causes damage and few production centres have the transport or organisational infrastructure to deliver directly to schools. Transport and freight costs are generally in the region of 10 per cent of the cost of kits. There are huge demands placed on vehicles in provincial education centres so long delays are common. Commercial transport firms could greatly add to the cost of supplying schools with kits thus defeating the objective of low-cost provision. In most countries transport is severely limited at provincial centres and has to be shared by many users. Even so, it is remarkable that bundles of examination papers, often as bulky as science kits, always get to their destinations on schedule. If the same importance was attached to the distribution of science equipment the quality of science education would be greatly improved. It is important that there is a holistic approach to the distribution of science kits so that they get from production or assembly centres to the classroom with the minimum of delay. Planners will need to review existing transport services at provincial or district level and augment these with cheap commercially contracted transport where appropriate. Careful planning and scheduling could ensure that kits are distributed during science teachers' meetings. Above all, there is a need to promote awareness at district and provincial levels so that the special needs of science education are appreciated.

2. Responsibility

In many countries it is the state or regional centre and not individual schools which orders from suppliers. The effectiveness of such systems can only be as good as the links between schools and districts, and between district and central supplier. In a decentralised system there are many individuals with responsibility for distribution and plenty of scope for 'buck-passing' when things go wrong.

The SEPU in Kenya sells directly to schools and has a salesman to persuade schools to buy SEPU kits rather than imported equipment. The salesman is a science educators and is able to demonstrate the kit in action. Many centres have found that bulk delivery of chemicals is cheaper than schools buying directly, but packing and distribution problems are incurred. Some countries have a network of science teacher resource centres, *e.g.* the Awraja Pedagogical Centres in Ethiopia, and these have the potential to assist in the distribution of equipment. There are also regular meetings of science teachers' associations.

Although most countries are still centralized, decentralization of the administrative function in education is becoming an almost worldwide tend, influenced by a perceived need for increased efficiency, a need to adapt to local conditions, and a need to provide greater responsibilities to local groups. But a centralized system usually has its most qualified and experienced personnel at the administrative centre and not in the districts. Decentralization of administrative functions rarely includes the decentralization of qualified human resources. Hence, officials at the local level are unlikely to be sensitized to the specific needs of science education and appreciate the need to keep schools well supplied with science teaching materials.

Orpwood and Werdelin (1987) note that the delivery system of science education exerts a direct influence on the outputs of science education and can be manipulated more easily than other variables such as curriculum structure and content. They discuss the restrictions, constraints and difficulties for the renewal of science and technology education in terms of:

- external resources (equipment, laboratories, books);
- internal resources (qualification of teachers and administrators);
- internal preparedness (flexibility, support, attitudes);
- external preparedness (socio-economic factors, scientific literacy).

It is possible that the more obvious constraints such as those concerned with resources may blind us to the influence of the more pervasive constraint, the level of preparedness. The Hoshangabad project provides a model of what can be done in a decentralized system through effective local clusters of schools, clearly articulated areas of responsibility, and regular meetings.

3. Equity of Supply

Schools vary a great deal in terms of their needs for science equipment. Some are old established schools with an experienced science staff; others are small newly established schools in remote areas with in many cases inexperienced new graduate teachers. In Papua New Guinea there was an attempt to cater for such variation by developing a formula to determine the quantity of kit material to be supplied to individual schools. Schools were categorized according to the age and needs of the school and plans were made to assemble large, medium and small kits. However, the planned system was abandoned in favour of kits of uniform size. While this has made distribution easier (uniformly sized kits are easier to store and transport), it has probably disadvantage large schools. Another disadvantage is that as newly established schools only need some of the equipment immediately, the equipment for higher grades may lie unused for several years. Papua New Guinea now plans to put out tenders for grade specific kits and to stockpile supplies of these. Despite organisational difficulties, it is important to ensure that supplies match school needs.

If the full benefits of science kits are to be obtained the distribution system must cater for the needs of remote schools. It is important that a distribution system applies the principle of *'putting the last first'*; it must give first priority to the needs of remote schools. Systems which result in 'science equipment mountains' in regional and district offices give unfair advantages to the more urban schools and fail the more disadvantaged rural schools which have little access to the centre.

4. Storage in Schools

There have been reports about loss of equipment in schools attributed to lack of adequate storage facilities. There are also reports about theft and misuse of apparatus both by teachers and students. For instance, in Zimbabwe, there were reports of misuse by school staff, with clocks, cassette players and batteries regularly disappearing. Care has to be taken to avoid the kind of problems encountered in India and Zimbabwe by avoiding flimsy kit boxes which get easily damaged in transit and which are difficult to store securely. There are reports of donor-supplied mahogany containers being used to store kits in Tanzania which ended up in the hands of local artisan carvers. While this may have enriched the art world it did little to improve science education! It is sometimes not possible to store kits in the classroom and so they are stored in the Headmaster's office. The science teacher may not have access to the office, it may be locked or the Headmaster may be concluding a meeting. The Hoshangabad project has recognized the importance of storage in schools and insists that all schools participating in the project have kit storage facilities (almirah) attached to each classroom.

There are many ideas for school storage in the literature, e.g. mobile trolleys to accommodate stacks of colour coded plastic (or wooden) trays containing equipment for special topics or levels. There are now many examples of suitable storage containers. For example, many United Kingdom science kits now come in a heavy duty plastic container which is lockable, portable and insect proof. But there can be disadvantages in providing lockable cabinets for science kits given the propensity for teachers and technicians to lose keys. The Sri Lankan Mini-Lab incorporates many good storage ideas but is relatively expensive. It claims to be a 'complete science laboratory for rural schools'. The Mini-Lab is transported directly from the manufacturer to schools, installed, provided with equipment, and handed over. It requires only an existing classroom, 20ft long x 10ft wide. Water on tap, electricity from sunlight and a heating facility are provided in the Mini-Lab without the need to connect to mains supplies. All cupboards and drawers may be locked.. All instruments and frequently used equipment are inventoried. In Ghana and Thailand, teacher demonstration kits have been designed with teacher mobility in mind, and come in easily transportable form. This is especially important for student-teachers on teaching practice, who may not be familiar enough with the school to know where various items are kept. Kit producers could assist schools by providing more ideas on storage such as inventories for school checking. The moveable assets inventory recommended for use in Zimbabwean schools would help in the management of consumable resources.

5. Replenishment

Replenishment of kits and kit items has to be part of any science kit project. In Papua New Guinea all provincial high schools have now been supplied with science kits and the Department of Education has introduced a reimbursement scheme as part of the recurrent budget, to assist schools to replenish science kits on a regular basis. While there is some doubt whether the scheme will be able to keep pace with inflation it should at least provide for the annual replenishment of consumables. Since there are no in-country stocks of permanent kit items, replacement components will have to be ordered from overseas. Nevertheless, bureaucratic procedures for ordering replacements have been greatly simplified so that delays should be minimised. After the last Zim-Sci kit has been dispatched, CDU in Zimbabwe proposes to sell items from a catalogue as single units in order to provide for the re-supply of consumables, replacement of broken/stolen items, the supply of large school needing multiple kits and the supply of schools wishing to supplement conventional apparatus. The Hoshangabad project provides for the regular replenishment of science kits through its system of local committees. Each local committee (*Sangam Kendra*) makes regular checks on availability and conditions in participating schools, calculates the kit replacements needed and maintains up-to-date kit records for each school. There are regular meetings of participating schools which also serve as distribution centres for kits and replacements. The small number of manufacturers involved in the production of kit items has obviated the need for numerous quotations, so that paper-work is reduced and delays are uncommon. The Principal of each *Sangram Kendra* has additional supplies of kits.

The cost of equipment is generally higher in kit form because of the additional costs of packing and freight. Most production centres now cater for the supply of single-items as well as kits. In countries without production centres there is a role for local entrepreneurs to cater for the replenishment needs of schools by procuring and building up supplies of everyday kit items. For instance, in the United Kingdom, there are agencies which buy bulk supplies of items such as batteries, gears, pulleys, bulb holders, connecting wire etc. These can be quickly supplied to schools and bulk buying by schools is also encouraged.

6. Repair

> "In any country, and especially in one with foreign exchange problems, one of the best investments that could be made by the Ministry of Education would appear to be a school equipment and repair service."
>
> *Commonwealth Secretariat, 1982.*

Tropical conditions are notoriously unkind to kit items such as lenses and electronic components; high humidity levels and insects conspire to peel off the labels from chemical reagent bottles; student science kits are especially vulnerable to the kind of damage done through regular contact with pairs of little hands. Hence the need for hard-wearing materials requiring the minimum of repair and replacement. A major consideration in the design of science kits is the durability of components *versus* the cost of replacement. For instance, dry cells become quickly depleted and have to be regularly replaced. Following reports from teachers that dry cells were often 'dead' on arrival, the Zim-Sci project decided to supply the more expensive and more durable Nicket-Cadmium rechargeable cells. The more durable the item the less replacement needed.

The directory of local production centres (British Council, 1979) lists a number of centres which at that time provided repair facilities, and the majority were either in operation or planned. The Federal Science Equipment Centre in Nigeria was one of the first centres to recognise the importance of providing a repair service. It provides teams of mobile technicians equipped to effect repairs of electronic and optical equipment, etc. Equipment can be repaired on the spot, taken to the nearest state centre for equipment repair, or taken to the national centre. In Botswana the Teaching Aids Production Unit (TAPU) has a mobile section dealing with the repair of general school equipment. The Curriculum Development Centre in Malaysia has mobile teams located at various centres throughout Malaysia which carry some equipment-repair and in-service training. NCERT in India has a repair and maintenance workshop and provides training for teachers and technicians.

Laboratory technicians have an important role in the maintenance and repair of apparatus. It has been estimated that 25 per cent of laboratory technician time is taken up by the repair and cleaning of science equipment. Apparatus is particularly vulnerable when it lies unused for long periods of time and where there is rapid turnover of teaching staff. Opportunities for the transfer of technicians are much more limited than those for teachers. Hence, technicians have the advantage that they are on the spot at all times. But school-based technicians suffer from low prestige, are poorly paid and many have to earn additional income by 'moonlighting'. Technicians must be integrated into the science education team and not just be seen as 'add-ons' there to do the teachers' bidding. It has been reported that technicians fail to operate effectively because of a perception of low status in the science education hierarchy (Pullan, 1991), and that for this reason they tend to await the orders of their superiors in the teaching force. Greater levels of teacher-technician co-operation and less attention to hierarchies of responsibility would help to reduce some of the problems caused by equipment deterioration and high levels of teacher turnover. Mobile teams of repair technicians could also provide role models for school-based laboratory technicians. National and regional facilities exist in many countries for the training of technicians and should be fully exploited to ensure that more technician support for science kits is provided. Skilled technicians are more likely to be effective if there is a review of pay scales and of carrier structures.

In most schools there is no laboratory technician and little likelihood of acquiring one. Repair and maintenance is therefore likely to remain the responsibility of the teacher. Many science kits include a set of tools for the teacher as well as repair manuals and hints on the maintenance of equipment. There is also a need to train science teachers in simple repair techniques so that they can more effectively use these tools and interpret maintenance and repair manuals.

7. Implications

The distribution of science kits is a major but not unsurmountable problem. Bundles of examination papers rarely fail to reach schools on time. With similar levels of preparedness at local level science kits could also be more effectively distributed. There is a need for central warehousing facilities, including permanent distribution staff and an efficient stock control and transport system. Planning therefore requires a holistic approach involving not only central production or assembly staff but also officials at local or district level. Wherever possible, a decentralised system for school supply is preferable because kit content can be more closely based on actual school needs and the kits have a better chance of reaching remote and disadvantaged schools. Some schools may not have adequate storage facilities necessitating kit modification. These and other special needs are best catered for by a decentralised system of distribution. Wherever possible advantage should be taken of existing local science teachers groups, school clusters and educational resource centres to provide for temporary storage and distribution of new equipment.

Planners need to ensure that there is adequate provision for replenishment and repair. Various options and combinations of options can be considered:

- establishing surplus buying agencies;
- introducing annual reimbursement schemes;
- providing for single-item supply;
- providing inventories and check-lists for science kits;
- assisting science teachers to categories kit items;

- providing advice to schools on the best way of obtaining replacements;
- making science equipment catalogues easier to use;
- improving school budget flexibility;
- providing tools and instructions in science kits;
- obtaining supplies of cheap, durable items and stock-piling these;
- keeping supplies of consumables to an absolute minimum;
- providing technician training and career incentives to improve status;
- establishing mobile teams of repair technicians.

7

Uses

A recent Commonwealth Secretariat seminar (1987) discussed the role of experiments and demonstration materials in the learning process in enabling the progression from the concrete to the abstract formulation of ideas. Situations identified by participants which provide opportunity to learn science include:

- children handling materials;
- children designing, making or manipulating apparatus using a variety of materials;
- children moving around freely and finding the materials they need;
- children trying to work out for themselves;
- children comparing ideas and observations with those of others. (adapted from the Commonwealth Secretariat 1987:91).

It would be dangerous to allow children to 'move around freely' in many traditional school science laboratories and, even if they could, the chances of them 'finding the materials they need' would be remote given the nature of many of those materials. If children are to handle materials safely they must include a large proportion of the materials with which they are already familiar.

Despite the apparent lack of a firm research basis for any positive impact of practical work there is little enthusiasm for dropping practical work. In fact more and more countries are beginning to recognise its importance, at least as judged by the rhetoric of curriculum statements. It is the aims, content and implementation of practical work in science that have to be reviewed. If science kits are to have an important impact they must cater for more than the development of manipulative skills, they must provide encounters with everyday materials in familiar as well as unfamiliar situations, they must provide opportunity for students to explore their ideas not only in classrooms and laboratories but also outside. Care must be taken not to base kits on the kind of activities found in recipe approaches to science practical work.

In order to determine the extent to which these requirements are met this chapter reviews the information currently available on the integration of science kits with existing material, the intended and actual use of science kits, constraints to effective use of equipment, and their impact on attitudes and learning.

1. Linkage

Linkage of science kits to other materials can be achieved through references in teachers' guides, student worksheets, textbooks and examinations. Properly planned, such integration can ensure that kits are not just seen as add-on bits and pieces to standard equipment lists.

In some countries science kits are based on equipment lists and science activities which have been in place for a number of years in existing material such as teacher' guides. For instance, in Papua New Guinea, despite a science-for-all orientation in more recent curriculum rhetoric, the science kits are really collections of subject-specific conventional science equipment and materials to support existing curriculum material. Because the teachers' guides (including specimen worksheets) were published long before the provision of kits they contain no references to the kits. New textbooks are being developed for science but this activity was not linked to the provision of kits.

The Zimbabwe secondary school science project teachers' guides (Zimbabwe, 1987) mention the Zim-Sci equipment, but teachers are also advised that they can adapt modules for more conventional apparatus where this is available. More recently, the need for an additional instructional pamphlet has been recognised so as to advise teachers how kit materials are to be integrated with existing materials. The absorption of the Zim-Sci project in recurrent curriculum development activities might create further linkage possibilities.

In Kenya, the early SEPU kits were not linked to any particular philosophy of science education: the kits were designed in such a way that they could be easily adapted to any one of the then common learning-by-doing programmes. However, this flexibility proved a problem for inexperienced teachers. In later phases of production science kits were re-designed for specific individualised practical work and were accompanied by material such as worksheets. Teacher demonstration kits also included audio tape and slide packages. In Thailand, the IPST production of science equipment for trial schools proceeds concurrently with textbook development and teacher training.

The Hoshangabad Science Teaching Project (HSTP) in India is an example of a local curriculum development project where there are effective links between the development and distribution of science kits, the development of student workbooks and teacher training. The creation of a district level administration model incorporating follow-up and regular feedback ensures that the science kit is constantly evolving to meet local teacher and student needs. The follow-up programme comprises monthly visits from senior science teachers who observe the curriculum in action and report on any observed difficulties. Workbooks which are designed to accompany the science kits are not stores of facts but instructions for science activity and questions to encourage thinking. There are also kinks with examinations to enhance positive backwash effects on student learning. Rather than test the recall of information, practical and written examinations have been developed to test observational skills, data analysis, logical thinking and creativity. Thus, the HSTP provides a model for the development of an integrated educational package based on science kits.

2. Additional Resources

Some kits provide a minimum of very basic materials and equipment and have to be supplemented using locally available materials. Other kits leaving nothing to the whim of teachers, provide all requirements including consumable items such as cotton thread, kitchen roll and matches, as well as detailed instructional booklets and tools. Still others provide some form of radio support. All teachers need advice on the storage and management of science kits, especially where there are many classes using the same materials. If they are to augment the kits they need knowledge of local resources, time to organise collection teams, practical skill in the use of tools as well as a positive attitude towards promotion and respect for local materials. All of this implies a need for regular contact between schools, equipment production centres and in-service training personnel. There is a need for such personnel to closely monitor the use of kits in a wide variety of different situations. While the additional resources required might be readily available in urban schools (*i.e.*, those normally used in trials), this is not necessarily the case in the more remote schools.

3. Intended Use

In Zimbabwe science kits are intended to emphasize child-centered learning and enjoyment of science teaching:

> "By using the study guides, teachers' guides and low-cost apparatus, you the teacher can become the organiser and manager of a child-centered learning environment so that you can enjoy teaching science."
>
> *Zimbabwe, 1987:iii.*

The Zim-Sci kits have been designed to meet the needs of rural day high schools which often have no conventional laboratory facilities. The kits are intended for use by students working in pairs but there is also a small demonstration kit for teacher use. The Papua New Guinea science kits are really no more than packages of additional or replacement subject-specific materials which can be used by both teacher and student in the activities of the teachers' guides. The HSTP kits are designed for groups of four students and emphasize hands-on approaches and environmentration work in rural schools but can be adapted for student use. SEPU kits (Kenya) are produced in student and teacher form. Generally, the emphasis at primary level is on teacher demonstration kits, while at secondary levels there is increased emphasis on science kit for groups of students.

Science kits intended for teacher demonstration have to be designed to reduce the kind of problems resulting from overcrowded classrooms or laboratories and teacher reluctance to use equipment. In Malawi, Mhlanga (1984) reports that because of the acute shortage of laboratory equipment, about half of the practical work is carried out by the teacher. But classes are too large for students to see what is happening in teacher demonstrations and the groups are too bit to allow everyone to have an opportunity to handle the apparatus. In Thailand, it was recognised that while student-teachers were provided with an opportunity to carry out practical science activities as part of subject-specific course work, they were not provided with training opportunity to demonstrate such activities to others in a classroom situation. Warren (1971) discusses the need for a science education laboratory/workshop course to train student-teachers with a demonstration carrying case to help in teaching practice. Such training can help to uncover real problems in demonstration activities and encourage the search for solutions.

4. Actual Use

It is regrettable that despite the abundance of information on the content of science kits, modes of manufacture and availability in schools, there is almost nothing on the use of science kits. This is not really surprising given the lack of information on the use of equipment generally. What little information there is comes from the reports of kit manufacture or from reports of in-service sessions designed to introduce kits (see chapter 8). Even in cases where donors have been involved in the supply of science kits there is an alarming lack of information on the kits in action. Most donors seem satisfied with the fact that the kits have been supplied. Many evaluations consist of 'gut response' statements like the provision of science kits should improve the conditions of science learning in schools or "give students and teachers more access to relevant practical science". There are a few accounts of teachers' reactions to the science kits but these are generally concerned with defects, complaints and suggestions for improvement (see below). What is needed is an unobtrusive study of the way in which teachers and students actually use science kits, and the extent to which patterns of use reflect the stated intentions of science kits. Such an independent study on the use of science equipment and kits in Papua New Guinea secondary schools is now in progress (Waldrip, 1991) and might provide some useful insights.

Preliminary findings based on Waldrip's questionnaire survey of 38 grade ten science teachers suggest that teachers are now doing more experiments than before the introduction of kits. It is important to ensure that all science kit development project include a detailed evaluation of equipment in use.

5. Impact

There have been a few surveys on the impact of science kit son teacher attitudes. There is evidence from Zimbabwe that teachers felt that Zim-Sci kits promoted a watered-down image of science, *i.e.* not real science. The emphasis on low-cost equipment in the kits seemed particularly upsetting to the more qualified and experienced 'O' level teachers. There were also reports that some equipment was inadequate for the purposes intended and that teachers had to search for alternatives. In Papua New Guinea, primary teachers are taught to improvise at college but they still expect to find the 'real thing', *i.e.* conventional science apparatus, when they get to schools.

Two issues emerge from these considerations. The *first* concerns the nature of low-cost materials and the *second* concerns the training of teachers. The term 'low-cost' is often associated with 'low value' and 'low prestige'. In the context of science kits, 'low-cost' means using locally available resources and local technology *wherever these are appropriate.* It does not imply low quality. If a science experiment requires high precision calculation then a low-cost home-made pH meter may not be appropriate; on the other hand for many qualitative experiments such a pH meter would be quite appropriate, provided it was well-made. In many cases, teacher-produced improvised equipment is indeed low quality and generally breaks down after a short time. It is important that low-cost items are finished properly and subjected to the same rigorous quality control as other more costly items. The use of low-cost equipment must not be seen as an attempt to provide a watered-down science education. But this can only be achieved by convincing teachers and administrators through the demonstration of low-cost equipment in action. With care and attention to design, low-cost equipment can be used to enhance understanding of many scientific principles in everyday contexts. There are many examples of low-cost equipment in the literature which could easily be produced by commercial companies or at teacher workshops. Teachers trained to produce their own low-cost apparatus have been found to develop a sense of ownership and an appreciation that such apparatus can be more relevant and user-friendly than highcost imports. There is a need to make teacher educators more aware of the value of low-cost equipment so that they can impart confidence in and enthusiasm for such equipment.

6. Constraints

Williams and Buseri (1988) paint a familiar picture of contemporary science teaching when they report that:

> "the accepted picture of science teaching in Nigeria as being highly expository, teacher dominated, short on explanation but high on assertion and totally lacking in planned opportunity for students to exercise initiative."

The lack of involvement of students in science lessons has been attributed by the teachers themselves to a lack of resources in schools as well as to their own inadequate science education. However, there are too many reports of underutilised but well-equipped laboratories to support the lack of resources argument. Schmidt (1986) argues that it is not shortage of equipment that constrains practical activity in science but psychological barriers to internalising the teaching styles implicit in many imported and adapted curricula. The most important of these barriers is teacher preference for frontal style delivery which results in science lessons orientated towards the acquisition of facts rather than the development of understanding. Modern science curricula with their emphasis on discovery learning, pupil centeredness and hands-on experience in practical activity are in conflict with traditional cultural norms which stress the authority and centrality of the teacher, and discourage the questioning of adults by children. In teacher-student relationships it is the integrated group rather than the individual which matters, and open debate on controversial matters is not encouraged. Adopting the foreign teaching styles implicit in curriculum materials and equipment (including science kits) threatens the culturally sanctioned relationship between the teacher and the taught. The adaptation of curricula originating in another country is unlikely to be satisfactory if the cultural gap between the two societies is too great. The curriculum reform of earlier decades has not been accompanied by an equivalent reform of teaching style. Many argue that curriculum reform should be based on the empirical reality of teaching style rather than the aspirations of curriculum developers and teacher trainers orientated towards external value systems. (Guthrie, 1983)

Preference for exposition and frontal-style delivery is to a large extent endorsed by objectives-driven curricula and time pressures on teachers to cover the work of the syllabus for all-important terminal examinations which stress the acquisition of facts, even although these facts are only required by a handful of students destined to specialise in science. Added to this is the lack of science background in many teachers and poorly developed scientific thinking skills. For example, Ehindero (1980) argues that the lack of formal operational thought in students might be due to a similar lack in teachers. Notwithstanding the cultural constraints, the lack of science background means that teachers are not equipped to respond effectively to the kind of questions expected to emerge as a result of discovery learning approaches.

The organisation of practical work requires the teacher to take responsibility for class safety and for the proper care of equipment. Many inexperienced teachers fear that they or their students might break expensive apparatus which will be difficult to replace, thus threatening the teacher's prestige in the hierarchy of the school. In addition, there are fears that groups of students will be difficult to manage, especially in large classes, causing disruption and a threat to teacher authority. Teachers often lack the skills required for demonstration experiments and fail to use the experiment to illustrate important concepts and stimulate questioning. Although they may have performed the experiment before as students and student-teachers they may never have benefited from an objective appraisal of their demonstration skills. Teachers can therefore become concerned of losing face and looking foolish when the experiment goes wrong, does not happen at all, or produces the wrong results. As Schmidt (1991) has noted there are rational and objectively verifiable reasons for continuing to teach through lecturing and drilling rather than through experimental practice.

Science teaching requires different strategies to those used in other subjects and the development of these in teachers can be hindered by a variety of compounding factors inhibiting the use of equipment in science lessons. If science kit are to become the basis for science teaching then to avoid the fate of existing equipment they must be designed to reduce the psychological barriers discussed above. This implies a review of the practical content of the curriculum as well as a review of teacher training. The cultural contexts for science education differ substantially and science and scientific ideas are perceived differently in different cultures (see for example, Wilson, 1981). Much curriculum development has been based on the assumptions of a Western rationalist perspective. Teacher training has to encourage reflection on different perspectives of science—implicit in their own cultures as well as in the West—in an attempt to enable trainees to understand what various curricula are intended to achieve and how they might develop appropriate teaching styles.

7. Implications

> "The most optimistic view that can be offered involves the use of carefully designed, integrated packages involving kits of equipment closely linked with curriculum materials which allow the teacher to demonstrate experiments and to offer occasional practical experiences for the students."
>
> *Allsop, 1991:40.*

The design of a science kit must be an integral part of a whole planning, production and distribution process. Science kits will only be effective if they are closely linked to curriculum development, textbook writing and teacher training. But matching must not be so inflexible that change makes a science kit useless. Efforts have to be taken to ensure greater levels of acceptance of low-cost components by improving the quality of finished products, and by effective teacher training. There has to be a review of the nature and value of practical activity in science teaching within the social and cultural context of the teacher. The provision of teacher demonstration kits and adequate training in use would be a useful first step in generating a more practical based approach to science. Examination reform measures would also help promote acceptance and effective use of kits by reducing emphasis on the acquisition of facts and increasing emphasis on understanding the concepts science kits are intended to illustrate. This implies a need for more curriculum sensitive item-writing to ensure that examinations reflect more of the everyday applications of science, publicize illustrations of low-cost equipment and base questions on the kind of activities in kit worksheets. But efforts are needed to overcome resistance from traditional groups who favour a more conventional approach to written science examinations. Above all, there is a need for planners to ensure that evaluation is an integral part of any science kit development project.

8

Teacher Training

The importance of teacher training in the use of science equipment has been stressed in many seminars and workshops on local production.

> "Clearly, local production of science equipment should be much more concerned with issues of teacher development than with the idea of saving money and foreign currency, even if one adopts the priorities of the financiers rather than those of the educators."
>
> *Commonwealth Secretariat, 82, 18.*

> "From an external point of view no general recommendation can be made as to what should be put into a science kit, what it should cost, how long it should last and what it should perform. This must be done at a national level considering available budget, means of production and distribution and not least the means of introducing science kits through teacher training."
>
> *DSE, 1986.*

This section is concerned with the nature of pre-service and in-service provision on the use of science kits, the participants involved in such training and its impact on them.

1. Training Provision

There is wide variation in the pattern of provision. Workshops and seminars have been conducted for student-teachers, teachers teacher educators, inspectors, technicians, local administrators and equipment development staff. Workshops have varied in length form 1 day to about 3 weeks, with most being short 3-5 day duration. Training is provided by a variety of personnel such as :

- equipment production unit staff;
- teachers' college lecturers;
- curriculum developers;
- international experts in low-cost and improvised equipment;
- science resource centre tutors.

There have been pre-service as well as in-service training strategies. Each of these will be discussed.

Pre-service

Prasarnmitr Teachers College in Thailand has attempted to improve demonstration skills and improvisation skills in student/teachers by establishing a science education laboratory/workshop with the following student-teacher objectives :

- to use apparatus to demonstrate certain teaching points;
- to use apparatus critically in a variety of situations;
- to construct apparatus from simple, cheap, readily available materials;
- to able to use questions to develop understanding;
- to become aware of new curriculum material;
- to use natural material to promote understanding and observation skills in students.

Students teachers are provided with portable science demonstration kits containing some of their own improvised equipment which they take to practice lessons.

In Ghana, it is argued that college should prepare the teachers for the school by helping them develop their own individualised science kits. Based on the kind of ideals exposed in the German Cultural Institute workshops, the kit will provide a nucleus of simple one-session experiments and all kits will be made by student teachers. It is felt that this strategy will help to develop a personal commitment among teachers (Jarvis, 1991).

Recently, a guide for teachers on the improvisation of apparatus for a continuously evolving home-grown science kit has been published (Ghana, 1991). The 20-page guide presents a rationale for practical work together with notes on resources, how to use them and advice on how to deal with any problems which might arise. The box part of the kit serves many functions and it can be filled gradually and becomes the teacher's property. In this way it is hoped that a pre-service initiative will be extended after the student teacher has joined the teaching force. In addition, there are new procedures for the continuous assessment of student teachers in practical work, including their use of kits.

Schmidt (1986) outlines a number of strategies for improving pre-service training such as showing teachers how to manage small group work using science kits of inexpensive materials. To implement these strategies it will be necessary to address the serious issues of curriculum overload and the skills of teacher educators in pre-service colleges. In the light of Schmidt's experience in pre-service training, *the most efficient method, from both the economic and subject-related points of view, is the production of standardized basic kits as part of pre-service teacher training*. (Schmidt : 1986:2).

In-service

Some production centres provide advisory services to teachers on the use of equipment and run short workshops aimed at developing skills in using handtools for making teaching aids. Longer vacation workshops have been held in Guyana, Nepal and Singapore. There are also many regional centres involved in promoting quality science education through the use of kits, *e.g.* the State Institutes of Science Education in India. Many teachers' colleges have resource centres attached which include workshops for student teachers and teachers in surrounding schools.

The Goethe Institute has sponsored in-service workshops in many developing countries, including Bolivia, Ecuador, Ethiopia, Ghana, Nicaragua and Tanzania. These have been aimed at identifying cost-effective, feasible and motivating ways to improve science teaching. The involvement of student-teachers and teachers in these courses helps to promote a sense of ownership of the equipment as well as giving confidence in its use. As far as possible there are follow-up activities after the workshops.

Baldwin (1990) reports on a recent workshop for 30 teacher educators in Tanzania designed to identify teacher needs with respect to science kits. The potential and limitations of science kits in overcoming problems due to general lack of apparatus and common teacher difficulty in teaching certain science concepts was demonstrated. During the two-day workshop participants were provided with an opportunity to handle the apparatus in the kit and to complete some problem-solving exercises.

2. Nature of in-service

There is a great deal of paper provided in various handbooks, manuals, teachers' guides, resource centre newsletters and journals of science teachers associations which, if properly organised and supported, could promote the use of science kits through in-service training. One of the most widely used sourcebooks of ideas for in-service training in science is the UNESCO handbook on science teaching which contains many ideas on the use of everyday materials in science teaching. The book lists a number of items such as plastic bags, candles, metal foil, sandpaper, straws, marbles, polystyrene foam, which could be used in science lessons or to effect repair. Over 20 other basic guidebooks on improvising science teaching equipment are listed in the UNESCO handbook. Without active support from the Education Department a great deal depends on the energy and goodwill of individuals.

One of the most common approaches has been to link training to the production of low-cost equipment in teacher workshops. Typical activities of Goethe workshops are the production of small-scale hand-experiments, the development and testing of practical activities and models, the production of a science kit and the preparation of source books for teachers. Workshops have provided technical working instructions for the production of kit items, devised experiments to use the kits and generally concluded with some discussion on advantages and disadvantages.

In some cases there have been attempts to provide in-service by means of radio, television and video. For instance, in Papua New Guinea the Radio Science Pilot Project for primary science provided weekly evening radio broadcasts for teachers in order to provide background information and hints on using kits in its science lessons broadcast the following day.

The Hoshangabad programme considers training, field experiences of the teachers, followed by analysis and synthesis as an integral part of internalising the method by the teachers. There are initial orientation camps, refresher courses, follow-up and teachers' monthly meetings. HSTP has created a special resource group consisting of teacher educators, scientists, science teachers, engineers. The group has developed over the years and is continually being broadened. HSTP regards follow-up as essential for maintaining impact; during follow-up feedback and ideas for improvement are collected; there is opportunity for information exchange; teachers have a chance to discuss their own strengths and weaknesses. In addition there are monthly forums for sharing common experiences and problems and getting feedback about administration problems.

Workshops have also been run for technicians. The Regional Centre for Education in Science and Mathematics (RECSAM) in Malaysia was established in 1967 to meet the training needs of its eight Member Countries. In 1974 RECSAM decided that the centre :

> "should develop the necessary materials only to the stage of educational prototypes, and that the emphasis should be on the training of personnel who would be likely to be employed as designers in national equipment workshops."

It conducts Secondary Science/Maths Apparatus Workshops designed for 2-4 participants over 10-20 weeks. These workshops are product oriented and provide realistic exposure to the techniques of mass production, so are more suited to those who have been selected to lead local production efforts. Of particular concern to RECSAM is the nature of working relationships in developing equipment and special workshops for administrators are designed to further strengthen the link between production and use of equipment.

3. Evaluation of Training

Most in-service sessions are followed by reports. However, many of these reports are little more than lists of what equipment and printed materials have been produced. They also contain expositions of the advantages of science kits and training as perceived by the organisers. A few have some recommendations based on the perceptions of participants. One of the major criticisms of these approaches is that while they succeed in promoting awareness of the value of improvisation among participants, the length of sessions and lack of follow-up in schools prevents any lasting impact.

Schmidt (1986) claims to have evaluated the results of different approaches, and has found that three basic types of seminar have proved practicable :

- compact seminars of one to two which provide general orientation and suggestions;
- weekly seminars which provide extended practical advice;
- extended seminars which provide two to three weeks for the production of kits.

The German experience has found that science kit development is more feasible at pre-service levels because there is usually sufficient time. But it is still possible through in-service through extended seminars of 2-3 weeks aimed at the production and use of equipment. It is claimed that teachers have successfully produced their own materials and carried out experiments. Extended seminars need a workshop and work best for groups of 15 to 20 teachers. It is recognised that not all science can be taught using low-cost equipment and so part of training is on the use of the imported equipment which might be found in kits. One result of such extended seminars is that teachers have developed their own kits during pre-service training and taken them to their first posting.

Zimbabwe provided special training programmes for teachers on the use of Zim-Sci kits, but there are reports that many of the teachers are no longer working in zim-Sci schools. Until 1984, regular and large in-service courses were held to support kits and encourage teachers to adopt the 'hands-on' Zim-Sci method. Following a reduction in the number of people in the Zim-Sci team it has not proved possible to maintain this effort. Most teachers in a recent survey (Zimbabwe, 1990) had not participated in Zim-Sci in-service. The possibility of training through teachers' colleges and the University is being considered.

In Nepal there have been a number of workshops aimed at developing simple experiments which teachers can carry out using simple low-cost equipment which they produce at workshops. However, as Mali (1981:52) reports :

> "notwithstanding the beauty of the principles emphasized during the workshop, lack of continuing reinforcement and follow-up in the school of participating teachers, however, seem to be leading toward gradual dilution and dissolution of the enthusiasm gathered during the workshop period."

Maranga (1984) has evaluated in-service activities in Teacher Advisory Centres (TAC) in one district of Kenya. Short one-day courses were the norm with about 120 teachers attending at one time. The provision of UNESCO-supplied equipment attracted teachers to attend the workshops. Teachers produced materials such as drawings of improvised science equipment and teaching aids. However, they reported that the general lack of textbooks and equipment in TACs, the poor organisation of courses, and the lack of follow-up by tutors, reduced the impact. They also reported resentment for the practice of using these workshops as a means of rubber stamping curriculum materials which they had no hand in producing.

Baldwin (1990) reports that the most lasting impression gained from a recent Tanzanian workshop for teacher educators was the change of attitude in participants as a result of their gaining confidence in using kit apparatus. Participants reported that they felt motivated by being able to use apparatus in such a structured way and also motivated by exposure to new and exciting apparatus. Recommendations from the workshop included ideas for expanding kits, producing add-on kits for special topics and rewriting of support materials. There is no doubt that the United Kingdom science kit suppliers attending the workshop also learned a great deal from watching teacher educators handle the equipment. Because this workshop was targeted at teacher educators and the colleges were provided with kits there is likely to be more lasting impact.

4. Implications

The implications for training in the use of science kits are that training should help teachers to internalise the aims and objectives of curriculum so that they can appreciate the role expected of science kits; training should help enhance the quality of teacher-centered approaches at the same time as giving encouragement for more student-centered approaches; training should be aimed at reducing the reliance on over-prescriptive teachers' guides and encourage exploration of new ideas.

Large-scale production and teacher training have to be separate activities; their needs are not compatible. There are opportunities for developing low-cost equipment at pre-service level, provided teacher adductors are involved from the beginning, and given the necessary training beforehand. Student teachers can be trained to improvise simple low-cot equipment for illustrative experiments, and encouraged to develop their own constantly evolving kits. There needs to be opportunity for students to demonstrate practical skill and a system for its continuous assessment. Training is also required in small group management to encourage teachers to provide student learning experiences based on science kits. At the in-service level there is a continuing role for paper in-service through books, manuals and newsletters, but there needs to be a system of evaluation and follow-up. The main problem is effective follow-up and competing priorities for in-service. As the HSTP experience shows, it works it followed through. There is a need for active support for science teachers' associations and for teachers with special skills.

9

Costs

The cost of providing fully-equipped laboratories varies enormously, not only between developing countries, but also within the same country. For example, in Kenya a laboratory which costs $32,000 in the capital may cost up to $80,000 in the more remote areas. There are also additional costs in maintaining laboratories, in procuring regular supplies of expendables, and in supplying gas, electricity and water. Changes in the foreign exchange rate and inflation can greatly modify the cost of both local and imported equipment from month-to-month. The following table is based on costs estimated for the IIEP study on science provision and refers to the US$ costs in 1990 of providing a physics laboratory with preparation room and equipment.

The cost of providing a fully equipped specialist science laboratory ranges from $19,250 in Chile to $144,120 in Botswana. General laboratories or specially modified classroom are less costly. For a basically-furnished junior science room in Botswana the cost is $51,500 with equipment costs of $7,900. About 75 per cent of equipment is imported. Gas, water and electricity are supplies at the teachers' desk and at four separate stations for students. To cover replacements and consumables junior secondary schools are allocated $5.28 per student per year. Thus, for a school with enrolment of 500 students the total annual cost of a junior science laboratory is about $62,000 (excluding services). (see *Table 1)*

Table 1. Estimated cost of a fully-equipped physics laboratory with preparation room (1990)

Country	*Laboratory cost*	*Equipment*	*Total*
Argentina	35 000	10 000	45 000
Botswana	132 000	12 120	144 120
Burkina Faso	21 400	6 700	28 100
Chile	13 000	6 250	19 250
Jordan	16 000	31 000	47 000
Kenya	32 000	9 400	41 400
Korea	43 500	21 900	65 400
Morocco	29 000	93 723	122 723
Papua New Guinea	95 000	20 000	115 000
Senegal	56 500	14 000	70 500
Thailand	24 300	3 500	27 800
Average	45 245	20 781	66 027

Source: Caillods, F.; Gottelmann, G. IIEP, 1991, mimeo.

1. The Basic Costs of Science Kit Provision

It is not surprising that several countries have sought less costly alternatives to the provision of fully equipped science laboratories. For instance, in January, 1984 the Botswana government provided a science kit which could be used in an ordinary classroom. The IIEP country monograph (Kann; Nzonunu, 1992) provides no details of cost but 33 per cent of the kit can be bought locally. It was found possible to keep the costs of the Botswana Science Kit to a minimum by designing a curriculum which relates science to everyday life and everyday materials, by limiting the use of expensive laboratory glassware, by using standardised equipment and by locally manufacturing simple wooden and metal items. The kit is modelled on the Zim-Sci kit developed in Zimbabwe.

Thailand produces a general science kit for lower secondary and specialised science kits for upper secondary. Each kit is portable and can be used to meet the needs of five classes. Only specialised classrooms are required. According to a report in the mid-1970s, 75 per cent of items for the physics and chemistry kits were being purchased locally while 23 per cent of the biology kit was locally purchased. The total cost of a chemistry kit for each trial school was Bhat 9,753 ($5,852).

According to recent reports (Obura, 1992) Kenya produces biology, chemistry and physics kits each costing $600. Thus, $1,800 would be required to meet the needs of three specialised science courses. Many of the items fulfil more than one function and it is possible for schools to purchase mixed kits and replacement components. The kits are designed for student use and require the services available in a general science laboratory or specialised classroom.

In India, the Hoshangabad Science Teaching Programme (HSTP) provides general science kits to 350 middle schools spread over seven districts in Madhya Pradesh. Each kit is designed for groups of four students. The average cost including transportation to a middle school of 120 students is Rs. 1,200 ($47) with annual recurrent cost of Rs. 1.5 per student. It has been possible to reduce costs by using locally available materials (Eklavya, 1985).

In Sri Lanka the Mini-Lab is a complete science laboratory for rural schools. The Mini-Lab requires only an existing classroom, 20 ft. long x 10ft. wide. All equipment, materials and facilities required for teaching-learning the science syllabus from year 1 to year 11 are included in the Mini-Lab kit. Water on tap, electricity from sunlight and a heating facility are provided in the Mini-Lab without the need to connect to mains supplies. Mini-Labs, are transported to schools and installed by the manufacturers who claim that it costs less than 10 per cant of a conventional laboratory and can be easily maintained. The Mini-Lab is designed for demonstration purposes but could accommodate a group of five students. The Mini Lab kit is an extension of the Mini Lab Unit with additional furniture designed to accommodate up to 20 students.

The United Kingdom (1991) cost of a Primary Teaching Kit exported to Tanzania is £85 ($146). Many companies in Britain now produce thematic kits to support the new national curriculum materials. These range in range price form about £20 to £100. Schools would require several kits. Various surplus buying agencies supply schools with replacement items such as motors, pulleys, gears, dry cells, etc. at a fraction of the cost of the same items in kit form. For example, a pack of 4 pulley can be bought for 50 pence ($0.90), a battery charger costs £5.50 ($9.80), materials science kit costs £1.75 ($3.10). These services are currently only available to schools in the United Kingdom.

Table 2. Costs of providing science kits in Papua New Guinea, in local currency, (1984-1988)[1]

Equipment	*1984*	*1985*	*1986*	*1987*	*1988*	*Cost per school*
Biology kits (112)[2]	107 995	–	–	–	–	964.24
Physics kits (120)	–	102 224	–	–	–	851.87
Chemistry kits (120)	–	–	105 600	–	–	880.00
Geology kits (125)	–	–	–	107 937	–	863.50
Assorted science kits (125)	–	–	–	–	57 519	460.15

Note: The above costs do not include transport and freight costs.

[1. 1 Kina = $1.0421 (1/8/91).

2. Numbers in brackets refer to the number of kits; one kit was distributed to each school.]

Table 2 shows the costs of providing science kits in Papua New Guinea for the period (1984-1988). In Papua New Guinea, the cost of supplying all five kits was K4,019.76 ($4,189) per school. However, the actual cost of the imported kit was found to vary with the year of purchase. In each year additional kits (not shown in *Table 2)* had to be bought for recently-opened schools. Transport and freight costs amounted to about 6 per cent of purchase costs. Annual reimbursement grants of $700 per school are now provided to ensure that kit items are replaced.

The Papua New Guinea science kits contain sufficient equipment for student work and teacher demonstration. The kits are really based on the equipment lists provided in existing teachers' guides for lower secondary science. They require the use of a general science laboratory and storeroom, but in some cases the kits are being used in new schools which do not yet have fully-equipped laboratories. Although it was found that inflation increased the cost of kits over the five-year period, considerable saving was possible through bulk buying and local kit assembly. Local supply companies competed for the tender but could not match the costs quoted by overseas suppliers. For instance, a local supply company produced a Hudson light box kit for K254 compared to K55 charged by overseas suppliers.

Science kits produced by teachers in pre-service or in-service training seminars can be much less costly than locally manufactured or imported kits. For instance, at a recent workshop held in Morogoro, Tanzania, participants developed and tested experiments and activities which could be organised economically and within a very short preparation time by secondary school teachers to cover the basic physics concepts at lower secondary level. Another result of the workshop was the production of illustrated source books. Prototypes of basic physics concepts at lower secondary level. Another result of the workshop was the production of illustrated source books. Prototypes of basic teaching kits for specialised science were produced and it is claimed that these can be assembled from prefabricated parts at less than $20 each kit, (the Goethe Institute, 1991). However, it is widely reported that the quality of such teacher-produced kits can vary.

In most cases the above kits do not require the provisions of the kind of furniture and fittings used in specialised laboratories. Storage is simple so that there is no need for elaborate preparation rooms. While details of current costs are in many cases not available they do provide for a considerable saving over the conventional approach of providing and maintaining fully equipped laboratories.

2. Additional Costs

There are additional costs associated with science kits which have to be considered at a national level. As stressed many times in this review, the kit approach has to be an integral part of currinulum and teacher training. This implies a need for research and evaluation, particularly where kits are to be developed to suit local conditions and make use of local manufacturing capacity. These additional costs also vary from country to country. In Thailand, for instance, in-service training has been estimated to require $5.64 million for 23,500 teachers, i.e. $240 per teacher, allowing 3 training sessions in 5 years.

The Hoshangabad Science Teaching Project (Eklavya, 1985) has considered the financial implications of the kit approach to science teaching to take account of the basic kit material, annual replacement, follow-up and feedback mechanisms and a continuous teacher training programme. The figurers shown in *Table 3* are based on the US$ costs of the kit approach in an average district of Madyha Pradesh in India. The 1985 costs in rupees have been converted at current exchange rates ($1 = Rs 25.83).

Table 3. Cost of science kits in Madyha Pradesh, India (1985)

School level	*Capital $*	*Recurring $*	*Cost per school $*
Primary (1 000 per district)	39 300	11 790	51
Middle secondary (200 per district)	9 825	5 895	79
Higher secondary (40 per district)	15 720	7 860	590
Total	64 845	25 545	720

Source: Eklavya, 1985.

Capital costs refer to the initial purchase costs of science kits, including transport to schools. Recurring expenditure includes kit replacement, follow-up and teacher training costs. Higher secondary estimates assume that schools are already equipped with science laboratories; capital costs refer to the cost of refurbishing these for the HSTP kit approach and recurring estimates are over and above that normally provided Recurrent costs can be up to 60 per cent of the initial capital costs. The estimates do not include infrastructure expenses like construction and improvement of school buildings and the provisions of services.

In Viet Nam there are proposals to supply all secondary schools with specialised science kits by 1995. *Table 4* shows the funding scheme in US dollars for the production of biology and chemistry kits in the period 1990-1995 (Viet Nam, 1990).

Table 4. Cost of producing biology and chemistry kits in Viet Nam (US$)

Year	*Develop/design*	*Pilot production*	*Large scale production*
1990	40 000	40 000	-
1991	50 000	50 000	-
1992	50 000	50 000	1 500 000
1993	50 000	50 000	1 500 000
1994	50 000	50 000	1 700 000
1995	40 000	40 000	1 700 000
Total	280 000	280 000	6 400 000

Sources: Viet Nam, 1990.

These estimates are based on the supply to 15,000 lower secondary schools and 1,500 higher secondary schools in Viet Nam. Thus the project aims at supplying virtually all secondary schools in Viet Nam with the basic facilities required for the teaching of the new biology and chemistry syllabi, *i e.* about $422 per school. Development and design includes the provision of in-service training for teachers on the use of kits.

3. Implications

It is not easy to obtain reliable estimates of costs for cross-country comparisons; it is not always clear what the published costs refer to and on which year the estimates are based; exchange rates can fluctuate widely even over short periods of time. *Table 5* shows the costs (US$) of providing a fully-equipped specialist science laboratory in various countries compared to the cost of providing science kits.

Table 5. Cost of laboratories and science kits in US$ (around 1990)

Country	*Science laboratory costs*	*Science kit costs*
Botswana	144 120	n.a.
Hoshangabad (India)	n.a.	46.50 (1 kit)
Kenya	41 400	1 800 (3 kits)
Papua New Guinea	115 000	4 180 (5 kits)
Sri Lanka	19 040	1 785 (1 kit)
Thailand	27 800	5 852 (1 kit)
Viet Nam	n.a.	422 (2 kits)

n.a. = not applicable
Source: IIEP monographs on the condition of science education.

The data shown in *Table 5* requires careful interpretation. In some cases science kits are provide in *addition* to fully equipped laboratories, *e.g.* in Papua New Guinea the kits are intended to supplement existing laboratory equipment. The advantage of providing kits in Papua New Guinea is that it makes ordering easier and bulk buying under tender has helped to reduce the costs of equipping laboratories. On the other hand, a much greater saving is possible using the kind of kits provided in Hoshangabad and Thailand because these do not require laboratories and use low-cost, locally-manufactured components. In Viet Nam the costs refer to kits for biology and chemistry only but include training and evaluation costs.

Despite the difficulties in cross-country comparisons of this kind, it is possible to draw some general conclusions from the above data. The provision of science kits is less costly than building and equipping a conventional science laboratory, but there are additional costs which have to be considered. Science kits have to be an integral part of a whole curriculum strategy and so provision has to be made for teacher training in the use of kits, for follow-up and evaluation, as well as for replacement and repair. These additional costs can be up to 60 per cent of the initial capital costs of providing science kits. Planners have therefore to consider all aspects of science kit provision in the light of initial capital and the expected recurring costs.

10

An Appraisal

Before providing an appraisal of science kits it is important to appreciate the realities of the educational setting in which quality enhancement measures have to operate. *Firstly,* there is increasing recognition of the need for science-for-all for the majority and science-for-continuation for a minority. *Secondly,* the image of science is changing and this is reflected in new emphases on technology, the environment and problem-solving. *Thirdly,* the influence of constructivist theories of learning in science are likely to have a significant impact on future curriculum development. *Fourthly,* the realities in many countries are that teacher-centered teaching styles, selection systems based on examinations, crowed classrooms and limited funding for quality enhancement are likely to continue.

The implications for practical activity in science is that it should reflect the everyday experiences of teachers and students, that equipment should be low-cost and user-friendly, and supported by teacher-training and examination reform. There are also alternative low-cost approaches to practical work which can provide students with the process skills involved in the planning and design of experiments, data collection, data analysis, and prediction.

The literature is replete with information on the production and distribution of science kits but very sparse on the evaluation of the use of science kits in schools. This final chapter provides a summary review of what is known about science kits in order to develop a framework for the evaluation of science kits. Finally, this chapter will attempt to address the important question of whether science kits are a worthwhile investment, and if so, under what conditions.

What science kits are intended to achieve?

The rationale for science kits has an economic as well as an educational dimension. The cost of providing science kits can be considerably lower than the cost of providing fully-equipped laboratories, and there is further scope for reducing costs in the design of kits. The emphasis of the curriculum on technology and environment call for more effective means of providing hands-on experience for students in practical science. Science kits are also intended to overcome the psychological barrier teachers have in the use of science equipment.

What kind of science kits are currently available?

There are now many different examples of science kit in use throughout the developing world. They come in a variety of forms and have been designed for integrated as well as specialist science and have been targeted at teachers and students and at primary, secondary and independent learners.

What kind of items do science kits generally contain?

Science kits include a mixture of conventional science apparatus and locally obtainable items. The need for hard-wearing, multi-functional and user-friendly components has largely been recognised by designers. Science kits are often supported by teachers' guides, worksheets, construction manuals and tools.

How are science kits produced?

Some science kits are manufactured locally in specially-designed production centres using locally-produced and imported components. Local production centres are generally under government control and self-sustainable in situations where market demand can be maintained. Other kits are assembled locally from a variety of imported and locally-available components. Others are produced by teachers and student-teachers during workshops.

How are science kits distributed to schools?

Centralised and decentralised distribution systems exist with schools ordering direct from suppliers or through the district education office. Because of their compactness and size, science kits are easier to distribute than conventional apparatus. Nevertheless, there are problems caused by inadequate storage and transpiration as well as administrative apathy at local level. The establishment of local committees or school clusters can help to reduce constraints at local level.

What procedures exist for the replenishment of science kits?

There have been many examples of one-off kit supplies which did not cater for replenishment. Most production centres now include options for single-item supply. There are problems caused by the rapid depletion of consumables. More can be done to assist teachers by providing check-lists, by introducing more flexible school budgeting and simple reimbursement schemes.

What provision is made for the repair of kit items?

Most production centres have recognised the need for a repair service, especially for optical and electronic equipment. This is provided through mobile teams of technicians, or through teacher and technician workshops. Many kits include a set of tools and construction ideas. The provision of more durable items can reduce the need for repair.

What uses are made of science kits?

There have been many reports of science kits lying unused. There have been few studies of science kits in use. Classroom observational studies have shown that although teachers use kits they often do not use them in the manner intended, *e.g.* to develop questioning skills in students or to promote discussion. In some cases the fault lies in the design of the kit itself; in other cases it lies in the lack of internalisation in teachers of the curriculum goals which the kit is designed to match. There are also reports of teachers failing to supplement kit materials with materials of their own, despite advice on how to do so. Where teachers have produced their own kits there are reports that they develop confidence, a sense of ownership and can use them effectively. Teachers have reported that the provision of science kits made teaching easier; others have reported that the kits are unsuitable for some practical activities. Where they have been designed to illustrate specific science experiments and teachers have been trained in their use, science kit have been found effective. There is a 'general feeling' that science kits are useful, usually based on preliminary trials in pilit schools.

What training and support is provided in the use of science kits?

At pre-service level it has been found possible to train student-teachers to improvise simple low-cost equipment to illustrate experiments, and to encourage them to develop their own constantly-evolving kits. Training has also been provided to improve science demonstration skills. In-service training is generally in the form of workshops but there are reports that these have limited long-term impact, largely because they are too short and there is seldom provision for follow-up in schools. In some cases kit use is supported by practical and written examinations focusing on the kind of process skills being developed by practical work based on science kits.

1. Science Kit Evaluation Framework

How is a school or local administrator to determine whether a particular science kits is appropriate? *Firstly,* there is the question of *cost.* How much is the kit and how many kits would be required? What are the hidden costs in terms of storage, replenishment and repair? *Secondly,* is the question of *intentions.* What is the target user group and how is this group intended to use the kit? Is the kit intended for demonstration or for student groups? Is the kit intended to illustrate particular scientific principles are these clearly defined? What learning environment is required (classroom, laboratory, outdoor activities)? What teacher training has to be provided? *Third,* is the question of *user-friendliness.* Is the equipment student-friendly—is it likely to motivate students? Does it match learning styles? Does it reflect the interests of girls as well as boys? Does it cater for students from a wide variety of socio-economic backgrounds (rural/urban/remote)? Does it cater for the needs of different abilities? Is it safe and easy to use in the normal student environment? Is it teacher-friendly in terms of handling, replacement, ease of procurement, fit to teaching style, preparation time required for practical? *Fourthly,* is the question of kit compatibility with existing curriculum and assessment patterns? Does the kit reflect the aims and objectives of the syllabus? Does it match the kind of practical activities in student textbooks? Does it provide for comprehensive coverage of the whole course or does it need to be supplemented? Is it likely to cater for school-based currinulum development initiatives? Is it likely to assist in the assessment of students?

At a national level, planners and administrators have to consider strategies of production, distribution, replenishment, repair and support. Local production will be a costly undertaking requiring large amounts of capital outlay, regular supplies of raw material, skilled technical staff, quality control, marketing skill, guarantee and service warranties and a facility for repair. Full local production is unlikely to be sustainable unless long-term demand can be maintained. A feasible study will first be necessary to investigate small-scale industry capability and support systems as well as a survey of the expected market demand for products. Production costs can be reduced in some cases by importing light-weight components and assembling these as kits within the country using the existing resources of vocational institutes, small industries, rehabilitation centres, or educational materials resource centre personnel. Such a strategy will be more feasible provided it is effectively managed and organised to ensure that kits are developed in close co-operation between curriculum developers, textbook writers and teacher trainers, that all components can be procured on a regular basis; that the components from different sources are compatible; that effective quality control measures are in place; that effective warehousing and distribution systems are established. There is scope for business entrepreneurs to establish surplus buying agencies to ensure that kits can be easily replenished. It is also possible to import science kits provided overseas suppliers are sympathetic to the needs of the system and work together with local science educators. Often, import costs are high due to heavy tariffs levied by government: there is a need for science education centres to lobby for tariff reduction with regard to the import of science equipment. It is probably true to say that specialised science courses for university entrance will continue to require a considerable amount of the more traditional and expensive science laboratory apparatus. There are possibilities for cost-reduction through sharing of expensive equipment or by using video recordings of expensive equipment in action and by considering alternatives to practical work. It is most important to continue supporting centres devoted to the pursuit of excellence in science.

Support for science kits has to be provided at pre-service and in-service levels. For this reason teacher educators should be involved in science kit development projects from the beginning. Large class size and low qualifications of teachers are likely to remain features of most delivery systems. There is a need to review existing teacher training courses so that provision is made for training in demonstration skills and small group management. Improvisation of resources by teachers requires a thorugh background and understanding of the scientific principles which equipment is designed to illustrate. There may be a need to first train the teacher-educators. Reliance on one-off efforts by international specialists in a short-term strategy benefiting a few teachers and can only be as effective as the multiplier-effect. Teachers need to be psychologically prepared to improvise as well as to have the necessary practical skills to do so. It is important not to attempt to develop improvisation skills in a vacuum: skills must be related to developing particular concepts in science with the resources normally available in a minimally-equipped school. Student-teacher can be trained to develop their own kits but may need to supplement these with more traditional science apparatus and local materials. In-service courses are best organised at local level and must incorporate an effective means of follow-up and feedback. National examinations can be reformed to lend further support to the use of science kits. For example, questions can be illustrated with items from science kits and thinking skills based on the kind of activities carried out using science kits.

2. Are Science Kits a Worthwhile Investment?

Science Kits Can

- help to reduce the cost of science education;
- be locally produced or locally assembled;

- be designed to match a variety of science curriculum orientations;
- be user-friendly for teachers, students and the learning environment;
- be designed to illustrate important scientific principles.

And therefore a Potentially Good Investment, Provided

- they are carefully integrated for use with existing curriculum materials;
- they are designed to match local conditions in schools;
- they are supported by training and examination reform;
- they can be easily replenished and repaired;
- they are carefully evaluated at all stages in development.

The implementation of a science kit project requires extensive design and development, to include the testing of prototypes and small production runs for trial schools, in-service training of teachers before full-scale production can be attempted. There are therefore many associated costs. For instance, Viet Nam plans to spend about $7 in the period 1990-1995 on the full-scale production of biology and chemistry kits for its secondary schools.

The need for evaluation cannot be over-emphasized. Pilot schools involved in science kits projects usually receive a fair measure of professional support through regular (and much publicized) visits of kit development specialists and are often located in more accessible regions. They can be a far cry indeed from the more minimally resources schools further afield. Any development project aimed at providing science kits must include an on-going evaluation component to incorporate studies of the kits in use in a wide variety of school situations.

Conclusions

Despite the abundance of information on the design and provision of science kits it would be unwise to recommend the use of science kit at this stage in their development, other than to say that they have attractive features in that they contain basic equipment and can be designed and packaged in such a way as to encourage use in a variety of learning situations. Each country has first to examine the philosophy of science education, the appropriateness of practical science activities patterns of use of existing equipment, levels of teacher preparedness and the national capacity for quality-controlled local production or assembly, distribution, replenishment and repair. Until this is done there is little point in taking stop-gap measures: there is sufficient evidence that kits provided as a form of 'relief-aid' gather dust and do not meet long-term needs because they are rarely taken up by national authorities.

It is important that strategies aimed at encouraging the effective use of existing resources are developed *before* embarking on strategies aimed at the local production or assembly of science kits. If existing equipment, however meagre, lies unused there is no point in providing science kits unless it can be shown that they assist teachers to overcome reluctance in using equipment and that they assist student learning. Some of the commonly reported reasons for under-utilisation have been discussed in this review but there are likely to be others related to local conditions. These must be identified.

A full review of the nature of science learning activities is a necessary precursor to the development of science kits. In particular, it is important to review the expected and actual role of practical work in science, and to distinguish between the needs of those who continue with formal science education and those who do not. There is a need to involve teacher training institutions, curriculum developers and resource material developers in such a review. The review should encompass a survey of the science resources currently available, the nature of practical activities recommended in teachers' guides and texts, the scope for lower-cost experiments, and the use made of these by teachers.

Having identified needs, strategies should be developed aimed at encouraging teachers to make more use of appropriate science equipment, whether imported, locally-produced or improvised. This can be done through pre-service and in-service strategies aimed at improvisation skill development and resource management. Local and national administrators must also be involved in order to familiarise them with the special problems of science education and to increase levels of preparedness to support current developments and possible innovations such as science kit provision. The use of regional networks can also assist and there are international aid agencies with access to appropriate human resources.

Finally, it is important to note that while the nature of practical work is under review there is an opportunity to examine less costly alternatives such as group work, simulation exercises, peer teaching, 'thought' experiments and reformed examinations. It is not intended that these replace practical work but they could supplement existing provision of practical work and ease the demand for costly equipment and teacher reluctance to use equipment. While it is beyond the scope of this review to examine these strategies in more detail, further investigation by local science education review personnel could prove profitable.

3. Some Planning Needs Related to Science Kits

1. There is a need for an integrated approach to science kit development involving curriculum developers, textbook developers, teacher educators and teachers as well as science equipment manufacturers.
2. There is a need to review the nature of practical experiences provided in existing curriculum materials with a view to identifying lower-cost alternative experiences which could be provided through the use of science kits.
3. There is a need to enhance the capacity of developing countries to develop their own science kits from a variety of imported, locally-manufactured and teacher-produced components, especially for primary and secondary integrated science kits.
4. There is a need for teacher training in the use of kits to improve demonstration skills, improvisation skills and the management of student practical groups.
5. There is a need to address the problem of low prestige if kits are going to contain substantial amounts of low-cost and improvised equipment.

6. There is a need to support science kits through examination reform.
7. There is a need for evaluation to be an integral component of science kit development and use.
8. There is a need to continue supporting the equipment needs of upper secondary and pre-university specialised science courses.

APPENDIX 1:

Source of Information

The Commonwealth Secretariat reports of the 1970s provide an abundance of information on early developments. In addition, publications of organisations such as UNESCO, including its regional offices, the British Council, the German Foundation for International Development (DSE), the CABS Rural Development Abstracts, the Asian Development Bank, the Swedish International Development Authority (SIDA), the United Kingdom Overseas Development Administration, UNICEF, the World Bank and various government and university publications and journals of education have been searched for information on the production and provision of low-cost equipment for science teaching. A Dialog computer search of the following database was carried out: (i) British Education Index Database (BEI)[1]; (ii) the ERIC database[2]; (iii) the Social Science Research Database[3] using search distributors such as the following: equipment, kit, developing, laboratory, science, secondary, primary, Third World, biology, chemistry, physics. The Dialog search was limited to material published since 1980 and found a total of 14 items. Other sources of information include:

Bangladesh Journal of Extension Education
Boleswa Educational Research Journal
Comparative Education Review, Index, 1957-1989
EKLAVYA Publications *(India)*
Geneve-Afrique *(Switzerland)*
Journal of Education and Social Change *(India)*

Journal of the Ghana Association of Science Teachers
Pakistan Journal of Distance Education
Philippines Education Quarterly
West African Journal of Education
Zambia Educational Review
Zimbabwe Journal of Educational Research

Department of Education *(Kenya)*
Department of Education *(Malawi)*
Department of Education *(Malaysia)*
Department of Education *(Nigeria)*
Department of Education *(Papua New Guinea)*
Department of Education *(Sri Lanka)*
Department of Education *(Thailand)*
Institute of Development Studies *(Sussex)*
National Research Institute *(Papua New Guinea)*
Nepal, Education and Development
Research Centre for Educational Innovation and Development, Tribhuvan University *(Nepal)*
Swaziland Institute for Educational Research

There have been several conferences, workshops and seminars on the production of science equipment. Among these are the following:

- Science Education in Africa, Report of Sixth Levershulme Inter-University Conference, Malawi, 1968.
- Science Teaching Equipment, Material and Facilities; Workshop for Science Education Programme Planners in English-Speaking African Countries, Nigeria, 1971.
- Problems of the Promotion and Production of Teaching Materials in Developing Countries, DSE, Germany, 1971.
- Problems of the Promotion and Production of Teaching Materials in South-East Asia. SEAMEO/DSE, Singapore, 1972.
- Regional Seminar on School Science Equipment, New Delhi, India, 1972, Report: UNESCO, 1973.

- Production of Low-Cost Teaching Materials for Primary level Science and Mathematics, SEAMEO/DSE, Malaysia, 1973
- Low-Cost Science Teaching Equipment Regional Seminar/Workshop, Commonwealth Secretariat, Bahamas, 1976.
- Low-Cost Science Teaching Equipment Regional Seminar/Workshop, Commonwealth Secretariat, Tanzania, 1977.
- Low-Cost Science Teaching Equipment Regional Seminar/Workshop, Commonwealth Secretariat, Papua New Guinea, 1979.
- Resources for Science Teaching : report of a survey in the Commonwealth Caribbean, Commonwealth Secretariat, 1982.
- Low-cost Equipment for School Science and Technology Education, UNESCO, Kenya, 1985.
- Teaching of Science : Report and Recommendations of the National Seminar on Science Teaching held at Bhopal, EKLAVYA, November, 15-17, India, 1985.
- The Use of Media in Science Education, DSE, Germany, 1987.

REFERENCES

1. BEI attempts to list every significant article of permanent educational interest appearing in over 250 English-language periodicals published in the British Islesand in certain internationally published periodicals.
2. Educational materials collected by the Educational Resources Information Centre of the USA—750 *journals and serial publications.*
3. International mlti-disciplinary indexes to the literature of the social, behavioural, and related sciences, produced by the Institute for Scientific Information from indexed journals are selected according to citation analysis.

APPENDIX 2:

A Summary of Activities in Developing Countries

A Survey of Science Kits

Afghanistan

Afghanistan has imported *primary* science kits from India, and has a National Science Centre.

Arab World

Lowe (1981) reports that laboratory apparatus is mostly imported with some attempts to use local resources in Iraq, Bahrain, Jordan, Qatar, Kuwait and Egypt. New curricula in Qutar include activities and suggestions for the involvement of students and teacher in the production of simple apparatus utilising raw material from the environment.

Bangladesh

The government has established the Bangladesh Educational Equipment Development Bureau (BEEDB) under the administrative control of the Directorate of Technical Education; produces prototypes designs to promote local manufacture; provides advisory design and training services to equipment manufacturers and teachers. An ADB supported project on secondary science is in progress in Bangladesh which includes support for the production of science kits.

Bolivia

Chemistry kits designed with DSE (Germany) support; with 100 source books on hand-experiments.

Botswana

The Department of Curriculum Development and Evaluation includes a Teaching Aids Production Unit; established in 1976/77; has mass produced science eduction aids such as electric circuit board, electromagnets, terrarium, weather station and balances; has also mass produced 14,000 teaching aids on Wildlife Conservation for the Ministry of Local Government and Lands. In 1982 Andringa reports that MOE, Brigades, BEDU and TAPU have been approached to assist in an investigation of the possibilities of production of local science equipment for secondary schools; recommends implementation of Science Equipment Service Unit. The Appendix to Andringa's report contains 62 items for possible local production. In 1984 Botswana introduced science kits at junior secondary level, with 33 per cent local content.

Brazil

In 1963-64 a UNESCO Pilit Project on the Teaching of Physics was introduced. This developed and produced 200 lots of 8 kits on the topic, Light. Also FUNBEC kits were developed with accompanying booklets—50 kits in pocket -size boxes, simple equipment but which can be used in an advanced way; each kit is associated with the work of a particular scientist; made generally available through marketing by street vendors.

Cambodia

The Division of Pedagogic Services attempts to supply equipment on a small scale, and also runs courses for teachers. Cambodia sends trainees to RECSAM in Malaysia.

Cameroon

IPAR-BUEA produces teaching aids in Observational science and Village Technology. Allsop (1991) reports on an alternative approach to the use of kits which has developed from the work of regional groups of physics teachers. They have prepared workbooks for students which aim to provide an indirect experience of practical science, sometimes through data analysis, sometimes through comprehension of completed experiments, sometimes through 'thought' experiments. Impact remains to be evaluated.

Caribbean Region

Various Commonwealth Secretariat reports (1977, 1982) discuss activities in the region. These reports identify items such as solar stills, biogas generators, power packs, electronics teaching kits, physics application models which have been produced by local science educators. Commonwealth Caribbean governments were requested to establish a production unit to provide materials for curriculum renewal. The general view is that curriculum renewal has not been properly supported by equipment production strategies despite the considerable human resources in science education available in the Caribbean region.

Colombia

A DSE-aided in-service teacher training seminar took place in Bogota, Colombia in 1984.

Costa Rica

There is some early doubts about the commercial viability of local production. The Programme Conjunto Gobierno-UNESCO-UNICEF produce some drawings and prototypes. The country is considering using low-cost Japanese plastic mini-science kits.

Dominica

The Dominica Science Project (1974-77) produced a low-cost apparatus handbook. All apparatus was built and tried out in schools.

Ecuador

Integrated science kits developed with DSE aid.

Ethiopia

Ethiopia has its own science equipment production unit (EMPDA); establishment in 1977-78; has adapted SEPU materials for primary level. In 1981 a project for the production of 110 science kit was launched. A contract to produce 6,000 kits in 1987-89 has been signed between EMPDA and the World Bank. Also about 5,000 School Pedagogical Centres have been established to support schools with materials. DSE has supported the development of chemistry kits with accompanying source books on hand experiments.

Ghana

The United Kingdom ODA supplied JSS Science Kits worth £1 million. Recent reports (1991) stress the need for simpler materials than those found in commercial kits, e.g. heat source; they emphasize that imported kits are often not used. A guide for teachers to improvise apparatus and prepare a science kit box for use in Junior Secondary Schools has been recently published. 20-page pamphlet on rationale for practical work, provision of resources, use of resources, problems, improvisation. The box part of the kit serves many functions and it can be filled gradually; it also contains various booklets on contents (electricity, magnetism); also worksheets for continuous assessment of student teachers in practical work.

Guyana

There are plans of an Equipment Production Centre. The Science Teachers Association of Guyana Journal (quoted in UNSECO handbook) has indicated one approach to developing science kits—teacher produced thematic kits. The aim is to eventually develop a series of specific thematic kits and scope for kit exchange possibilities.

Hong Kong

A series of science kits (Simplex') were produced in the 1970s as an independent business venture. However, the kits are no longer produced.

India

The National Council for Educational Research and Training (NCERT) established the Central Science Workshop in 1965 to begin designing and developing science kits in 1968. The NCERT operates a government-run production unit but uses local companies to make some kits under contract; has a team of inspectors responsible for quality control. In the mid-1970s the CSW had 100 staff and an annual budget of 500,000 rupees for the 1975/76 fiscal year with an additional 50,000 rupees for research and development. 60 per cent of the production budget was allocated to the purchase of raw materials. The CSW was expected to become self-supporting from the sale of kits. The kits were purchased by each state. In the mid-1970's there was no direct purchase by schools and no means of obtaining spares. There were two types of kit—one for teacher demonstration use and the other for groups of 4-6 students. States were encouraged to set up State Institutes of Science Education to provide in-service and science kit orientation for teachers.

The Hoshangabad Science Teaching Programme (HSTP) provides science kits to 350 schools spread over seven districts in Madhya Pradesh. Each kit is designed for groups of four students and costs about $47. The HSTP started as pilot project in 1972 and covers an entire district; it has plans to expand to eight more districts in 1986. The HSTP started as pilot project in 1972 and covers an entire district; it had plans to expand to eight more districts in 1986. The HSTP is implemented through district-level committees with a follow-up and feedback system, kit distribution mechanism, in addition to curriculum development and teacher orientation. Each kit has permanent, temporary and consumable components and part of the kit is purchased locally.

The following shows the distribution of kits in the period 1969 to 1976. The cost of these kits in 1976 ranged from about $20 (primary) to $40 (chemistry).

Subject	*69/70*	*70/71*	*71/72*	*72/73*	*73/74*	*74/75*	*75/76*
Primary	-	760	188	155	61	110	47
Physics 1	69	426	130	116	40	68	25
Physics 2	-	-	351	213	57	124	67
Physics 3	-	-	-	175	437	44	35
Biology 1	-	468	129	108	4	-	-
Biology demonstration	-	-	350	211	56	129	65
Chemistry demonstration	-	-	350	214	57	129	65
Physics student	-	-	467	1 571	-	480	-

Source: The NCERT, 1972.

Krishna Sane of Delhi University conducts workshops on the production of chemical instrumentation for senior chemistry students: products include pH meters, calorimeters and conduct meters. The approach has been widely replicated, with evaluation suggesting that quality control can be maintained, and that product costs are of the order of 10 per cent of commercial equivalents for comparable performance. (Sane, cited in Woolnough, 1991).

Indonesia

In the 1970s the government had proposals to spend oil revenue on science equipment. Over the years there has been a lot of help from external agencies but teacher were found to be reluctant to use apparatus. Some prototypes of apparatus and kits are designed at the science teaching centre in Bandung and there is also one small commercial manufacturer. DSE has recently helped develop and produced science kits for primary science.

Jamaica

A common wealth secretariat report (1982) list 11 items made by one teacher of physics and integrated science circuit boards, pinhole, camera, optics kit, resistance box, rheostats, magnetic effect apparatus, electrical effect kit, galvanometers, liver kit, balances. But these are really improvements on commercial equipment.

Kenya

The science equipment production unit (SEPU) is part of Kenya institutes of education. The (SEPU) operates commercially but as a non-profit making venture. Its directors are appointed by government bodies. It sells direct to school and has salesmen to promote marketing. Workshop construction started in February, 1970 and production started in September the same year. The total initial capital cost (buildings, machines, tools) was £32,500; non-salary costs (1971) £5,960; salary costs (1971) £7,150. In 1972 there were two expatriates and seven Kenyans on staff. The SEPU financed by a joint Kenya/Sweden project until mid-1979.

Each SEPU science was designed for individualised practical work, accompanied by written material (worksheets) with sides and tapes. Radio support was provided for biology kit. SEPU found it possible to cut down costs by combining chemistry and physics materials. The basis of the chemistry kit was a pegboard stand on which it was passible to mount all components of a piece of an experiment set-up so that the relationship between components could be clearly seen. About 50 per cent of the kit consisted of glassware and flexible plastic tubing was supplied rather than fixed glass joints (this obviated the need for beehive shelves and other apparatus). Many of the item fulfilled more than one function. When not in use, the apparatus could be stored in plastic mould or inside a cardboard box. A wooden box was also available to store several kits.

SEPU output by April, 1976 is shown as follows:

Physics	*Chemistry*	*Biology*
547	-	-
443	-	-
381	162	-
436	353	13
159	152	112

Republic of Korea

Most laboratory equipment is produced locally by different companies. Student science centres have basic facilities to develop science laboratory equipment and public company to produce laboratory experiment is in operation. The Republic of Korea provides fully equipped laboratory than kits.

Lao PDR

lAO PDR trained its teachers to make science equipments. The directorate of materials and educational productions produces some very simple materials but has plans for more. Lao PDR PARTICIPATES IN RESCAM workshops. School Inspectors demand initiative from teachers and improvisation is encouraged.

Leostho

There is an instructional Materials Resource Centre at the National Teacher Training College which develops and produces teaching and learning materials for revised curricula, including some prototype charts. There is no local production of equipment as yet. The junior Certificate Integrated Science scheme includes as in-service component where teachers construct apparatus. The Swaziland Conference (Swaziland, 1979) recommended the establishment of a Maths/Science centre to procure equipment for all schools. Apparently a suitable building is available but there are needs for design and developmental skills. The conference called for co-ordination of activities, school surveys, surveys of transport, maintenance facilities and training assistance. Babolo *et al* (undated) report on the design of an inexpensive unit which permits use of ordinary classroom in science teaching-tea trolley idea—could be made by school handyman.

Malawi

Malawi institute of Education (Domasi) is responsible for designing, preparing and piloting appropriate educational materials and equipment for primary education; it has carpenters' workshops but no facilities for mass production. There are also Educational Resource Centres for training and distribution of materials.

Malaysia

Malaysia already manufactures more than half of its secondary school needs. The curriculum development centre in Kuala Lumpur is an example of a nationally-established centre for prototype equipment research and production. CDC was established in 1973 and UNESCO help. Its workshop produces prototypes in wood, metal and plastic. Once designed, prototypes are tendered to commercial manufacturers for construction and marketing. Training is provided to key personnel so that there is a multiplying effect in the states. CDC has mobile teams located at various centres throughout Malaysia which carry some equipment-repair and in-service. Malaysia has a National equipment Centre for the design, development and distribution of equipment.

Mali

The 'Section Sciences Biologique' in Bamako has interests which include the production of low-cost scientific materials based on local resources.

Republic of Mauritius

At primary level, science is part of a multi-disciplinary subject, Environmental Science, introduced in 1981. Teachers are encouraged to produce their own teaching aids. Some aids such as thermometers, mirrors and magnets are provided in a science kit distributed by the Ministry of Education and Culture.

Myaanmar

In 1964 the Rangoon Arts and Science University started to make science equipment for education and production began in 1965. The RASU was one of the first centres of local production in the region. It provide to be very influential in the region as a model for other countries.

Nepal

The Science Equipment Centre (part of the Janak Education Materials Centre, JEMC) in Kathmandu was initially set up as a distribution centre, but has plans to develop and produce equipment for schools. An ADB-aided project on local production is currently in progress. Mali (1981) reports on the Science Teacher Preparation Programme (STPP) and the use of mobile teams which organise workshops on the use of local resources at secondary level. The Centre for Educational Research, Innovation and Development also runs courses for teachers on the utilisation of low-cost simple material.

Nicaragua

DSE has helped develop kit for integrated science.

Nigeria

In 1970, the Fedral Ministry established a Science Equipment Centre in Logos with UNDP/UNESCO support until 1976. There are now branches in Enugu, Jos and Abraka. SEC is responsible for the design and production of prototypes of school science equipment, repair and maintenance, in-service, advisory service. A review of SEC activities in 1975 found that the most urgent needs were for equipment repair. Mobile teams were set up each with seven technicians, tools, test instruments, glassworking equipment for the repairs of microscopes, electronic equipment etc; has a network of educational services centres. The Products Development Agency (PRODA) which is based in Enugu develops local materials for science equipment on pilot basis. The Federal Government has directed that MOE and PRODA set up a Science Equipment Manufacturing Unit for post primary, and has approved 5 million naira for the project. According to the guidelines of the fourth National Development Plan (1981-85) the Nigerian Educational Research Council is one of the key institutions expected to contribute to the attainment of 100 per cent local production of school texts and other instructional materials for primary and post-primary. NERC is the implementing agency for the National Primary Science and Mathematics projects; has procured science kits for 906 pilot schools all over the country, trained teachers to use the kits; the project reached the teacher-trainer re-orientation phase in 1986. There are reports on a Science Equipment Workshop in Bendel State. (It has produced a 111 item kit for primary and was commissioned to produce 1,560 kits over the period 1976-79). Kwara State College has a production unit involving students and proposes the establishment of a Production Services Unit on a commercial basis.

Pakistan

The Science Educational Equipment Technical Assistance Centre (SEETAC), Lahore was established in 1964 (sponsored by government and the Ford Foundation) to design and promote the local manufacture of science equipment. It cost R 2 million for local non-recurrent expenditure with 0.6 million in aid. Has its own quality control laboratory and tests showed that locally produced equipment was comparable to imported equipment? By 1975, when the federal government took over responsibility, the renamed National Equipment Centre had developed 200 different items, as well as a comprehensive 95-item kits for primary. NEC has also produced a primary teachers' tool kit covering science, mathematics, social studies and Urdu. The centre trained 2,200 master-teacher trainers, who in turn, were expected to trained 200,000 more teachers in the use of the primary kit. The science Education Centre at the University of Punjab develops innovative kit for science. An Asian Development Bank-aided project on local production in currently (1991) in progress.

Papua New Guinea

Papua New Guinea has foreign exchange but a lack of technological skill. It therefore tends to import rather than locally produce. UNICEF provided primary science kits to accompany the Three Phase Primary Science Project, which was introduced to all schools in 1972, but the original kits have now been depleted and schools have to order their own equipment. The basic kits were available from UNICEF Packing and Assembly Centre (UNIPAC) in Denmark at a 1982 cost of $128 (basic) and $56 replacement. An evaluation of TPPS (Wilson, TMMC Report 14, 1970) found that in many cases it was the teacher-supplied items that were missing from lessons, A $5.5 million project funded by USAID, the Radio Science Pilot Project (1986-1990), developed radio science programmes to support upper primary science education. It was found that many of the trial schools lacked the basic equipment to implement the programme. Consequently, trial schools were each supplied with basic science kits. This project also attempted to improve teachers' confidence by broadcasting background notes (including equipment ideas) for teachers in the evening before the school broadcast.

Papua New Guinea used a boys' reformatory to assembly imported components for electricity kits. This had a workshop and made a modest profit. But equipment production needs a huge cash flow which was apparently lacking. In 1984, the Department of Education in Papua New Guinea under a loan agreement with the World Bank, provided science kits for biology, chemistry, physics, geology and assorted science. These kits were all imported. There are several lessons to be learned from the PNG experience with importing science kits:

- the imported secondary science kits are more suitable for science for continuation rather than science for all;
- there have been delays due to failure of overseas companies to supply components on time;

- the cost of the kits increased each year; a biology kit purchased in 1984 cost K964 whereas it cost K1,375 in 1986;
- newly established schools initially do not need all of the materials in the kit; special 'start-up' kits for early grades would have been a better strategy;
- while the tendering system generally worked well, there were problems with one overseas supplier, where materials either failed to problems with one overseas supplier, where materials either failed to arrive or were faulty; such problems can incur considerable legal costs;
- the decision to supply uniformly size kits regardless of school-size may result in problems for large schools. Material and timetabling constraints might result in an emphasis on demonstration activities rather than individual student activities.

Philippines

The Philippines has a National Science and Technology Authority which has supported various science equipment efforts. There are one or two equipment firms but output in small. Some private technical schools make apparatus but it is not widely available. The School Science Equipment Development Project involved the National Science and Technology Authority, Ministry of Education, UNDP and UNICEF, but barely alleviated the plight of the elementary and secondary school science teacher since, assuming one kit per school, approximately 30,000 kits would have been needed and only 8,486 elementary science kits were distributed (Lockheed *et al,* 1989). The Science Education Centre at the University of Philippines has produced an elementary school science kit guide to accompany the comprehensive kit for grades 1-6; it was designed and developed in accordance with the University of the Philippines Science Education Centre.

Sierra Leone

The country paper presented at the DSE seminar (1986) mentions some problems encountered in science education in Sierra Leone—such as processes of science not appreciated, low status for science, lack of encouragement for hands-on approach, expensive teaching aids. The Science Curriculum Development Centre undertakes the development of low-cost school teaching science equipment with the prospect of inspiring local production.

Singapore

All apparatus is bought locally. Quasi government industrial agencies help in design and production. The Curriculum Development Institute of Singapore offers a 30-hour in-service course on developing skills in primary science teaching which includes developing and implementing low-cost experiments. CDIS has mass produced large numbers of educational packages.

South Pacific

The South Pacific regional Environment Programme has developed a Coral Reef Kit (1989) and resource book with references to local names; 150 sets of the coral reef kit are planned for secondary schools in the region. The Solomon Islands use UNICEF kits at primary level but import apparatus for secondary. See Papua New Guinea.

Sri Lanka

In the 1960s NOSTRAD kits for teaching heat, light etc. were distributed to 'O' level schools under a UNESCO aid programme. At present the Mini lab produced in Sri Lanka is recommended by government for the teaching of 'O' level general science. The 1988 cost of the Mini lab is Rs. 75,000 and schools can purchase with funds from aid agencies, *e.g.* ADB. In 1985 and 1986 the Goethe Institute organised meetings where appropriate; cheap media for chemistry and biology teaching were produced.

Swaziland

At secondary level, the Junior Certificate Integrated Science Scheme includes an in-service component where teachers construct apparatus for their own immediate use. A Curriculum Development Centre for primary and secondary levels was completed in 1976, and has a fully-equipped Production Unit which is used mainly in the production of general prototype materials for use in pilot schools. A Science Education Centre was established in 1979, but according to a report dated 1986 (Ward) there were still not plans for the local manufacture of simple items of laboratory equipment. Another 1986 report states that the Science Production Unit was being hampered by lack of finances to purchase supplies and materials.

Tanzania

There are a number of proposals for small-scale production which do not need large capital investment and have minimum transportation costs. Self-reliance activities were expected to meet 25 per cent of the recurrent costs of each school (Malekela, 1989). Improvisation is therefore strongly encouraged. There have been attempts by some organisations at prototype development for either industrial use or as aids for schools. In every district there are about four science kits shared by primary schools. A workshop on the teaching of physics to beginners with locally-available materials was help in Morogoro from 15-26 July, 1991. The workshop was organised jointly by the Ministry of Education and the Goethe Institute. During the workshop, the participants developed and tested experiments and activities which could be organised economically and within a very short preparation time by secondary school teachers to cover the basic physics concepts at lower secondary level. These kits can be assembled from prefabricated parts at less than US$20 each during in-service and pre-service training courses.

Thailand

The Institute for the Promotion of *Teaching* Science and Technology *(Govt./UNDP)* designs and makes prototypes and small-scale production runs of apparatus. The IPST is autonomous within MOE, and entrusted by MOE to produce prototypes of equipment which are simple, made of locally available materials and low-priced. Prototypes are then marketed by the Business Organization of the Teachers Council (branches in each province) on a commercial scale for nationwide distribution at low prices. Schools are required to buy local equipment. The IPST produces both teacher demonstration and student kits for general science, chemistry, biology, physics and physical and biological science. The kits require no specialised laboratories and can be easily moved from class to class. Reports from supervisors indicate problems with the purchase of expendable materials due to enrolment Increases without corresponding budget increase for equipment. IPST-designed equipment is cheap but some of its breaks easily, and cannot be repaired by schools. Warren (1971) discusses the need for a laboratory to help train student teachers to demonstrate science activities. The laboratory has since been established in one teachers' college and student-teachers are provided with demonstration kits.

Trinidad

Has firms to service and repair microscopes but local production for secondary science is unlikely (1982)? Has recognised the need for primary science kits?

Uganda

The National Curriculum Development Centre (NCDC) is responsible for the development of low-cost teaching aids and the training of teachers in their production.

Viet Nam

The Science Education Equipment Project (SEEP) started in 1981, as a co-operative venture between the National Institute of Educational Science in Viet Nam and the Komtee Wetenschap en Techniek (KWT) based in the Netherlands, on the design and production of science education equipment for the basic general schools in Viet Nam. The project has had several phases: (i) the revision of existing equipment and teachers and students instruction; (ii) try out of materials in several schools; (iii) the development of prototypes of kits of equipment; (iv) production of biology and chemistry kits; (v) distribution of kits and instructions. Plans for the fourth phase involve the production of 500 kits for grade 6 biology and 500 kits for grade 8 chemistry. There is a plan for continued co-operation during the years 1990-1995. At the same time there is in-service teacher training in key schools. The project aims to supply virtually all (16,500) secondary schools in Viet Nam with the basic facilities required for the teacher of the new biology and chemistry syllabi, *i.e.* about $422 per school.

Zimbabwe

The Zim-Sci project which started in 1981 is designed to provide 'hands-on' science education for the increasing numbers of schools and pupil enrolments since Independence. The provision of basic, low-cost science equipment in the form of kits has always been an integral part of the Zim-Sci programme. The kits are designed for use by students working in pairs but there is also a small demonstration kit for teacher use. Science kits are assembled from pieces of equipment supplied by different suppliers, both local and overseas. The Zim-Sci project has now been assimilated into the Ministry of Education and the concept is bring extended to the 4th year of secondary science education on an experimental basis. A report by the Curriculum Development Unit recommended that Zim-Sci should attempt to reduce the number of items ordered from outside. The distribution of new 'O' level kits started in October 1987, with a Zimbabwe Junior Certificate (ZJC) tender for 150 kits for new schools opened in 1986. Future plans are for the continued procurement of kit for new schools, the production of learning/ teaching materials and orientation workshops. By the end of 1990 all schools should have been provided with a ZJC kit and most with 'O' level kits. Staff reduction in the Zim-Sci team meant that it was not possible to maintain the level of support for teacher in-service. The Curriculum Development Unit has produced the specifications for 'A' level Physics kits which are currently being assembled both in Zimbabwe and Germany under an Aid agreement. The Harare Generator (Seminar) took place in Harare from 12 January to 2 February, 1991, in order to show developments from around the world following the Bangalore conference of 1985. Among the items produced was a low-cost micro-electronics kit (Chinyanga, 1991).

APPENDIX 3:

List of Abbreviations

ADB	Asian development Bank
BC	British Council *(United Kingdom)*
BEEDB	Bangladesh Educational Equipment Development Bureau (Bangladesh)
CDC	Curriculum Development Centre (Kuala Lumpur)
CDIS	Curriculum Development Institute of Singapore *(Singapore).*
CSW	Central Science Workshop *(India)*
DSE	Deutsche Stiftung für Internationale Entwicklung *(Germany)*
EMPDA	Educational Materials and Distribution Agency *(Ethipopia)*
GTZ	Deutsche Gesellschaft für Technische Zusammenarbeit *(Germany)*
HSTP	Hoshangabad Science Teaching Project *(India)*
IEA	International Association for the Evaluation of Educational Achievement.
IIEP	International Institute for Educational Planning
INISTE	International Network for Information in Science and technology Education
IPAR	'Institut de Pédagogie Appliquée à Vocation Rurale' *(Cameroon)*

IPST	'Institute for the Promotion of Teaching Science and Technology *(Thailand)*
JEMC	Jank Education Materials Centre.
KWT	Komitee Wetenschap en Techniek *(Netherlands)*
MOE	Ministry of Education
NCDC	National Curriculum Development Centre.
NEC	National Equipment Centre
NERC	Nigerian Educational Research Council
NCERT	National Council for Educational Research and Training, *(India)*
ODA	Overseas Development Administration *(United Kingdom)*
PNG	Papua New Guinea
PRODA	Products Development Agency *(Nigeria)*
RASU	Rangoon Arts and Science University *(Myanmar)*
RECSAM	Regional Centre for Education in Science and Mathematics, *(Malaysia)*
SEC	Science Equipment Centre (*Lagos*)
SEEP	Science Education Equipment Project *(Viet Nam)*
SEETAC	Science Educational Equipment Technical Assistance Centre
SEPA	Science Education Programme for Africa
SEPU	Science Equipment Production Unit *(Kenya)*
SIDA	Swedish International Development Authority *(Sweden)*
SSA	Sub-Saharan Africa
STPP	Science Teacher Preparation Programme
TAC	Teacher Advisory Centre *(Kenya)*
TAPU	Teaching Aids Production Unit *(Botswana)*
TPPS	Three Phase Primary Science *(Papua New Guinea)*

UNDP	United Nations Development Programme
UNESCO	United Nations Educational, Scientific and Cultural Organisation
UNICEF	United Nations International Children's Educational Fund
UNIPAC	UNICEF packing and Assembly Centre
USAID	US Agency for International development
ZJC	Zimbabwe Junior Certificate

Bibliography

Ahmed, R. 1977. "Science education in rural environment". In *Science education in the Asian region*. Bangkok: UNESCO.

Allsop, T. 1991. "Practical science in low-income countries". In Woolnough, B. (ed.) *Practical science*. Milton Keyes, United Kingdom: Open University Press.

Apea, E.; Lowe, N.K. 1979. *Development and production of school science equipment: some alternative approaches*. London: Commonwealth Secretariat Education Division.

Baldwon, N. 1990. *Report of the Rooper's science orientation workshop*. Tanzania: Marangu Teachers' College.

———. 1986. *Science for living*. (Sayansi Ili Kuishi). United Kingdom: Roopers Export Sales Ltd.

Bangladesh. 1975. Publicity material. Dhaka: Educational Equipment Development Bureau.

Botswana, 1980. Ministry of Education, the Teaching Aid Production Unit (TAPU), Curriculum development and evaluation.

Bowker, M.K.; Hunk, A.R. 1968. *Making elementary science apparatus*. Nelson—Africa.

Bredderman, T. 1983. "Effects of activity-based elementary science on student outcomes: a quantitative synthesis". In *Review of educational research*, 53, pp. 499-518.

British Council, 1979. *Directory of Educational Equipment Production Centres*, British Council.

Brophy, M.; Dalgety, F. 1981. "Curriculum diffusion and adoption : a West Indian experience". In *Education for development*, 6(4), pp.53-62.

Caillods, F.; Gottelmann-Duret, G. 1991. *Science provision in academic secondary schools: organisation and condition*. International Institute for Educational Planning, UNESCO.

Campos, M. 1989. "Science teaching integrated in the socio-cultural context with some hints from ethnoscience and ethnoastronomy". In Dias, PV (ed.) *Basic science knowledge and universalisation of primary education*, pp.95-124. Frankfurt, Paedagogik: Dritte Welt, Johann Wolfgang Goethe-University.

Carelse, X.F. 1985. *The local production of equipment for teachers (Zimbabwe)*. Paper presented at a UNESCO seminar, Nairobi.

Carrol, M. *et al*. 1975. "The KSTC chemistry kit: a teaching aid for a developing country". In *School science review*, 57(199), pp.254-264.

Chinyanga, C. 1991. "What was the Harare generator? In *Education in science, ASE*, No. 144, p.14.

Cole, M.J. 1975. "Science teaching and science curriculum in a supposedly non-scienctific culture". In *West African Journal of Education*, Vol. XIX No. 2, pp. 313-322.

Commonwealth Secretariat. 1987. *Primary science teacher training for process-based learning*. UNESCO.

————. 1985. *Interrelating science, mathematics and technology education: a basis of general education for all*. London.

————. 1979. *Low-cost science teachng equipment: 3, report of a seminar-workshop, Papua New Guinea, 19-30 March, 1979*. London.

————. 1978. *Low-cost science teaching eqipment: 2, report of a seminar-workshop, Tanzania, 20-30 September, 1977*. London.

————1977. *Low-cost science teaching equipment: report of a seminar-workshop, Bahamas, 16-26 November 1976*. London.

————. 1970. "Education in the development countries of the Commonwealth". In *Research register 1*. London.

Crellin, C.T. 1979. "Low-cost materials for science and mathematics teaching". In *Second ICASE-Asian symposium on low-cost equipment for integrated science education at all levels*.

ICASE. Dias, P.V. (ed.) 1989. *Basic science knowledge and universalisation of primary education*. Frankfurt, Paedagogik: Dritte Welt, Johann Wolfgang Goethe-University.

Dock, A. 1983. *The ZIM-SCI project: Zimbabwe secondary schools science project*. progress report No. 2. Harare: Ministry of Education and Culture, Department of Curriculum Studies.

Driver R. 1983. *The pupil as scientist*. Miltion Keynes (United Kingdom): Open University Press.

Duncan, W.A. 1988. *Engendering school learning: science attitudes and achievement among girls and boys in Botswana.* Stockholm: Institute of International Education, University of Stockholm.

Ehindero, O. 1980. "Relationships between actualising concrete and formal science teaching intentions and the levels of cognitive development among some prospective teachers in Nigeria". In *Science Education*, 64(2), pp.185-193.

Eklavya. 1985. *Teaching of science: report and recommendtions of the national seminar on science teaching held at bhopal,* India.

Elliott, F. 1988. "Mobilising adaptive technology potential in the sector of African economies". In Menck, K.W. (ed.) *Challenges for science and technology promotion in Africa: problems, priorities and actions.* German Foundtion for International Development.

Eshiet, I.T. 1988. *Using local resources in teaching, education in chemistry.*

Fiji. 1981. *Report onthe meeting of permanent education secretaries and directors of education to establish a South Pacific Equipment Centre.*

Gallagher, J.J. 1987. "A summary of research in science education." In *Science Education*, 71, pp. 277-284.

George, J.; Glasgow, J. 1989. *Some cultural implications of teaching towards common syllabi in science : a case study from the Caribbean, SSR* 71(254).

George, T.C. 1990. *The condition of science provision in academic secondary eduction in Papua New Guinea.* Country monograph prepared for IIEP.

German Cultural Institutes. 1990. *Ethiopian chemistry teachers sourcebook.*

————. 1990. *Tanzanian chemistry teachers sourcebook.*

————. 1989. *Ghanaian science teachers sourcebook.*

Ghana. 1991. Resource Production Centre. *The science kit box : a guide to teachers to improvising apparatus and preparing a science kit box for use in junior secondary schools.* Accra : Tacher Education Division, Education Department.

————. 1991 Resource Production Centre. *The science kit box : a guide to teachers to improvising apparatus and preparing a science kit box for us in junior secondary schools.* Accra: Teacher Education Division, Education Department.

————. 1991. Resource Production Centre. *Worksheepts for continuous assessment in practical work in science.* Accra. Teacher Education Division, Education Department.

Giffould, G.D. Undated. *Education and intermediate technology*. Botswana: Ministry of Education.

Gupta, A. 1989. "Using day-to-day common objects for understanding principles of science". In Dias, P.V. (ed.) *Basic science knowledge and universalisation of primry education*, pp. 158-165. Frankfurt, Paedagogik: Dritte Welt, Johann Wolfgang Goethe-University.

Guthrie, G. 1983. *An evaluation of the secondary teacher training system*. Boroko (Papua New Guinea): National Research Institute, ERU Report 44.

Guyana. 1977. Ministry of Education, Social development and Culture. *The production teacher vacation course, 1977*. Report.

Haddad, W.D. 1986. *Role and educational effects of practical activities in science education*. Washington D.C.: The World Bank. (Education and Training Department).

Hakansson, C.S. 1979. "Design and production of low-cost equipment on a national scale". In *Second ICASE—Asian symposium on low-cost equipment for integrated science education at all levels*. ICASE.

Harlen, W. 1983. "New trends in primary schools science education". In Harlen W. (ed.), Vol. 1. UNESCO.

Hawes, H.; Stephens, D.C. 1990. *Questions of quality*. Longman group. Hawes, H. 1979. "The curriculum of teacher education". In Gardner, R. (ed.) *Teacher eduction developing countries: prospects for the eighties*. Commonwealth Secretariat.

IEA, 1991 and 1992. (International Asociation for the Evaluation of Educational Achievement). *Second international science education project*. Oxford: Pergamon Press. [See individual entries in this bibligraphy under Rosier; Keeves. (Vol. 1): Postlethwaite; Wiley. (Vol.2): Keeves. (Vol. 3)].

Jarvis, A. 1991. *Personal Communication*, Ghana.

Kalbag, S.S. 1990. "Vigyan Ashram : A novel experiment in taking modern science to the countryside". In *Journal of Education and Social Change.*, Vol 4(3), pp.33-46. Indian Institute of Education.

Kamariah, H.; Rubba, A.; Tomera, A.; Zurub, A. 1988. "Jordanian and Malaysian science teacher's prominent perceived professional needs : a comparison". In *Journal of Research in Science Teaching* 25(7), pp.573-588.

Kassenally, K. 1985. *Low-cost equipment for school science and technology education (Republic of Mauritius)*. Paper presented at a UNESCO seminar, Nairobi.

King, K. 1985. *Low-cost equipment for school science and technoly education (Republic of Mauritius).* Paper presented at a UNESCO seminar, Nairobi.

King, K. 1985. "Education science policy, research and action : a review paper". In King, K. (ed.) *Science, education and society : perspectives from India and South-East Asia.* Ottawa: International Development Research Centre.

Krasilchik, M. 1979. "Biology teaching in Brazil : a case for curricular transformation". In *Joural of Biological Education,* 3(4), pp. 311-314.

Kreitler, H.; Kreitler, S. 1974. "The role of the experiment in science education". In *Instructional science* 3, pp. 75-88.

Layton, D. 1973. *Science for the people : the origins of the schools science curriculum in England,* Allen and Unwin.

Lewin, K.M. 1992. *Science education in developing countries: issues and perspectives for planners.* Paris: International Institute for Educational Planning, UNESCO.

Lockard, J. 1972. *Guidebook to constructing inexpensive science teching equipment.* Vol. 3, USA : Physics, Science Teaching Centre, Maryland University.

Lockheed, M.E.; Fonacier, J.; Bianchi, L.J. 1989. *Effective primary level science teaching in the Philippines.* Washington D.C.: Population and Human Resources Division, The World Bank. (Working Papers, No. 208).

Lowe, N.K. 1983. *Recent developments in the production of school science equipment,* London: Commonwealth Secretariat.

————. 1981. *Practical developments in the production of school science equipment.* London: Commonwealth Secretariat.

————.1981. *Practical proposals for the development of technology and technical education in the school system in Qatar.* British Council, Mali, G.B. 1981. "Science teacher preparation program : an analysis" In *Education Quarterly,* Vol. 26(1-3). Nepal : Institute of Education, Tribhuvan University.

Maranga, J.S. 1984. "The role of teachers advisory centres in the education of teachers and parents : a case study of Machokos district". In *Journal of Education,* 1(1), pp. 46-68.

McLeod, S. 1985. *Primary science development project.* Booklets 1-8. Edinburgh : Scottish curriculum development service.

Melton, R.H. 1972. *Elementay economic experiments in physics.*

Vol. 1-4. CEDO, British Council.

Menck, K.W. 1988. "Problems of development and domestication of science and technology in developing countries". In Menck, K.W. (ed.) *Challenges for science and technology promotion in Africa: problems, priorities and actions.* German Fondation for International Development.

Mhlanga, A. 1984. *Problems of teaching MCE physical science practicals in secondary schools in Malawi.* Bonn: Deustsche Gesellschaft für Technische Zusammenarbeit (GTZ); Nairobi: African Curriculum Organisation. (African Studies in Curriculum Development and Evaluation, No. 158).

Moon T.; Lowe, N. 1979. *School science equipment in the Third World : a tape/slide program with script and background notes.* United Kingdom: British Council.

Mundangepfupfu, R.M. 1985. *The use of laboratories in teaching secondary school science.* Washington D.C.: The World Bank. (Economic Development Institute).

Murray Thomas, R., (ed.) 1990. *International comparative education: practices, issues and prospects.* Pergamon Press.

NCERT. 1972. *Improvising science teaching kits for schools,* India.

Nigeria. 1972. *Outline suggestion for the proposed Western State Science Equipment Centre.*

Nxumalo, M. 1985. *Consultation on low-cost equipment for school science and technology education (Swaziland)".* Paper presented at a UNESCO seminar, Nairobi.

O' Brien, A. 1987. "Country report on the National Curriculum Development Centre in Sierra Leone". In Schirmer, A. (ed.) *Science education: the case of Arican countries.* Germany: DSE.

Ohikhena, T.O. 1974. "Introducing elementary technology into secondary eduction in Nigeria". In *West African Journal of Education,* Vol. XVIII No. 1, pp.25-32.

Orpwood, G.; Werdelin, I. 1987. *Science and technology in the primary school of tomorrow.* UNESCO.

Osborne, C. (ed.) 1986. *International Yearbook of educational and instructional technology : 1986/87, association for educational and training technology,* Kogan Page/eichols.

pakistan. 1973. *Science Educational Equipment Technical Assistance Centre.* Instructional Manual Vol. 1. Punjab, Lahore.

Papua New Guinea. 1990. Ministry of Education. *Secondary schools science laboratories guide.*

————. 1988. *Curriculum statement for science in provincial high school.* Port Moresby: Department of Education.

Papua New Guinea. 1987-1989. *Workshop reports of the community schools science advisory committee.* Department of Eduction.

————. 1987-1989. *Workshop reports of the provincial high school.* Port Moresby: Department of Education.

————. 1982 *Community school science equipment handbook.* Department of Education.

Payne, R.D. Undated. Setting up a low-cost materials production unit. Popalzai, M. 1985. *Development of low-cost equipment in Pakistan.*

Paper presented at a UNESCO seminar, Nairobi.

Pullan, M. 1991. *Report to high eduction group re-visit to UDSM.* Tanzania.

Qubain, F. 1965. *Education and science teaching :·repot of a survey in the Commonwealth Caribbean.* Commonwealth Secretariat.

Sargent, R.A. 1986. "Projections and policies in Swaziland's education system". In *The Swaziland Institute for Educational Research.* No. 7, pp. 1-15.

Schirmer, A. 1987. *Science education : philosophy, media assessment, teaching and learning—the case of African countries.* German Foundation for International Development.

Schirmer, A. 1986. *Curriculum development programs in Africa.* German Foundation for International Development.

Schirmer, A. 1986. *Curriculum development programs in Arica.* German Foundation for International Development.

Schmidt, H. 1991. *Teaching and learning in a conflict of cultures: reforming natural science teaching in the Third World.* Draft.

Schmidt, H. 1986. *Cost-effective ways to make teaching of natural science by experiment accessible.* Gate, No. 3.86. Deutsches entrum für Entwicklungstechnologien.

Sharifah, Maimunoh. 1991. *Science education provision in general secondry schools in Malaysia.* A preliminary report on an on-going research. Mimeo. IIEP.

Simpson, R.F. 1979. "Producing low-cost science equipment for developing countries". *In Second ICASE-Asian symposium on low-cost equipment for integrated science education at all levels.* ICASE.

Srivastava, P. *et. al.* 1985. "Development of low-cost, locally produced laboratory equipment : an international initiative". In *Journal of Chemical Education,* 65(5), pp. 428:430.

Swaziland. 1979. *Low-cost production of school equipment*. Manzini.

Swift, D.G. 1983. *Physics for rural development : a soruce book for teachers and extension workers in developing countries*. New York: John Wiley and Sons.

Tanzania, 1990. *Tanzanian chemistry teachers sourcebook.*

Tasker, R. 1981. "Children's views and classroom experiences".

In *Australian Science Teachers Journal,* 27(3), pp.33-37.

Thailand. 1975. Institute for the promotion of teaching of science and technology. *Information pamphlet,* IPST. Bangkok.

Thomas, R.M.; Kobayashi, V.N. (eds). 1987. "Educational technology : its creation, development and cross-cultural transfer". In *Pergamon Comparative and International Education Series.* Pergamon Press.

Tobon, R. 1988. "Low-cost materials for science and technology education". In Layton, D. (ed.) *Innovations in science and technolgy education,* Vol. II, pp. 223-39. Paris: UNESCO.

Towse, P.; Anamuah-Munsah, J. 1991. *Directory of science education resources in anglophone Africa,* in preparation.

Udwin, M.; Manjoro, P. 1987. "Country paper on the curriculum development unit in Zimbabwe". In Schirmer, A. (ed.) *Science education: philosophy, media assessment, teaching and learning: the case of African countries.* German Foundation for International Development.

UNESCO. 1987. *Low-cost science and technology materials at kindergarten level.* UNESCO/National Commission for UNESCO of Korean Ministry of Foreign Affairs.

————. 1987. *Low-cost science and technology materials at the primary school level.* UNESCO/National Commission for UNESCO of Korean Ministry of Foreign Affairs.

————. 1987. *Low-cost science and technology materials at the senior middle school lower grade levels.* UNESCO/National Commission for UNESCO of Korean Ministry of Foreign Affairs.

————. 1985-1986. "Low-cost equipment for science and technology eduction". In N.K. Lowe (ed.), Vol. 1 and 2.

————. 1980. *UNESCO Handbook for science teachers.* Heinemann.

————. 1980. *Meeting of experts on the incorporation of science and technology in the primary school curriculum.* Final Report, Paris.

————. 1973. *School science equipment : a report of a regional seminar in Asia held in India, in December, 1972,* Bangkok.

————. 1969. *Planning for science teaching improvement in Asian schools : report of regional workshop.* Bangkok.

UNESCO-UNDP. 1972. *Feasibility study on the production of school science equipment in the Philippines.* Crunden, Hakkanson and Crellin.

UNESCO-UNICEF. 1971. *Planning for integrated science education in Africa: report on regional workshop, Nigeria.*

Viet Nam. 1990. *Science education equipment project : a report on 10 years of co-operation between KWT (Amsterdam) and NIES (Hanoi) on the design and production of science education equipment for the basic general schools in Viet Nam.* KWT/Committee Science and Technology for Vietnam, Amsterdam.

Wa Kuk Lee. 1992. Ministry of Eduction. *Condition of science education in academic secondary schools.* Monograph of Korea, UNESCO, IIEP.

Walberg, H. 1991. "Improving school science in advanced and developing countries". In *Review of Educational Research.* Vol. 61(1), pp.25-69.

Wanchoo, V.N. 1979. "Local production and distribution of school science equipment in India". In, *CASE-Asian symposium on low-cost equipment for integrated science education at all levels.* Philippines: Manila.

Warren, K. 1971. *Suggestion concernig the setting up of a laboratory/ workshop at Prasarnmitr College, Bangkok: report to CEDO,* (available in British Council Science Education Library).

Warren, K. & Lowe, N.K. 1978. *Technology from toys.* Bangladesh: UNICEF.

————. 1975. *The production of school science equipment: a review of developments.* London: Commonwealth Secretaiat. White, R.T. 1988. *Learning science, Basil Blackwell Ltd.* Oxford.

Whittel, J. 1975. *Local production : principles and practice, school science, Review,* 56(197), pp. 669-684.

Wilailak, W., 1992. Ministry of Education. *Condition of science education in academic secondary schools.* Monograph on Thailand, UNESCO, IIEP.

Wilson, B. 1981. *Cultural contexts of sciene and mathematics education : a bibliographic guide.* Leeds : Centre for Studies in Science Eduation. university of Leeds.

Wilson, M. 1972. *An evaluation of Papua New Guinea's three phase primary science project.* Teaching Methods and Materials Centre, University of Papua New Guinea. (Research Report No. 14).

Woolnough, B. (ed.) 1991. *Practical science.* Open University Press. World Bank/British Council. 1989. *Educating for capability: the role of science and technology education,* Vol. 1.

World Bank. 1988. *Education in Sub-Saharan Africa.* Washington DC.

Yager, R.E.; Engen, H.B.; Snider, B.C. 1969. "Effects of the laboratory and demonstration methods upon the outcomes of instruction in secondary biology". In *Journal of Research in Science Teaching.* Vol. 6, pp. 76.86.

Yoloye, E.A. 1986. "The relevance of educational content to national needs in Africa". In *International Review of Education,* 32(2), pp. 149-172.

Zimbabwe, 1990. *Report on Zim-Sci kits questionaires, secondary science team.*

Zimbabwe, 1988. *Projects and aid unit-planning division.* Report of the mid-term review on SIDA funded projects for the two Ministries of Education, 1987/88. Harimare.

———. 1987. *'O' level teachers' guide: science in energy uses: module 1: energy sources.* Harare: Curriculum Development Unit, Ministry of Education.

Zymelman, M. 1990. *Science educaion and development in Sub-Saharan Africa.* Technical paper No. 124. Washington: World Bank.